SCIENTIFIC PUBLICATIONS
OF
CHARLES WILKINS SHORT

This is a volume in the Arno Press collection

BIOLOGISTS AND THEIR WORLD

Advisory Editor
Keir B. Sterling

Editorial Board
Kraig Adler
Armin Geus
David M. Knight
E. Gorton Linsley
Hans Querner
Ronald L. Stuckey

*See last pages of this volume
for a complete list of titles*

SCIENTIFIC PUBLICATIONS OF CHARLES WILKINS SHORT

Edited with an Introduction by
Ronald L. Stuckey

ARNO PRESS
A New York Times Company
New York • 1978

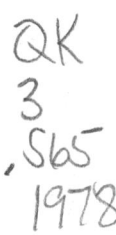
QK
3
.S65
1978

Editorial Supervision: MARIE STARECK

Reprint Edition 1978 by Arno Press Inc.

Arrangement and Compilation Copyright © 1978 by Arno Press Inc.

Introduction Copyright © 1978 by Ronald L. Stuckey

BIOLOGISTS AND THEIR WORLD
ISBN for complete set: 0-405-10641-6
See last pages of this volume for titles

Manufactured in the United States of America

Publisher's Note: The selections in this anthology were reprinted from the best available copies. In "A Third Supplementary Catalogue of the Plants of Kentucky" pages 436-440 appear as pages 336-340 and in "Instructions for the Gathering and Preservation of Plants for Herbaria," page 62 was omitted from all available copies. The texts are correct.

Library of Congress Cataloging in Publication Data

Short, Charles Wilkins, 1794-1863.
   Scientific publications of Charles Wilkins Short.

   (Biologists and their world)
   Bibliography: p.
   1. Botany—Collected works. 2. Botany—Kentucky—Collected works. I. Stuckey, Ronald L. II. Title. III. Series.
QK3.S56   1978   581   77-81125
ISBN 0-405-10721-8

3869868

INTRODUCTION

As a scientist, Dr. Charles Wilkins Short (1794-1863) is best known for his pioneering floristic studies of Kentucky and for his well-prepared, prolific plant collections, that he liberally distributed to botanists throughout the world. A quiet, calm, modest and dignified gentleman, he was a most industrious botanist and an effective promoter of botany in the United States through his teaching, writing, and correspondence with over 75 of the world's botanists.

Dr. Short was born in Greenfield, Woodford County, Kentucky, to Peyton Short, the son of a well-to-do Virginia planter. Dr. Short's mother was the eldest daughter of John Cleves Symmes, a Revolutionary War Colonel, later a congressman and judge, who was also a colonizer of vast areas of "military land" between the Miami Rivers in Ohio. Charles Wilkins Short's early education was completed at the Joshua Fry School, near Danville, Kentucky, and at the age of 13 he entered Transylvania University, where he remained four sessions (1807-1811) and graduated with honors. He studied medicine with his uncle, Dr. Frederick Ridgely, and then entered the University of Pennsylvania in 1813 and took his degree in medicine in 1815. While there he developed an interest in botany and was much influenced by Dr. Caspar Wistar, Abbe Jose Francisco Correa da Serra, and Dr. Benjamin Smith Barton. Upon graduation, Dr. Short was selected to filll the chair of Materia Medica and Medical Botany in Transylvania University, which he at first accepted, but soon declined before beginning his duties because he believed the newly founded medical department had little chance to succeed. He began a medical practice in Lexington in July of 1816, but that city was overcrowded with physicians. Unable to make a living at his profession, he moved in the spring of 1817 to Hopkinsville, in western Kentucky, where he practiced for eight years. During these early years of medical practice he found time to begin correspondence with several botanists which was instrumental in bringing him to the forefront of the development of botany in the midwest by the 1830's.

It was in 1825, shortly before Constantine Samuel Rafinesque left Transylvania University, that Dr. Short was again called to the chair of Materia Medica and Medical Botany in the Medical Department of Transylvania University, a position he now accepted, having previously declined twice. By this time, Transylvania University was under the presidency of an outstanding educational thinker and organizer, Dr. Horace Holly, and the Medical Department was greatly improved, being the second largest in the nation. While at Transylvania University, Dr. Short continued his practice as a physician, and during the first two years he devoted most of his time to preparing his lectures on *materia medica* and medical botany. These lectures were written out in full and were said to be read with a good voice and correct emphasis to his students. His style was described as chaste, concise, and classical, and his manner always grave and dignified.

By 1827, Dr. Short was actively studying the plants of the Lexington area in the field. During the decade to follow, he diligently surveyed the flora of Kentucky, with emphasis on preparing herbarium specimens, maintaining his voluminous correspondence with botanists throughout the world, and writing scientific papers. Dr. Short's major published writings were few, totalling only 30. These publications, appearing between the years 1828 and 1845, were on the flora of Kentucky, botanical nomenclature, botanical history, bibliography, biography, and public lectures to medical students. His publications were thorough, well-written, and certainly represented the largest amount of published knowledge on scientific botany of the western country. Most of these papers were published in *The Transylvania Journal of Medicine and the Associate Sciences*, which he and his colleague, Dr. John Esten Cooke, founded in 1828 and edited jointly for the next four years. Dr. Short's first major work was a "Prodromus" and a "Florulae Lexingtoniensis" published in 1828-1829. This work was a descriptive catalogue of the spring flora of the Lexington area. Although never completed, it is a unique item for it is the only local flora known to me that has the plants arranged according to the time of their flowering. Information provided about each plant included the scientific binomial, the common name, the Linnaean sexual classification name, the diagnostic generic and specific characters, and a lengthy paragraph of observations.

Among other botanical contributions were a "Catalogue of the Native Phaenogamous Plants, and Ferns of Kentucky" published in 1833, co-authored with his medical colleague, Dr. Robert Peter, and their field companion, Mr. Henry A. Griswold. Additions to the "Catalogue," descriptive notes, and descriptions of new species were published four times from 1834 to 1840. Other now classic papers were his "Instructions for the Gathering and Preservation of Plants for Herbaria" (1833), the first of its kind written in the western country, a "Bibliographica Botanica" (1835), the first bibliographic listing with comments or annotations on the major botanical works and floras of the United States, and "A Sketch of the Progress of Botany in Western America" (1836), the most thorough account by a resident botanist of the history of botanical exploration west of the Allegheny Mountains. His paper on the "Observations of the Botany of Illinois, . . ." gives vivid on-site descriptions of the autumn prairie flora when much of that landscape was yet virgin territory. He wrote three biographical sketches, one on Dr. Frederick Ridgely, his uncle under whom he first studied medicine, Hazekiah Hulbert Eaton, his first field companion with whom he planned to write a "Natural History of Kentucky," and Dr. Clarendon Peck, a former medical student. Three lectures to medical students were also published. In his "Introductory Address to a Course of Lectures on Materia Medica" (1833), Dr. Short pointed out the importance of the study of botany to the physician and showed its close relationship to the study of medicine.

The papers cited above, as well as four others, are reprinted here to bring together in one volume all of the principal writings of Dr. Short. These papers, mostly published in the *Transylvania Journal*, are difficult to obtain because few copies still exist, and those that do are mostly in medical libraries. Some of these libraries do not even have a complete set of the journal, and so the availability of his papers is even further reduced. As brought together here, Dr. Short's principal writings may now be read and studied as a unit to enhance our understanding of the flora of Kentucky in the 1830's and our knowledge of the field of medical botany in the frontier country.

With his literary ability, his broad knowledge of western botany, and considerable leisure at his disposal, one wonders why Dr. Short did not publish more. Unlike other leading botanists of the period, he failed to assemble his botanical research into a major publication. Ample evidence from his letters exists to show that he intended producing a major work on the "Flora of Kentucky," but it was never realized. Dr. Short was certainly capable of such a work for he was intelligent, a careful observer, and accurate in his statements. It has been suggested that his distaste for writing and publication, his timidity in placing his research before his contemporaries, the expenditure of his energy in writing out his lectures in full, and the voluminous number of letters he sent to relatives, friends, and scientists, doubtless took much of his time and energy. In latter years poor health must have been a factor in his lack of productivity.

As a professor in the medical schools, Dr. Short's reputation must have been high among his colleagues, for he served as Dean of the medical departments at Transylvania University from 1828 to 1837 and as Dean of the Louisville Medical Institute from 1838 to 1849. In these roles, he certainly was in a position to keep *materia medica* and scientific botany at the forefront of the medical curriculum. His retirement from teaching in 1849 coincided with the death of his uncle, William Short, who earlier in life was America's first appointed foreign diplomat when the United States government was organized under George Washington. Dr. Short inherited half of his uncle's estate, his share being $250,000, and retired to a country estate, Hayfield, located about five miles south of Louisville. Here he curtailed his writing, shrank from public life, worked in his garden and herbarium, financed botanical expeditions, and entertained friends and relatives. He died 14 years later.

As a summary of Dr. Short's botanical contributions, Professor Asa Gray of Harvard University, the foremost contemporary authority on American botany, probably summarized Short's botanical contribution best. At the time of Dr. Short's death, Gray wrote:

> He was a very industrious botanist, and an effectual promoter of our science in this country. His great usefulness in this field was mainly owing to the extent and the particular excellence of his personal collections, and to the generous profusion with which he distributed them far and wide among his fellow-laborers in this and other lands. He was the first in this country to prepare on an ample scale dried specimens of uniform and superlative excellence and beauty, and in lavish abundance for the purpose of supplying all who could use them . . . The vast improvement in the character of the dried specimens now generally made by our botanists may be mainly traced to the example and influence of Dr. Short.

In addition to the vital statistics that appear on Dr. Short's tombstone in Cave Hill Cemetery, Louisville, is this message:

> During a long period of his life, he devoted the riches of a well stored mind, to instruction in medical science, directed toward that branch, which was ever his favourite study, Botany.
>
> In all the relations of domestic life no one ever lived more faultless. To the circle of those who enjoyed his friendship he was ever true and faithful. To his God, he has rendered a good account of the talents committed to his keeping.

. . .

Dr. Short's botanical work is today documented by (1) the plant specimens of his own great herbarium that survive in the herbarium of the Academy of Natural Sciences of Philadelphia, (2) the letters he wrote to botanists and friends that are housed in many of the libraries of the world, principally those in the United States at the Filson Club, the American Philosophical Society, the Academy of Natural Sciences, the Library of Congress, and the Cincinnati Historical Society, and (3) the published papers and unpublished manuscripts about his life. Most of the papers known to this author are cited below. The reader will find those written by Ahlquist (1947), Davies (1945), Gross (1865), and Short and Richardson (1843 and 1879) to be the most complete and informative.

Ronald L. Stuckey
Associate Professor of Botany
The Ohio State University
Columbus, Ohio
October 1976

References

Ahlquist, Irving Frederick. 1947. Ohio Valley Culture as Reflected in the Short Family, 1700-1860. Ph.D. Dissertation, University of Illinois, Urbana. 344 pp.

Anonymous. 1866. Charles Wilkins Short, M.D. Proc. Am. Acad. Arts & Sci. 6:135-136.

Bayless, George Wood. 1866. Reminiscences of the Medical College: Being an introductory address delivered before the Medical Department of the University of Louisville. Courier Printing Co., Louisville. 50 pp.

Bowe, Charles, 1961. Rafinesque and Dr. Short. Filson Club Hist. Quart. 35: 28-32.

B[radford], T[homas] L[indley]. 1912. Charles Wilkins Short (1794-1863), pp. 370-371. In Howard A. Kelly. Cyclopedia of American Medical Biography Comprising the Lives of Eminent Deceased Physicians and Surgeons from 1610 to 1910. Vol. II. W. B. Saunders Company, Philadelphia & London. 545 pp.

Bradford, Thomas Lindley. 1920. Charles Wilkins Short (1794-1863), pp. 1048-1049. In Howard A. Kelly and Walter L. Burrage, eds. American Medical Biographies. The Norman Remington Company, Baltimore. 1320 pp.

Bradford, Thomas Lindley. 1928. Charles Wilkins Short (1794-1863), pp. 1107-1108. In Howard A. Kelly and Water L. Burrage, eds. Dictionary of American Medical Biography; Lives of Eminent Physicians of the United States and Canada, from the Earliest Times. D. Appleton and Company, New York. xxx + 1364 pp. Reprinted, Milford House Inc., Boston. 1971.

Coker, W. C. 1941. Letters from the collection of Dr. Charles Wilkins Short. J. Elisha Mitchell Sci. Soc. 57: 98-168.

Core, Earl L. 1970. Charles Wilkins Short (1794-1863), pp. 34-36. In The Botanical Exploration of the Southern Appalachians, pp. 1-65. In Perry C. Holt with the assistance of Robert A. Paterson. The Distributional History of the Biota of the Southern Appalachians Part II: Flora. Research Division Monograph 2. Virginia Polytechnic Institute and State University, Blacksburg. 414 pp.

Davies, P. Albert. 1945. Charles Wilkins Short, 1794-1863: Botanist and physician. Filson Club Hist. Quart. 19: 131-155, 208-249.

Davies, P. A. 1948. First Louisville Natural History Society. Kentucky Naturalist 3(1): 9-10.

Davies, P. Albert. 1949. An unpublished Rafinesque letter [to Charles Wilkins Short]. Filson Club Hist. Quart. 23: 199-201.

Davies, P. A. 1950. Botanical history of Jefferson County, Kentucky. Kentucky Naturalist 5(1): 3-8.

D[idlake], M[ary] L[eGrand]. 1930. Charles Wilkins Short, pp. 127-128. In Dumas Malone. Dictionary of American Biography. Sewell-Stevenson. Volume 17. Charles Scribner's Sons, New York. 636 pp. Reprinted, 1935, 1946, and 1964 (in volume 9, Part 1).

G[ray], A[sa]. 1863. Dr. Charles Wilkins Short. Am. J. Sci. 86: 130-139. Reprinted and repaged, Collins, Philadelphia, pp. 33-36. 1865. Reprinted,

Scientific Papers of Asa Gray Selected by Charles Sprague Sargent. Volume II. Essays; Biographical Sketches 1841-1886. Houghton, Mifflin and Company, Boston. pp. 312-314. 1889.

Gross, S. D. 1865. Obituary of Charles Wilkins Short, M.D. Proc. Am. Philos. Soc. 19: 171-186 + photograph. Reprinted and repaged, Collins, Philadelphia. pp. 5-31. 1865.

Horine, Emmet Field. 1961. Charles Wilkins Short, pp. 329-330. In Daniel Drake (1785-1852): Pioneer Physician of the Midwest. University of Pennsylvania Press, Philadelphia. 425 pp.

Kelly, Howard A. 1914. Charles Wilkins Short, pp. 129-135. In Some American Medical Botanists. D. Appleton and Company, New York. 216 pp. Reprinted. 1929. Reprinted, Milford House Inc., Boston. 1973.

Kibbe, Alice L. 1953. A Biography of Dr. Charles Wilkins Short (1794-1863), p. 453. In Afield with Plant Lovers and Collectors Botanical Correspondence of the Late Harry N. Patterson with the Great Botanical Collectors and Distributors of America from 1870-1919. Published by the Author, Carthage College, Illinois. 565 pp.

Miller, Henry. --?--. In Memoriam. The late Charles Wilkins Short, M.D. [Original publisher not known]. Reprinted and repaged, Collins, Philadelphia. pp. 37-40. 1865

Perkins, Samuel E., III. 1938. Letters by Rafinesque to Dr. Short in The Filson Club Archives. Filson Club Hist. Quart. 12: 200-239.

Peter, Robert. 1905. Doctor Charles Wilkins Short, pp. 78-82. In The History of the Medical department of Transylvania University. Filson Club Hist. Club Publ. No. 28. 193 pp.

Rothert, Otto A. 1933. Three letters by Dr. L. P. Yandell, 1838 [to Charles Wilkins Short]. Filson Club Hist. Quart. 7: 148-153.

Rothert, Otto A. 1934. A letter by J. Cleves Short, 1829 [to Charles Wilkins Short]. Filson Club Hist. Quart. 8: 128-129.

Short, C[harles] W[ilkins], and Mary Churchill Richardson. 1843 and 1879. A Chronological Record of the Families of Charles Wilkins Short and Mary Henry Churchill, compiled from various authentic sources, by C. W. Short, Louisville, Kentucky, January 1843 and continued by his daughter, Mary Churchill Richardson, Ivywood, Jefferson County, Kentucky, 1879. Typewritten Manuscript. 196 pp. Copy seen in the Medical Library, University of Louisville, Louisville, Kentucky.

Titley, Joan. 1964. Dr. Charles Wilkins Short and the medical journals: 1820-1831. Stechert-Hafner Book News 19(3): 29-31.

Wilson, James Grant, and John Fiske, eds. 1888. Charles Wilkins Short. p. 5. In Appletons Cyclopaedia of American Biography, Vol. V. Pickering-Sumter. D. Appleton and Company, New York. 752 pp.

CONTENTS

[Gross, S. D.]
[Biographical Sketch]: Obituary Notice of Charles Wilkins Short, M. D. (Reprinted from *Proceedings of the American Philosophical Society*, Vol. X), Philadelphia, 1869

Scientific Publications
Part I: Floristic and Medical Botany

Prodromus Florulae Lexingtoniensis, Secundum Florendi Aetatem Digestae (Proposal for a Descriptive Catalogue of the Phaenogamous Plants Indigenous to this Portion of Kentucky) (Reprinted from *The Transylvania Journal of Medicine and the Associate Sciences*, Vol. I), Lexington, Kentucky, 1828

Florula Lexingtoniensis, secundum Florendi Aetatem Digestae; Or a Descriptive Catalogue of the Phaenogamous Plants Indigenous to this Portion of Kentucky, Arranged in the Order of Their Periods of Flowering, Fasciculi I-IV [Parts I-IV] (Reprinted from *The Transylvania Journal of Medicine and the Associate Sciences*, Vols. I and II), Lexington, Kentucky, 1828 and 1829

Short, C[harles] W[ilkins] and H. Hulbert Eaton
Notices of Western Botany and Conchology (Reprinted from *The Transylvania Journal of Medicine and the Associate Sciences*, Vol. IV), Lexington, Kentucky, 1831

[Short, Charles Wilkins, Robert Peter and Henry A. Griswold] A Catalogue of the Native Phaenogamous Plants, and Ferns of Kentucky (Reprinted from *The Transylvania Journal of Medicine and the Associate Sciences*, Vol. VI), Lexington, Kentucky, 1833

Short, [Charles Wilkins] and [Robert] Peter
A Supplementary Catalogue of the Plants of Kentucky
(Reprinted from *The Transylvania Journal of Medicine and the Associate Sciences*, Vol. VII), Lexington, Kentucky, 1834

[Short, Charles Wilkins and Robert Peter]
A Second Supplementary Catalogue of the Plants of Kentucky (Reprinted from *The Transylvania Journal of Medicine and the Associate Sciences*, Vol. VIII), Lexington, Kentucky, 1835

A Third Supplementary Catalogue of the Plants of Kentucky (Reprinted from *The Transylvania Journal of Medicine and the Associate Sciences*, Vol. X), Lexington, Kentucky, 1837

A Fourth Supplementary Catalogue of the Plants of Kentucky (Reprinted from *The Western Journal of Medicine and Surgery*, Vol. II), Louisville, Kentucky, 1840

Review of William Darlington's *Flora Cestrica* (Reprinted from *The Transylvania Journal of Medicine and the Associate Sciences*, Vol. X), Lexington, Kentucky, 1837

On the Cultivation of Certain Medicinal Plants (Reprinted from *The Transylvania Journal of Medicine and the Associate Sciences*, Vol. II), Lexington, Kentucky, 1829

Observations on the Botany of Illinois, More Especially in Reference to the Autumnal Flora of the Prairies—in a Letter to Daniel Drake (Reprinted from *The Western Journal of Medicine and Surgery*, Vol. III), Louisville, Kentucky, 1845

Instructions for the Gathering and Preservation of Plants for Herbaria; in a Letter to a Young Botanist (Reprinted from *The Transylvania Journal of Medicine and the Associate Sciences*, Vol. VI), Lexington, Kentucky, 1833

Part II: Botanical Nomenclature, History and Bibliography

Remarks on the Nomenclature of Botany (Reprinted from *The Transylvania Journal of Medicine and the Associate Sciences*, Vol. VIII), Lexington, Kentucky, 1835

A Sketch of the Progress of Botany in Western America (Reprinted from *The Transylvania Journal of Medicine and the Associate Sciences*, Vol. IX), Lexington, Kentucky, 1836

Bibliographia Botanica. A Notice of Some of the More recent Works on American Botany (Reprinted from *The Transylvania Journal of Medicine and the Associate Sciences*, Vol. VIII), Lexington, Kentucky, 1835

Part III: Biographical Sketches

Biographical Notice of Dr. Frederick Ridgely, Late of Lexington, Kentucky (Reprinted from *The Transylvania Journal of Medicine and the Associate Sciences*, Vol. I), Lexington, Kentucky, 1828

A Biographical Memoir of H. Hulbert Eaton, A. M., Late Assistant Professor of Chemistry in the Medical Department of Transylvania University. (Delivered November 10th, as an Introductory Address to the Medical Class, at the Opening of the Session of 1832-3). Reprinted from *The Transylvania Journal of Medicine and the Associate Sciences*, Vol. V), Lexington, Kentucky, 1832

Obituary [of Clarendon Peck, aged 25 years]. (Reprinted from *The Transylvania Journal of Medicine and the Associate Sciences*, Vol. X), Lexington, Kentucky, 1837

Part IV: Public Lectures to Medical Students

A Valedictory Address Delivered in the Chapel of Transylvania University, to the Medical Graduates at the Commencement on the 12th of March, 1828 (Reprinted from *The Transylvania Journal of Medicine and the Associate Sciences*, Vol. I), Lexington, Kentucky, 1828

An Introductory Address to a Course of Lectures on Materia Medica (Reprinted from *The Transylvania Journal of Medicine and the Associate Sciences*, Vol. VI), Lexington, Kentucky, 1833

Duties of Medical Students During Attendance on Lectures; An Introductory Address, Delivered at the Opening of the Session of 1845-6, in the Medical Institute of Louisville, No.. 3d, 1845, Louisville, Kentucky, 1845

[BIOGRAPHICAL SKETCH]
OBITUARY NOTICE
OF CHARLES WILKINS SHORT, M. D.

[S. D. Gross]

OBITUARY NOTICE OF CHARLES WILKINS SHORT, M.D.

Dr. Short was born at Greenville, Woodford County, Kentucky, on the 6th of October, 1794. His father was Peyton Short, of Surry County, Virginia, whose mother, Elizabeth Skipwith, was the daughter of Sir William Skipwith, Baronet. His own mother was Mary Symmes, daughter of John Cleves Symmes, who removed from Long Island to Cincinnati, where, after having occupied various offices of trust and honor, he died in 1814. Dr. Short had, beside a brother and sister who both died in infancy, one brother, the late Judge John Cleves Short, and one sister, the wife of Dr. Benjamin Winslow Dudley, the eminent Kentucky surgeon. He had also several half brothers and sisters, his father having married a second time.

The early part of Dr. Short's life was marked by no event of particular importance. It was noted chiefly for his exemplary conduct and love of Nature, to the development of which the wild scenery of his native village was eminently conducive. With the pleasant memories of this much-loved home of his childhood his heart was filled to his dying day. It furnished the theme for youthful poems and the picture for his boyish pencil. Greenfield was for many years the country residence of his father, being a farm of several thousand acres, in one of the most beautiful and romantic regions of Kentucky, so distinguished for the variety and grandeur of its scenery. It was here, no doubt, that he first imbibed his love for the particular science which he afterwards cultivated with so much ardor and success, and which contributed so greatly not only to his happiness but his reputation.

His primary education was obtained at the school of Mr. Joshua Fry, a celebrated teacher, under whose training were reared some of the most distinguished divines, physicians, lawyers, and statesmen of Kentucky. It was, in fact, for a long time the only male seminary of any importance in that State. What proficiency young Short made in his studies under the instruction of this gentleman, my information does not enable me to state; that it was highly respectable may be inferred, not only from the character of his mind and his habits of industry, but from the fact that, immediately after quitting him, he was admitted into Transylvania University at Lexington, where he was graduated, with considerable honor, in 1810. He was one of the speakers on commencement day, and his address on the occasion was very warmly applauded both by the faculty and the public.

Soon after the event just referred to, young Short began the study of medicine under his uncle, Dr. Frederick Ridgely, a gentleman of considerable scientific attainment, and for many years one of the leading practitioners of Kentucky. In 1813 he repaired to Philadelphia, where he became a private pupil of Dr. Caspar Wistar, Professor of Anatomy in the University of Pennsylvania. He remained in the office of this distinguished teacher until he was graduated in the Medical Department of this institution in the spring of 1815. The thesis which he presented on the occasion was on the medicinal virtues of *Juniperus Sabina*, and was treated with marked ability. During his residence in Philadelphia he was a diligent and zealous pupil, and devoted much attention to the study of botany, a branch of science in which he was destined to become so conspicuous. A warm attachment sprung up during this period between the professor and the pupil, which continued until the former died in 1818, universally beloved and honored, with a reputation coextensive with our continent. That such should have been the case is not surprising when we consider the character of the two men. Wistar was an eminently amiable man, of the most engaging manners and of remarkable conversational powers; he was the idol of his classes, and probably the most popular teacher of his day in this country. His social position was of the highest order, and he was the founder of the parties which have since borne his name, and which have contributed so much to the elevation of the social character of Philadelphia. His fondness for young men was proverbial; he encouraged them in their studies and aided them with his counsel and even with his purse. The letters which young Short brought with him from eminent citizens of the West secured him at once the *entrée* to his house; they saw each other constantly, and when the young backwoodsman at length left Philadelphia, his greatest regret was at parting with his beloved preceptor and friend. As a proof of this attachment, I may mention that Dr. Wistar presented to his pupil a cherished case of eye instruments, the trusty companions of a long lifetime, which now, that his own eye was becoming dimmed with age, he hoped would be of service in restoring the sight of the blind in the hands of his promising young friend after his return to the wilds of Kentucky.

In November, 1815, Dr. Short was united in matrimony to Mary Henry Churchill, only child of Armistead and Jane Henry Churchill, the latter of whom, after the death of her husband, became the second wife of Mr. Peyton Short. This circumstance occurred while Charles W. Short, the subject of this sketch, and Mary H. Churchill were children, who were thus brought into the same family circle. Of this alliance, in every respect one of supreme happiness, six children survive, one son and five daughters, all of whom, excepting the youngest, are married, and in a prosperous condition.

Soon after his marriage he returned with his wife to Kentucky, travelling the entire distance in a spring wagon. The journey, although tedious and fatiguing, was replete with interest, on account of the beauty of the scenery along the route, and often formed the topic of pleasant reminiscences in after years. He now settled at Lexington, in his native State, but, not succeeding to his wishes, he shortly after removed to Hopkinsville, where he entered into partnership with Dr. Webber, and very soon obtained a large practice. It was while living here, in a wild, hilly, and romantic region of country, now highly cultivated and densely populated, that he devoted himself, with all the ardor of an enthusiast, to those botanical researches which formed the basis of his future reputation and the great source of his future happiness. No plant, or shrub, or tree escaped his notice. His daily rides through the country, rendered necessary by his practice, were invariably productive of some botanical trophies, which, carefully dried and preserved, thus assisted in laying the foundation of one of the richest and most valuable private herbariums ever collected in this or any other country. The researches in which he was thus so assiduously engaged soon brought him into favorable notice with scientific men, and served to establish for him a certain degree of reputation, apart from that of the mere practice of his profession, for which he seems never to have had any particular fondness.

In 1825 he was called to the chair of Materia Medica and Medical Botany in Transylvania University at Lexington, his former home. This school, then recently organized, was rapidly rising into distinction, and was destined eventually, though only for a short period, to occupy a very prominent position in the public eye. A wide field of glory and usefulness now lay before him, and he was not slow in availing himself of its advantages. Most of his associates in the school were men of mark and merit. Dr. Benjamin W. Dudley, his brother-in-law, the incumbent of the surgical chair, had already achieved a high reputation as a teacher and an operator; patients flocked to him from all parts of the Mississippi Valley, and in a short time he became the great lithotomist of America. His only rivals were Physick and Mott; but, owing to the great distance which separated him from them, they were so only in name. He was literally, for a number of years, "monarch of all he surveyed."

Dr. Charles Caldwell graced the chair of the Institutes of Medicine. A resident of Philadelphia, a man of great and varied talents, well read in and out of his profession, his fame had preceded him to Lexington; and it is but justice to say that he contributed most largely, by his writings and teachings, to build up and give temporary *éclat* to its medical school. His tongue and pen were never idle. A more majestic figure on the rostrum could hardly be imagined. Tall and erect in person, with a noble head and a piercing black eye, he was the *beau ideal* of an elegant, entertaining, and accomplished lecturer. He was eloquent, but too artificial, for he had cultivated elocution too much before the mirror.

Dr. Daniel Drake, afterwards so distinguished as a teacher and a writer, had only a few years before made his debut in public. Emphatically a self-made man, he possessed genius of a superior order, and successfully coped with his colleagues for the highest place in the school. Of all the medical teachers I have ever known he was, all things considered, one of the most able, captivating, and impressive. There was an earnestness, a fiery zeal about him in the lecture-room, which encircled his person, as it were, with a halo of glory. The great work which he has left behind him on the "Diseases of the Mississippi Valley," attests his industry and talents, and forms a monument to his memory as enduring as the vast region of country whose maladies he has so glowingly and faithfully portrayed.

Dr. Holley, a man of brilliant talents, elegant accomplishments, and superior literary attainments, was President of the University; and, although not immediately connected with the medical department, nevertheless exerted considerable influence on its destiny. Lexington, emphatically the garden spot of Kentucky, was at that time justly regarded as the "Athens of the West;" its University had high pretensions; it was the home of Henry Clay; its bar was famous throughout the land; and its women were noted for their personal charms and great accomplishments.

With such men as his compeers, Dr. Short had every inducement for exertion; and there is reason to believe that, quiet and unostentatious as he was, he exercised no ordinary influence in sustaining the reputation of the University. His heart and soul were thoroughly in the work. The school soon rose to an unprecedented degree of prosperity, which it steadily maintained until the dissolution of its great Faculty in 1837.

In 1828 he founded, along with his colleague, Dr. John Esten Cooke, the "Transylvania Journal of Medicine and the Associate Sciences." With this publication, which for a long time wielded an important influence in moulding the opinions and practice of the great body of physicians of the Southwest, he continued his connection until the close of the fourth volume, zealously laboring for its interests and those of Transylvania University, whose prosperity it was more particularly designed to promote. In this periodical is to be found nearly everything that Dr. Short ever contributed to the public press.

In 1837, the Medical Department of Transylvania University, after a period of eighteen years of extended usefulness and remarkable fame, experienced a violent convulsion, which shook it to its very centre. Dissatisfaction of a serious character had existed for several years among some of the Faculty in regard to the manner of conducting its affairs. The school had grown too large for the place where it was located; there was a great dearth of anatomical material, and clinical instruction was, in great measure, neglected on account of the absence of hospital facilities. Owing to these circumstances a part of the Faculty withdrew, and accepted chairs in the medical school at Louisville, whither Dr. Short soon followed, although the Trustees of the University, upon reorganizing the Faculty, had reappointed him to his former situation.

In the University of Louisville, then a young but destined soon to be a gigantic institution, Short had the same chair as the one he had just vacated at Lexington. Here he quietly and unostentatiously pursued "the even tenor of his way," devoting himself to botanical researches and literary studies, and zealously co-operating with his distinguished colleagues, of whom the great Drake was again one, in promoting the interests and prosperity of the school, which soon rose to an extraordinary height, students flocking to it from all sections of the Mississippi Valley, until its spacious halls were completely crowded. The number of its pupils in 1847 was upwards of 400. Such rapid success had never before been witnessed in any medical university on this continent.

Becoming tired of medical teaching, Dr. Short dissolved his connection with the Louisville school in 1849, and retired to Hayfield, a beautiful and charming residence five miles from the city. A more lovely spot than this could hardly be imagined. The dwelling, the former abode of a gentleman of taste and refinement, was an elegant mansion, with all the conveniencies of a city house. It was furnished in the best Kentucky style, and overlooked a rich lawn of almost perpetual verdure, such as might have charmed Calypso and her nymphs. It was surrounded by stately elm trees; close by was an immense spring of the coldest and most limpid water; the rear was skirted by a beautiful piece of woodland; and at one side was an ample garden, set out in shrubbery and plants, native and exotic, many of them set out by Dr. Short's own hands. The farm, comprising several hundred acres, was highly cultivated, and stocked with Southdown sheep and choice cattle. It was here, in the bosom of his family, that he spent the evening of his life, in the enjoyment of an elegant leisure, diversified by literary and scientific pursuits.

The country for miles around Hayfield is bewitchingly beautiful; it is thickly settled, and in a very high state of cultivation. The traveller, as he slowly winds his way along its public roads, is instinctively attracted by the magnificence of the landscape. The wildness of the natural scenery has given way to ample fields, intersected by elegant fences, and dotted with groves and dwellings, buried in shrubbery, or reposing under the foliage of widespread elms, oaks, and beeches. Here and there is a large mansion, or the neat New England cottage, the abode of wealth and elegant refinement; the whole forming a grand tableau, well calculated to warm the imagination and inspire the soul of a pastoral poet.

It had always been one of the cherished objects of his life to have a house in the country, such were his love of nature and his distaste of city excitement. Even during his residence at Louisville, where his winters were occupied with his college duties, his summers were devoted to the improvement of a pretty little place on the Ohio River, near North Bend, which he called "Fern Bank," from the fact that it abounded in plants of that name. Here with his family around him, in the neighborhood of the residence of a much-loved and only brother, his time was spent much more in accordance with his tastes than in the noise and bustle of the city.

His only patrimony, in early life, was a good name; but by untiring industry and economy he eventually accumulated a moderate but independent fortune, which was considerably augmented, in 1849, by the death of his uncle, William Short, Esq., of Philadelphia, of whose estate he was one of the principal heirs. To this uncle Dr. Short was greatly attached ; he made him not only frequent visits but maintained a constant correspondence with him, his letters, down to the time of his death, numbering upwards of five hundred. From a memorandum now before me it seems that he was a native of Virginia, having been born in Surry County in that State in 1759. "His life, public and private," records the tombstone erected to his memory at Laurel Hill Cemetery, "was distinguished by ability, probity and industry never questioned. He received from President Washington, with the unanimous approval of the Senate, the first appointment to public office conferred under the Constitution of the United States; and from President Jefferson, whose affectionate friendship he always largely possessed, proofs of similar confidence." Mr. Short lived for a considerable time in France, first as secretary to Mr. Jefferson, and afterwards as a private citizen. He was at Paris during the most eventful period in the history of France, and, indeed, of all Europe. As a citizen of Philadelphia, he occupied a prominent position, and enjoyed the confidence and esteem of a large circle of acquaintances and admiring friends.

His botanical researches brought Dr. Short in relation with many of the most distinguished scientific men of Europe and America. Prominent, among the former, were Sir William Hooker, director of the Royal Gardens at Kew, near London ; De Candolle, of France ; Joachim Steets, of Hamburg ; Professor C. F. Meisner, of Switzerland ; Uzrelli, of Italy ; Thomas Nuttall and Mr. Wilson, of England. With Sir William Hooker, whose death at the age of eighty was only recently recorded, he was in constant communication for upwards of twenty years, and a large volume of his letters is now in the possession of the family. This correspondence, begun as a purely professional one, soon ripened into the most intimate intercourse, which manifested itself in various acts of kindness and the interchange of little mementoes, always gratifying to scientific men.

His American correspondents were too numerous to be mentioned. Among the most valued and distinguished were Asa Gray, Torrey, Darlington, Bachman, Agassiz, Engelmann, Audubon, Meade, Carey, Curtis, Lapham, and Durand. Dr. Gray was a warm friend of Dr. Short, and soon after his death he published in Silliman's Journal, a beautiful and appropriate tribute to his memory.

He was a member of various scientific societies, both foreign and domestic. After his death, a number of diplomas were found among his papers, but so retiring was he in his disposition and habits, and so modest in his intercourse with the world, that no little difficulty was experienced in hunting up these honors, for which he seems to have cared very little.

"As a lecturer," says one who intimately knew him as a friend and colleague—Professor Henry Miller, of Louisville,—"his style was chaste, concise, and classical, and his manner always grave and dignified. His lectures were always carefully written, and read with a good voice and correct emphasis. He never made the least attempt at display, nor set a clap trap in all his life." His courteous deportment made him a favorite alike with his pupils and his colleagues, the latter of whom he served for a number of years, both at Lexington and Louisville, as Dean, an office of no little importance in a medical school. He hated controversy, and never engaged in any of the medical quarrels at one time so rife at these two places.

In stature Dr. Short was of medium height, well proportioned, with light hair and complexion, blue eyes, and an ample forehead. His features, when lighted up by a smile, were radiant with goodness and beneficence. In his manner he was graceful, calm, and dignified; so much so that one coming into his presence for the first time, might have supposed him to be haughty and ascetic; such, however, was not the case. A kinder heart never vibrated in a human breast. Naturally mild and amiable, he had all of a woman's gentleness, with a mind of inflexible firmness upon all questions of duty. Of a sensitive, diffident disposition, he rather shunned than courted society, and never appeared to greater advantage than in the bosom of his own family, or in the midst of a few select friends. As he advanced in life, he grew more serious, but never was morose or even cynical. The sanctity of his heart was never invaded by such a feeling. He had studied God and man too closely; had enjoyed too great a degree of happiness and prosperity to cherish such a sentiment, or to exhibit such a trait in his intercourse with the world. I have the testimony of one who knew him well and intimately that he never saw any person who enjoyed more heartily an agreeable anecdote, or an innocent and amusing story. All his impulses, in fact, were of the noblest and most generous nature. The poor never knocked at the door of his heart without a prompt response. His moral character was untarnished. No one ever dared to impugn his motives, or to call in question the purity of his acts. As has been well observed by one of his scientific friends, he had an uncompromising sense of justice, and a keen hatred of everything mean and unworthy. He was a model man; a model philosopher; a model Christian. As a husband and father, his character reached perfection as nearly as is, perhaps, possible. His family not only loved, but revered him. His children often accompanied him in his botanical excursions, and assisted him in drying and arranging his specimens. One of his daughters, in referring to these labors, assures me that many of the happiest recollections of her childhood are connected with these excursions. "To those," she continues, "who met my father as colleagues, or as mere acquaintances, but little was known of his character in domestic life; only those who were the recipients of his deep affection, as wife and children, can form even a faint idea of his goodness. His home was truly his heaven on earth."

In his relation to those who were placed by Providence under his charge as servants, he was truly "the friend in need;" he treated them with real parental kindness, and spared no pains to improve their moral and religious character. Soon after he moved to Hayfield, three old negroes, once the property of his father, sought his care and protection, in order that they might die under his hospitable roof. Two of them had been free for thirty years.

In regard to his religious views, Dr. Short connected himself early in life with the Presbyterian Church, of which he remained a faithful and consistent member up to the time of his death. He made no ostentatious parade of his piety. The same retiring disposition, the same modesty and gentle demeanor that characterized his outer-life, attended him here. Without entering into details, it may be stated that there is every reason to believe that he rendered to his God a good account of the talents committed to his keeping. His very profession, as a practical botanist, brought him in daily communion with the Creator. A naturalist can neither be a skeptic nor a bad man. He finds a sermon in every plant, in every stone, in every living thing. The direct tendency of the study of the sciences, of botany in particular, is to refine and humanize our tastes, and to inspire us with love and reverence for the Deity. "Consider the lilies of the field how they grow; they toil not, neither do they spin; and yet I say unto you that Solomon in all his glory was not arrayed like one of these." Botany is emphatically the poetry of the sciences, or, as has been beautifully remarked by one of its most able and successful cultivators, "the amiable science."

When Dr. Short left the University of Louisville, the Board of Trustees, at once, as a just tribute to his long and faithful services, elected him Emeritus Professor of Materia Medica and Medical Botany; while his colleagues united in a complimentary letter, expressive of their warm personal regard, and of their hope that he might find in his retirement the ease and comfort for which he had so long sighed.

He was now in the fifty-fifth year of his age, with all his faculties, mental and corporeal, in full vigor. It was believed that one of the objects he had in view in quitting the school was to write a work on the botany of the Southwestern States, for which he had long been engaged in collecting material. His herbarium was one of the most extensive and complete in the country, and few, if any, were so thoroughly and intimately acquainted with its flora. With descriptive powers of a high order, with leisure at once elegant and refined, with a scholarly mind and independent wealth, he was capable of producing a work of the most profound interest and value, replete in originality and calculated to reflect vast credit, not only upon himself as an able and finished botanist, but upon the scientific character of the nation. He might, in a word, have effected for his favorite science what Wilson and Audubon so happily effected for ornithology. But, strange to say, he never accomplished his purpose. He seemed to be afraid to enter upon the task. Writing was distasteful to him, and his days and nights passed without yielding any scientific fruits. His vast collection of dried specimens, one of the richest of the kind in the world, is now in the possession of the Academy of Natural Sciences of Philadelphia; and other hands than his will, doubtless, ultimately delineate and describe it. It was originally bequeathed to the Smithsonian Institution at Washington, but as there was no suitable apartment for its preservation, it was fortunately sent to this city, whose scientific men cannot fail to appreciate its value and importance, and to render it ultimately available to the permanent fame of its author.

Most of Dr. Short's time during his residence at Hayfield, was spent in his herbarium, a model of elegance and neatness. It was, in fact, his daily study, absorbing nearly all his attention, especially in the winter. Here, year after year, he prepared, arranged and labelled his specimens, receiving and sending collections to all parts of the civilized globe, mainly through the hands of European botanists, and they through their colonies in more remote regions. In this labor, one of love and almost of necessity to him, he was often assisted by his daughters, many of whose happiest moments were thus spent in his presence, under circumstances of the most gratifying and delightful nature. The labels used upon his specimens were generally printed by their own hands by means of a small homemade press.

In summer his garden afforded him great delight in the planting and propagation of various plants and trees, which he often watched with the most tender care and the greatest interest. Neither Wilson nor Audubon ever watched a bird with more solicitude than he his flowers. His garden was spread over several acres, and few persons visited Hayfield without an introduction to it. For the more commonplace routine of his farm he had little or no taste, although it was one of the most magnificent in Kentucky. A general superintendence was all the attention he bestowed upon it.

Thus were his latter days passed—in the garden in summer, in the herbarium in winter—until about two years before his death; when he was seized with great debility and ennui, and seemed to have lost, in a great degree, his interest in things around him. His last illness was pneumonia, which soon assumed a typhoid form, and terminated his valuable life on the 7th of March, 1863, in the sixty-ninth year of his age. He sank away so quietly and calmly that the friends who watched him scarcely knew when the spirit fled. His remains repose in Cave Hill Cemetery, near Louisville.

The name of Dr. Short is commemorated by a number of plants, a list of which has been kindly furnished me by Mr. Durand, of this city, himself an able and accomplished botanist.

1st. *Genus Shortia*, founded by Professor Asa Gray, on a plant of the *Pyrola* family, discovered by Michaux on the mountains of North Carolina.

2d. A cruciferous plant, *Vesicaria Shortii*, described by Professor Torrey, and discovered by Dr. Short on the banks of Elkhorn Creek, Lexington, Kentucky.

3d. A leguminous plant, *Phaca Shortiana* of Nuttall, found in Missouri.

4th. *Aster Shortii*, so named by Boott, growing in Ohio, Wisconsin, and other regions.

5th. *Solidago Shortii*, of Torrey and Gray, discovered at the Falls of the Ohio.

6th. *Carex Shortiana* of Dewey, extending from Southern Pennsylvania beyond Illinois.

It will thus be seen that five eminent botanists have paid a just tribute to one whom they honored as an able and indefatigable laborer in the same field of science which they themselves have so earnestly and successfully cultivated. A stronger proof than this of the high appreciation and affectionate regard in which Dr. Short was held by them, could not be afforded. They seemed to have vied with each other to gratify him during his lifetime, and to perpetuate his name and fame after his death. Such acts are a beautiful reflection of the purity and unselfishness of the soul of science.

His love for his favorite science was so great, his desire for a diffusion of its knowledge so ardent, that he gave away not only all that he could spare from his own magnificent herbarium, but was a constant subscriber to all the North American collections within his reach. He planned and effectually aided several distant and difficult botanical explorations; and he purchased, at a liberal price, the rich herbarium of Berlandier, the fruit of extensive researches in Texas and Mexico.

He had a large and select library, containing about 3000 volumes, one-fourth of which were rare and costly botanical works, of which he was very fond. He possessed a fine literary taste, and always perused the choicest books. He had, however, a higher opinion of the authors of the past than those of the present generation, esteeming Fielding and Sir Walter Scott as far superior to the moderns. The latter was his great favorite; he had the best editions of his works, and a volume of them was always to be found upon his table. Several magnificent engravings of Sir Walter hung about the house, and he was very familiar with his life and character as drawn by Lockhart. Notwithstanding his love of classical and scientific knowledge, he was very fond of mechanical pursuits, and often amused himself in binding his loose papers into volumes, constructing the wooden cases for his plants, and making various little alterations and repairs about the place.

The writings of Dr. Short are extremely limited. If collected in book-form they would hardly fill a duodecimo volume of three hundred pages. They relate, for the most part, to botanical topics, and consist principally of articles contributed to the "Transylvania Journal of Medicine," of which, as already stated, he was for some time an editor. They all evince the accuracy and good taste which he carried into everything he attempted. In 1826, soon after his appointment to the chair of Materia Medica in Transylvania University, he commenced, in that journal, the publication of a series of papers designed to illustrate the nature of the vegetable productions of the neighborhood of Lexington and the circumjacent parts of Kentucky. He became particularly impressed with the want of such a guide while engaged, during the previous summer, in delivering, to a small class of students, a course of lectures on botany. His object was to furnish a complete local flora, similar in principle to that of Dr. Darlington, of the plants of West Chester, Pennsylvania. The only two systematic treatises on American botany then extant were those of the elder Michaux and of Pursh, the former published at Paris in 1803, the latter at London in 1814. The works of Bigelow, Barton, and Darlington, issued at a later period, were of a purely local character, and could therefore be of no special service to Western pupils. The papers thus commenced were continued until 1845.

The next article from his pen was one on the "Cultivation of certain Medicinal Plants," in which he drew the attention of the profession to the importance of cultivating various substances of the materia medica, such, for example, as digitalis, senna, poppy, and castor oil, with a view of securing a more reliable supply of drugs. The subject had engaged much of his reflection, and he expressed great confidence in our ability to furnish these and other articles of superior quality.

"Notices of Western Botany and Conchology,"—a paper jointly published by himself and Mr. H. Halbert Eaton—appeared in 1830, in the fourth volume of the Transylvania Journal. They comprise a brief account of the plants found between Lexington and the Ohio River, a distance of about eighty miles, traversed by the explorers for the most part on foot. As the season was unusually dry, an excellent opportunity was afforded them of examining the shells of this celebrated stream, and also of the contiguous portions of the Great Miami River. Hardly two years had elapsed from the time of this agreeable and instructive ramble when Dr. Short was called upon to mourn the death of his associate, a man of extraordinary promise as a naturalist, and universally beloved and esteemed for his amiable and social qualities. In an address, delivered at the opening of the session of the Transylvania University in 1832, Dr. Short pronounced a feeling and eloquent eulogy upon his life and character. Mr. Eaton was quite young at the time of his death. His zeal in the pursuit of science had early lighted the fire which consumed him. "Science' self destroyed her favorite son."

Soon after this he published an elaborate paper, entitled "Instructions for the Gathering and Preservation of Plants in Herbaria," in which he depicts, in glowing terms and at full length, the manual labor of a botanist in forming his collection, and in arranging and labelling his specimens. Appearing, as it did, at a period when very little was known upon those subjects in this country, it must have been of great service to the young men engaged in this pursuit, so delightful and invigorating alike to mind and body. What student of Nature is there that cannot appreciate the feeling so eloquently expressed by the great and good Elliott, one who himself so often worshipped at her shrine, in the following sentence: "The study of natural history," says he, "has been for many years the occupation of my leisure moments; it is a merited tribute to say that it has lightened for me many a heavy and smoothed many a rugged hour; that, beguiled by its charms, I have found no road solitary, rough or difficult, no journey tedious, no country desolate or barren. In solitude never solitary, in a desert never without employment, I have found it a relief from the languor of idleness, the pressure of business, and the unavoidable calamities of life."

In 1836 he contributed an article on Botanical Bibliography, comprising a notice of some of the more recent treatises on American botany. When this paper was published upwards of twenty years had elapsed since he had entered upon his favorite study with hardly any works to guide him. Now he was able to refer the young votary to the admirable productions of Torrey, Drummond, Hooker, Beck, Gray, and others; men who, like himself, have accomplished so much in diffusing a taste for the cultivation of this "amiable science," and whose names will be forever honorably associated with the progress of natural history in the United States.

The Bibliographia Botanica was speedily followed by "A Second Supplementary Catalogue of the Plants of Kentucky," a paper based upon his botanical explorations of that State in 1835, and embracing an account of nearly two hundred species added to the number previously described by him. A considerable number of these plants had either been unknown or had never been introduced into any of the systematic treatises on American botany.

Then followed a "Sketch of the Progress of Botany in Western America," a short but most instructive article, affording a full account of the improvements in our botanical knowledge since the commencement of the present century. The interest of the article is greatly enhanced by the fact that it is interspersed with brief sketches of the lives and services of our most distinguished botanists. Soon after this appeared his "Third Supplementary Catalogue of the Plants of Kentucky," comprising a brief description of the plants observed by him since the publication of his former contributions to the subject.

In 1845 he wrote a paper, entitled "Observations on the Botany of Illinois." It was addressed, in the form of a letter, to one of his colleagues, Dr. Drake, and was published in the "Western Journal of Medicine and Surgery," edited by that distinguished teacher and philosopher. It was, if I do not err, his last contribution to a medical periodical,—probably the last he ever composed. It was written with special reference to the autumnal flora of the prairies. In the journey which he undertook for the purpose, and which was performed in the latter part of summer, Dr. Short was accompanied by his brother and several intimate friends, on account of the interest they took in the objects of the tour. He travelled in a light covered wagon, purposely constructed for the accommodation of an extensive collection, and he was constantly on the lookout for everything of interest. He passed over a distance of nearly four hundred miles, including the best portion of the State of Illinois, and returned, late in the season, laden with botanical treasures. The emotions he experienced on beholding, for the first time, a large prairie, is thus graphically described : " On reaching the centre of one of these immense natural meadows, the view presented to the eye of a novice in such scenery is one of the most pleasing sort. But beautiful, imposing, and grand as is this spectacle, I must own that, in a botanical point of view, I was disappointed ! The flora of the prairies—the theme of so much admiration to those who view them with an ordinary eye—does not, when closely examined by the botanist, present that deep interest and attraction which he has been led to expect. The leading feature is rather the unbounded profusion with which a few species occur in certain localities than the mixed variety of many different species occurring everywhere." Certain plants seemed to monopolize, if such an expression be allowable, certain districts, extending, perhaps, over thousands of acres, and exhibiting the appearance of a vast flowering garden, of almost every shade of color, from the purest white to the deepest yellow, red, or purple. What particularly struck him was the remarkable absence of ferns, and the astonishing paucity of mosses, in these prairies. Of the former he did not meet with a single specimen of any species of the extensive tribe in the more open meadows,—a circumstance evidently due, as he supposed, to the want of shade and moisture in which most of these plants so much delight.

The above catalogue comprises, so far as I know, all, or nearly all, that Dr. Short ever wrote upon botany. His other writings consisted mainly, if not wholly, of medical cases and college addresses.

In 1830, he communicated to the Transylvania Journal of Medicine the particulars of a case, then considered as very curious, of spontaneous combustion of the human body. The subject was a female, of intemperate habits, upwards of sixty-five years of age. Without fully indorsing the idea of the possibility of such an occurrence, he expressed the opinion that it was an example of a more general destruction of the human body by caloric than could easily be explained upon ordinary principles, or the amount of combustible material present on the occasion. The whole question relative to this subject is still an open one.

A case of paralysis of the kidneys occurs in the third volume of the Journal. At the time this case was published only a few examples of this singular disease, described by Dr. John Mason Good, the celebrated author of the "Book of Nature," and of an erudite treatise on Medicine, under the name of *paruria inops*, had been recorded. The late Dr. George Hayward, of Boston, was the first to call attention to it in this country. An instance of it had previously been published by Sir Henry Halford, physician to George IV.

Another case of disease, deserving of brief mention, was one of polyp of the face, successfully treated by tartar emetic. The cure seems to have been perfect; for the woman, when last seen, three years afterwards, was entirely well. The tumor, apparently seated in the antrum, involved the upper jaw, and had assumed quite a threatening aspect when the patient was put under treatment, consisting of the internal use of a weak solution of tartrate of antimony and potassa, steadily persisted in for six months.

In 1824, Dr. Short had the misfortune to lose his venerated preceptor and early friend, Dr. Frederick Ridgely, of Lexington, Kentucky, and soon after this event he published a beautiful and well-merited eulogy upon his life and character. A native of Maryland, from which he had early emigrated to the West, Ridgely had been a surgeon in the Continental army, and for more than thirty years an eminent practitioner at Lexington. He was present at a number of the battles of the Revolution, possessed uncommon professional skill, had a well-cultivated mind and the most agreeable manners, and was especially noted for his charitableness to the needy and his unrequited services to the poor. Many of the most distinguished physicians of Kentucky, in his day, were his private pupils. Dr. Short was not only warmly attached to him, but loved him with filial affection.

In 1835, he published "A Brief Historical Sketch of the Origin and Progress of Cholera Asphyxia," based upon information mainly derived, as he himself states, from accounts of this disease in professed treatises and the reports of physicians and boards of health in various parts of the world. He traces the march of this frightful distemper from its first appearance in the Delta of the Ganges in 1817, to its irruption in June, 1833, at Lexington, whose population it completely decimated, carrying off more than six hundred persons in the space of a few weeks, in a city, which, up to that time, was regarded as so salubrious as to induce the belief in the minds of its most enlightened physicians that an outbreak of the epidemic would be a matter of impossibility.

SCIENTIFIC PUBLICATIONS

PART I

FLORISTIC AND MEDICAL BOTANY

PRODROMUS FLORULAE LEXINGTONIENSIS, SECUNDUM FLORENDI AETATEM DIGESTAE

ART. IV.—*Prodromus Florulæ Lexingtoniensis, secundum florendi ætatem digestæ.* By CHARLES WILKINS SHORT M. D. Professor of Materia Medica and Medical Botany in Transylvania University.

IT is proposed in the next and several succeeding numbers of this Journal, to give some account of the vegetable productions of the neighbourhood of Lexington and the circumjacent parts of Kentucky. The want of some such manual of practical Botany was much felt by the writer, whilst delivering a course of lectures during the last summer, to a small class of resident pupils, in the medical department of this school.

For, whilst *elementary* treatises on Botany are already numerous and daily multiplying, *systematic* works are comparatively rare; and as yet no local Flora of this section of country has been published. The Flora Boreali-Americana of the elder Michaux,[1] is so exceedingly scarce that I know of but one copy in the Western States; nor is Pursh's Flora Americæ Septentrionalis,[2] much more frequently met with. These, until very lately, were the only two standard works on American

---

[1] Published in Paris in 1803. [2] London 1814,

Botany, and although the excellent production of Mr. Elliott [1] has gone very far towards supplying the want of the two former, yet it does not altogether suit the Flora of this latitude. Moreover, works of this comprehensive kind are not so well suited to the capacity of beginners in the study, who, unaccustomed to the nice discriminations which distinguish one genus of plants from another, or the yet more minute shades of difference between the individual species, are confused and lost amidst the multiplicity of each which they meet with. "The Genera of North American Plants" by Mr. Nuttall, although invaluable to the proficient in the science and to the general botanist, is liable to the same objections for the mere tyro in the study.

It is true that in the Eastern States, many very cheap and good compendiums of systematic Botany have recently been published; as those of Drs. Bigelow, Barton, Darlington and Torrey. Of these the three first, however, are purely local in their character, being confined to an account of the indigenous productions found in the vicinities of Boston, Philadelphia and West Chester, Pennsylvania, and consequently are not suited to the investigation of those peculiar to this locality; whilst the last,[2] on account of its comprehensiveness, is liable to the same inconveniences attending the works of Michaux, Pursh and Nuttall.

To remedy in some degree these different objections to the otherwise excellent works just mentioned—works which no American Botanist should be without, is the object of the contemplated undertaking; which, at the same time that it will throw together, within a small compass, all, or the greater number of the plants of this neighbourhood, will do so without connecting them with associate genera and kindred species found in other parts of America. By this means, it is hoped that amateurs in the science throughout the Western country, but more especially the students of Botany in this institution, will

---

[1] A sketch of the Botany of South Carolina and Georgia in 2 vols. 8vo. by Stephen Elliott.—Charleston, 1821-24.

[2] Flora of the Northern and Middle States, by Dr. John Torrey of New York.

be facilitated in their acquirement of a practical knowledge of plants, by having their attention directed to a fewer number; and be enabled the more easily to identify and name the individuals, when met with in their excursions around this town; while distant Botanists may form, from the sketch here given, some general idea of the local Flora of this part of Western America.

It is well known that the greatest difficulty which presents itself to the Botanical student, at the onset of his inquiries, is that of the *nomenclature* of the science; more especially when he endeavours, by reference to books, to ascertain the systematic name of any particular plant before him. For although, from his previous knowledge of the elements of the science, he may be at no loss, by a mere inspection of the flower, in saying to which *class* and *order* in the Linnæan system it belongs, yet he must refer to systematic writings to discover its *genus*; and if, from some obvious and well defined character, he should be so fortunate as to ascertain its generic title, still a farther difficulty awaits him in fixing upon the *precise species* it may be: and if the genus should happen to be an extensive one, embracing a great number of species, his labour will be proportionably increased, before he arrives at a knowledge of the name of his plant.

In consequence of these difficulties attending the nomenclature of the science, all Botanists have regarded it, as a remarkable epoch in the history of their studies, when, unaided by the helping hand of a preceptor, they have first discovered the proper name of a plant, before unknown to them. The elder Barton,[1] whose name justly stands at the head of American Philosophical Botanists, has frequently dwelt, with peculiar delight, on his first achievement of this object; and I shall never forget the ecstacy with which, after wading through the voluminous class Pentandria, in the "species Plantarum" of Linnæus, I was enabled with certainty to designate an inter-

---

[1] Benjamin Smith Barton, M. D. late Professor of the Institutes and Practice of Physic, of Clinical Practice and Botany in the University of Pennsylvania.

esting little plant, the object of my search, to be the *Claytonia Virginica.*

It is in this manner then, that local Floras are especially useful to the student of Botany, in facilitating his acquaintance with the vegetable productions more immediately around him. In treatises of this kind, descriptive histories are given of those plants only which are found growing in particular districts of country, separate and apart from those, however nearly related to them, which are met with in other parts of the same country, or are found throughout the world. Thus in the "Florula Bostoniensis" of Bigelow, there are described *seven* species of the genus viola; in the work of Pursh, we find *twenty-two* species enumerated, as growing in different parts of North America; whilst in the latest and most comprehensive systems of general Botany, there are designated *seventy-eight* species of this generic family, now known in different parts of the world, and the number is still constantly increasing, as heretofore unexplored quarters of the globe are visited by naturalists. So comprehensive, indeed, is this humble genus, that Sir James Edward Smith does not hesitate to say, " that a full scientific botanical essay on Viola, might display as much skill and learning, and be made subservient to as much philosophical illustration of Botany, as any monographical subject that could be chosen." [1] It is then plainly apparent, that the Boston student would be enabled to ascertain and identify any one, or all the violets growing in the neighborhood of that place, by reference to the work of Dr. Bigelow, with far more readiness and certainty, than if he were to consult the extensive Flora of Pursh, or the yet more general systems last mentioned—the comparative difficulty in the latter case being as seventy-eight to seven. So with any other individual plant, and so with the whole Flora of any country.

For the purpose of aiding the student still farther in his first acquaintance with the scientific nomenclature of plants, some peculiarity in the arrangement of the subjects of his investigation, as well as in the description of each one, will be found in the proposed publication.

---

[1] Rees' Cyclopedia, vol. 28—article, Viola.

In the first place it is intended to arrange the plants described in the Florula Lexingtoniensis, neither according to the artificial system of Linnæus, nor the natural method of Jussieu; but in the *order of their seasons of flowering*, constituting it thus properly a Calendar of Flora. This disposition may be objected to by some, as being both unnatural and unscientific; since by following it, those plants most nearly allied botanically, may be widely separated: and even two species of the same genus, one of which may happen to bloom in March and the other in November, will necessarily be placed at the opposite extremes of the catalogue. The inconvenience is seen and the objection granted, but they are both willingly incurred for the purpose of promoting the object more immediately in view—that of facilitating an acquaintance with the science of Botany, by enabling its student in this institution to become familiar with its technicalities, in the easiest and shortest manner possible, and practically conversant with the vegetable productions of this neighbourhood, by offering him descriptions of the plants in the same order in which they are presented to him by the hand of nature. The advantages gained by this arrangement in acquiring the names of plants will, I hope, appear from a single example. The class Pentandria, the fifth of Linnæus, being by far the most comprehensive of the whole system, the species ranged under it must necessarily be numerous even in the most limited Flora, and in proportion to the number of descriptions which he has to examine, is it the more difficult for the Botanist to identify any particular one with the specimen before him; hence I have known many students, by no means deficient either in patient research, or the "ardor botanicus," to throw away a pentandrous plant, in utter despair of ever being able to distinguish it from among its numerous classmates. But if the individuals of this extensive tribe are separated, and present themselves one by one in the order of their inflorescence, the difficulty of encountering and naming them will be at once abridged. In farther evidence of the advantages of the plan proposed, I may observe, that even the *umbelliferous* subdivision of the 5th class is itself so extensive, and the individuals composing it, are characterised by such nice shades of distinction as to perplex even the veteran proficient in the study. The task must then be a hopeless one for an inexperienced novice; but if he finds amongst the snows of March one solitary species of the pentandrous class, and discovers it to be umbelliferous, and, on consulting his vademecum, he finds, at the beginning of the list, one only individual of the kind described under the name of *Erigenia bulbosa*, he has no hesitation in saying that this is the plant in question. In this manner are the vernal species easily distinguished from those which bloom in mid-summer, and these again from the autumnal.

In the next place, will be given the *derivation* of each *generic* name as the genera occur, and the fact will be stated when the name is gratuitous or its derivation fanciful, obscure, or unknown. It has been objected to the science of Botany, that its technical appellations, both in its elementary and systematic departments, are unmeaning, harsh and arbitrary, couched in hard latinity or yet more uncouth derivatives from Greek. To the language of the science in its elementary, anatomical or physiological branches, the present essay has no reference; a defence of these being more properly the province of the lecturer or writer on its elementary principles; but of the systematic names applied to individual plants, it is but fair to state, that this nomenclature, if not equally concise and explicit with that of modern chemistry, is much more so than the chemical vocabulary of the last century, and is as definite and intelligible to the novice as the language of anatomy, at this time, in describing the various muscles and other component parts of the human body; and yet no body objects to these anatomical names.

By giving, then, a few words of explanation in regard to the title of each genus, we hope in some measure to do away this objection to the science, and, at the same time, to impress more deeply these names upon the mind of the student. Thus the title given to a very beautiful and extensive genus of North American plants, some of which are medicinal, is *Asclepias;* which to the tyro might seem at first sight altogether unmeaning or arbitrary; but when he is informed that it is derived from

Æsculapius, the propriety of the dedication is at once seen, and is more likely to be remembered: and so with the most of those generic denominations obtained from proper names. Still more appropriate and intelligible are those afforded by some conspicuous property or character in the plants themselves, as in the Latin derivatives *Convolvulus*, *Sanguinaria*, *Lactuca*, *Sempervivum*, *Trifolium*, &c. or those of Greek extraction, as *Epidendrum*, *Hydrophyllum*, *Helianthus*, *Padophyllum*, *Cardiospermum*, *Dracocephalon*, *Polygala*, &c.

Thirdly.—The *class* and *order* of the genus in the Linnæan system will next be given; but as this treatise presupposes an acquaintance with the elements of Botany, or at least with the principles of the sexual system of that naturalist, no explanation of his system will be here attempted.

Fourthly.—The *description of the genus* will follow; but, as the arrangement proposed will necessarily lead to a separation of the different species of the same genus, to avoid repetition, the generic character will be given before the *first species* of that genus; and the genera and species being both numbered, the character of the former can easily be referred to, when any subsequent species present themselves.

Fifthly.—Next will follow some *particular species* of the genus under consideration, but as the different species of the same genus often bloom at very different seasons of the year, they will be met with in different parts of the Florula, according to the periods of their efflorescence. The distinctive names given to these different species are, for the most part, so characteristic, that their meaning is at once apparent, and requires no explanation; as Asclepias *tuberosa*, Lactuca *virosa*, Helianthus *annuus*, Trifolium *repens*, &c. Where, however, the sense of these specific appellations is more obscure, it will be explained.

Sixthly.—Then will be given, in as few words as are consistent with perspicuity, a *description of the species*, adding some of the more common synonyms by which the same plant may have been described in different books.

Seventhly, and in conclusion, some *general observations* will be made on the individual under review, noting any striking peculiarity, when such is offered, by which it may be at once distinguished from other plants, or from other species of the same genus—the particular locality in which it may be found—the exact period of its being first in general bloom—the duration of its florescence—the ordinary time of ripening its seed or fruit, and finally its application to œconomical, dietetic, or medicinal purposes.

It is by no means intended that this sketch shall embrace a complete Flora of the Lexington country; such an undertaking would very far exceed the limits which could be allowed it, in even four numbers of this Journal. The whole design of the proposed publication, is to aid the advances of the novice in the science, by presenting him with a manual or horn-book in Botany, which will point out to him in the clearest manner possible, those plants which are more commonly met with in excursions of a few miles around this place; and of these, those only will be described, which are more likely to obtrude themselves upon the notice of the observer. Hence many of our trees, whose blossoms are obscure, together with the greater number of the gramineous plants, and all the cryptogamous productions, will be excluded.

Such being the plan, and these the objects in view, it would be deemed superfluous to ask the indulgence of the scientific and minute Botanist for the numerous imperfections and omissions which will doubtless be detected in the ensuing numbers. It will be the groundwork merely—the bare outline of the natural history of this section of country, in one of its most interesting departments. At some future day, the work may assume a more imposing character, when the humble florula becomes, by farther observations and additional labour, converted into the more comprehensive Flora. In its forth-coming guise, as repeatedly observed, it is merely intended that *indocti discant*:—the *ament meminisse periti*, must be reserved for its future form.

FLORULA LEXINGTONIENSIS,
SECUNDUM FLORENDI AETATEM DIGESTAE;
OR A DESCRIPTIVE CATALOGUE OF THE PHAENOGAMOUS PLANTS INDIGENOUS TO THIS PORTION OF KENTUCKY, ARRANGED IN THE ORDER OF THEIR PERIODS OF FLOWERING

FASCICULI I-IV

ART. X.—*Florula Lexingtoniensis, secundum florendi ætatem digesta;* or a descriptive Catalogue of the Phænogamous plants indigenous to this portion of Kentucky; arranged in the order of their periods of flowering. By CHARLES WILKINS SHORT, M. D. Professor of Materia Medica and Medical Botany in Transylvania University.

FASCICULUS I.
For February, March and part of April.

1. GENUS.   ULMUS.   L.   (*Elm.*)

(*Derivation*—an old Latin name of obscure Etymology.)

Class 5th. *PENTANDRIA*—Order, *DIGYNIA.*

Generic Character. Calyx campanulate, 4 or 5—cleft. *Fruit* a *Samara,* compressed, encompassed by a membranaceous, alated border. *Stamina* varying from 4 to 8.—*Nuttall.*

Species 1st.—ULMUS AMERICANA.   *White Elm.*
Specific Character. Branches recurved, smooth; *Leaves* unequal at base, serratures hooked, acuminate; *flowers* pedicillate; *fruit* fimbriate.

Observations. A forest tree which is very generally met with throughout the United States, from New England to Carolina; but perhaps in this latitude, or in the more immediate vicinity of the Ohio river, it attains its greatest perfection. The Elm is particularly interesting from the circumstance of its being the earliest flowering tree in this country. In ordinary seasons its blossoms appear towards the middle or latter part of February, and on some occasions as early as the first of that month. The Elms in this neighbourhood are the favourite habitations of the missletoe, (*Viscum verticillatum*) whose clusters are so densely interposed among the branches of almost every Elm as to give to this tree a dusky verdure throughout the winter.

"There is a *variety* of this Elm with red branches, another with white, and a third more pendulous whose leaves are said to be smoother." *Smith.*

Florula Lexingtoniensis.

Species 2nd. ULMUS FULVA. *Slippery Elm.*

Sp. Ch. Leaves oval oblong, with a very long acumination, . pubescent on both sides; *buds* tomentose, with a thick, tawny wool; *flowers* sessile.

Obs. The slippery Elm has almost disappeared from the forest around Lexington in consequence of its destruction by cattle. In the more inaccessible situations among the cliffs of Elkhorn and the Kentucky river, it is occasionally met with, being readily distinguished from the preceding species, by its smaller size—its larger and more scabrous leaf. It blooms a few days later, but before any appearance of foliage in the tree. The inner bark is medicinal, being mucilaginous and demulcent.

Synonyms. U. Rubra. *Mich.* U. Campestris. *Walt.*

2. GENUS. CORYLUS. L. `(Hazel.)

(*Deriv.* Greek. *Korys,** a cap, or helmet—the fruit being invested by the calyx. *De Theis.*)

Class 21st. *MONOECIA—Order, POLYANDRIA.*

Gen. Ch. *Male florets. Ament* imbricate. *Calyx* a scale. *Corolla* none. *Stamens* about 8. *Female florets.* Calyx 2—parted, torn. *Corolla* none. *Styles* 2. *Nut* ovate, surrounded by the persistent calyx.

Species 1st. CORYLUS. AMERICANA. *Walt.*

Sp. Ch. Leaves nearly round, cordate, acuminate; *calyx* of of the fruit larger than the nut with the border dilated, many-cleft.

Obs. The Hazel bush although originally a native of this country, is no longer found growing wild in this immediate neighbourhood, yet it is frequently met with in gardens and shrubberies. In the western part of the state it abounds, often forming on the richest barrens almost impenetrable brakes. In these situations the bush attains the greatest perfection; its stems often measuring near the root more than an inch in diameter, rising 10 or 12 feet high, and bearing a profusion of large well-flavored nuts. The male flowers, formed during the preceding autumn, are evolved into blossom during February, in long pendent catkins, from the smaller branches; while the female flowers, much less conspicuous, occupy the extreme ends

---

* For want of Greek types, the Latin italics are used to explain derivations from the former language.

of the twigs. The fruit is too well known to need description. They ripen in September.

3. Genus.   CARDAMINE.   L.

(*Deriv.* Diminutive of *Kardamon*, the greek name for water-cress.)

Class 15*th*.   TETRADYNAMIA—*Order*, SILIQUOSA.

Gen. Ch. Pod long, opening elastically, with the valves revolute and equal with the partition. *Stigma* entire. *Calyx* expanding at the top.

Species 1st.   CARDAMINE VIRGINICA?

Sp. Ch. Small, *stems* partially decumbent: *leaves* pinnate, leaflets lanceolate somewhat auriculate; *pods* long, erect, strait.

Obs. This little plant excites no other interest than that arising from the early period at which it blooms; being here, as the *Draba verna* in the Eastern states, the earliest harbinger of spring. Root-leaves spread into a circle and densely aggregated, stem-leaves fewer and smaller, all pinnated. In the centre of its radical leaves. its minute white flowers first appear towards the last of February, and as the plant progresses in growth, the stems arise to the height of 6–8 inches, branch off and become somewhat procumbent; the flowers are succeeded by pods (siliques) 1 inch long.

In cultivated fields abundant: flowering from middle of February.

Syn. Nasturtium, bursæ pastoris folio.   Pluk.

4. Genus.   STELLARIA.   L.

(*Deriv.* from the latin *Stella*, a star; the corolla of bifid petals resembling a star.)

Class 10*th*.   DECANDRIA—*Order*, TRIGYNIA.

Gen. Ch. *Calyx* 5-leaved expanding; *petals* 5, two-parted. *Capsule* ovate, 1-celled, many seeded; Summit 6-toothed.

Species 1st. STELLARIA MEDIA.   *Chickweed.*

Sp. Ch. *Leaves* ovate, smooth; *stems* procumbent, with an alternate, lateral, hairy line.

Obs. An humble, unobtrusive annual plant, frequently flowering in this section as early as the 1st of March, and sometimes, in favourable seasons and situations, it is found in bloom in February. From that time its flowers are met with throughout the year. Whether native or introduced it is now found in every part of the continent. In this locality it prefers rich woods or cultivated places, frequently covering patches of considerable extent.

Syn. Alsine Media. L.

5. GENUS.   PACHYSANDRA.   *Michaux.*

(*Deriv.* From the greek, *pachus*, thick, and *aner*, a male, in allusion to the thickness of the stamens.)

Class 19th. *MONOECIA, Order. TETRANDRIA.*

Gen. Ch. Calyx about 4-leaved. *Corolla* none. *Filaments* subclavate. *Styles* 3. *Capsules* 3-horned, 3-celled: cells 2-seeded.

Species 1st. PACHYSANDRA PROCUMBENS.

Sp. Ch. Stem low and procumbent, *leaves* alternate, pubescent, stalked, entire at base, bluntly dentate towards the point; *spikes* nearly radical, lower part feminine; *flowers* bracteate.

Obs. The only species of this genus as yet known is the present one. It is rare in this neighbourhood, being only occasionally met with in that part of Fayette county bordering on the Kentucky river. In the western part of the state, and particularly on the rocky banks of Green river and its tributary branches it is profusely abundant. Its leaves partially retain their verdure throughout the winter, and towards the latter end of February or beginning of March its spikes protrude bearing a number of small inconspicuous flowers, for the most part distinctly male and female but sometimes hermaphrodite.

6. GENUS.   ERIGENIA.   *Nuttall.*

(*Deriv.* Greek. *Erigenia* a name of Aurora, the harbinger of day or the spring; in consequence of its flowering so early in the season.)

Class 5th. *PENTANDRIA—Order, DIGYNIA.*

Gen. Ch. Calyx none. *Corolla* uniform. *Petals* obovate, spreading, entire. *Styles* persistent, subulate, very long. *Fruit* oval, somewhat laterally compressed. *Seed* gibbously convex, marked with 3 striæ; commissure narrow, immarginate, flat. *Involucrum* none.

Species 1*st*. ERIGENIA BULBOSA. *Nuttall.*

Sp. Ch. Root a small globular tuber. *Caulis* simple, bifid, rarely trifid. *Leaf* solitary radical, lateral, 3-partite, segments multifid. *Scapes* furnishing a similar involucrate leaf. *Umbels* terminal from 3 to 5-flowered, flowers stellate.

Obs. This is the first of the umbelliferous tribe to bloom in this vicinity, and is met with most frequently in the rich alluvions of our larger streams. It is a very small plant conspicuous only from its precocity; its small white flowers appearing among the fallen forest leaves from the 1st to 15th of March, before its own leaves are fully evolved. The anthers are of a dark purple—when fully mature the whole plant does not exceed 6 inches in height.

Syn. Sison bulbosum—*Mich.* Hydrocotyle composita. *Pursh.*

7. GENUS. HEPATICA. *Willdenow.*

(*Deriv.* Greek, *Hepar;* the liver; the lobes of its leaves being supposed to resemble those of the liver.)

Class 12*th*. *POLYANDRIA—Order, POLYGYNIA.*

Gen. ch. Calyx 3-leaved. *Petals* 6 to 9.—*Seeds* naked.

Species 1*st*. HEPATICA TRILOBA. *Liver-wort.*

Sp. ch. Leaves cordate at base, 3-lobed, lobes entire, scape 1-flowered.

Obs. One of our most beautiful and earliest flowering plants, often blooming before its leaves have come up, and while the ground is yet covered with snow—The root is fibrous and perennial—Leaves all radical, on foot-stalks 3–6 inches long; flowers numerous, issuing from the root on peduncles 3 or 4 inches in length, for the most part of a purple colour, but rarely white. The whole plant when young is covered with fine silken hairs—when old, the leaves lose in some degree this appearance and become thick and coriaceous, they are partially sempervirent, and occasionally assume a dark purple hue.

Although the present is the only species of *Hepatica* known, yet two distinctly marked *varieties* occur—the one with obtuse-lobed leaves, the other having the lobes acute: the latter is more commonly met with in this section of country. Though rare in this immediate neighbourhood, it is sometimes met with on the rocky hill sides, bordering the Elkhorn, and more frequently among the cliffs of the Kentucky river in rich soils. Some attention has lately been drawn to this plant in pectoral diseases; whether it possesses any virtues in such I am not prepared to say, but I should judge it to be at least innocent.

Syn. Anemone Hepatica—*Willd. Mich. and Linn.*

8. GENUS.   ARABIS.   L.

(*Deriv.* An ancient Greek name of a plant; supposed to be a native of Arabia.)

Class 14*th.* TETRADYNAMIA—*Order,* SILIQUOSA.

Gen. ch. Pod linear, generally compressed, crowned with the sessile stigma, valves veined. Seed arranged in one row.— Calyx erect.

Species 1*st.* ARABIS RHOMBOIDEA.

Sp. ch. Leaves glabrous, rhomboidal, repand, toothed, the lower ones on long petioles; *root* tuberous.

Obs. Root a small tuber. Radical leaves few, roundish or sub-cordate, on slender flexuose petioles 3 to 6 inches long; stem-leaves of various forms; the lower on short foot-stalks and somewhat rhomboid, (whence the name of the species,) the upper sessile, narrower, acuminate and sparingly toothed. Flowers white or pale purple, about the size of those of the garden radish, in a terminal raceme, succeeded by linear pods on peduncles 1 inch in length. Found in moist rich woods, or on creek sides. Blooms about the 10th of March.

Syn. Arabis Bulbosa. *Muhl.*

Species 2*d.* ARABIS FALCATA.   *Sickle-pod Arabis.*

Sp. ch. Leaves lanceolate, narrow at each end, remotely dentate, hastate-sessile, alternate; *siliques* pendulous, compressed, falcate.

Obs. Root perennial, fusiform-fibrous, stem from 1 to 4 feet high. Leaves alternate; those from the root spathulate, petioled: of the stem linear lanceolate, sessile, amplexicaule, hastate, irregularly dentate, 4 to 6 inches long. Flowers in long terminal racemes. Corolla small, obscure white. Pods 2 to 4 inches long, linear, recurved, sometimes pendulous. Rocky shaded situations on North Elkhorn: flowers last of March and first of April.

Syn. Arabis canadensis. *Willd. Ell. Nutt.*

9. GENUS.   CLAYTONIA.   *Gronovius.*

(*Deriv.* Named by Gronovius in honor of John Clayton, an eminent botanist of Virginia.)

Class 5th. *PENTANDRIA—Order, MONOGYNIA.*

Generic character. Calyx 2-leaved. *Petals* 5. *Stigma* trifid. *Capsule* 1-celled, 3-valved, 3 to 5-seeded. *Seeds* uniform. *Nutt.*

Species 1st. CLAYTONIA VIRGINICA.   Gr.

Specific character. Leaves linear-lanceolate; *racemes* solitary; leaves of the *calyx* somewhat acute; *petals* obovate, retuse: *root* tuberous.

Obs. This delicate little plant adorns our meadows and pastures profusely in early spring. Several grass-like leaves arise in common with the stem, from a round small tuberous root. Stem-leaves two, opposite, linear, smooth, somewhat fleshy and connate at base. Flowers from 4 to 18, in a simple, curved raceme which becomes erect and straight as the flowers are evolved; their colour is white or a delicate pink, marked with lines of a deeper rose colour. It blooms generally from the middle to the 30th of March.

10. GENUS.   THLASPI.   L.

(*Deriv.* An old Greek word used by Dioscorides, to which he gives an obscure derivation.)

Class 14th. *TETRADYNAMIA—Order, SILICULOSA.*

Gen. ch. Pod emarginate, obcordate, many-seeded. *Valves* boat-shaped, keeled. *Ell.*

Species 1st. THLASPI BURSA-PASTORIS. Shepherd's purse.

Sp. ch. Hirsute; *pods* deltoid, obcordate; *root-leaves* pinnatifid; *stem-leaves* saggitate and amplexicaule at base.

Obs. This little weed, although originally exotic, is now met with abundantly throughout this section, in common with every other part of the Union. In early spring its lower leaves are used as greens; and about the 15th of March its minute, inconspicuous flowers appear, which are succeeded by a number of small obcordate silicles borne on a stem a foot or more in height: it continues blooming throughout the season, and is often met with in flower during the winter. Found every where in cultivated grounds.

11. Genus. ERYTHRONIUM. L.

(*Deriv.* Greek. *Erythros* red; in allusion either to the colour of the flower, which in some species is red, or to the purple stains on the leaves.)

Class 6th. HEXANDRIA—*Order*, MONOGYNIA.

Gen. char. Calyx none. *Corolla* campanulate, 6-petals reflected, and the 3 inner ones with a callous denture on each side near the base. *Capsule* superior roundish or eliptical, 3-celled.

Species 1st. Erythronium Americanum.   *Dogs-tooth Violet.*

Sp. ch. Leaves lanceolate, punctate; *petals* oblong lanceolate, obtuse at the point; interior ones bidentate near the base; *style* club-shaped; *stigma* entire.

Obs. This plant, the first of the lilliaceous tribe to bloom in this neighbourhood, is readily recognised by its two leaves, which are radical, elliptic-lanceolate, somewhat fleshy, and beautifully marbled with green and brown. The *flower* is yellow, solitary and drooping, on a naked scape. The root a small tunicated, brown, ovate bulb, situated 2 or 3 inches beneath the surface of the soil. Whole plant from 6 to 10 inches above it. Found most generally on the rich alluvial bottoms of streams. Blooms about the 20th of March.

Syn. E. lanceolatum. Pursh—*E. Dens Canis.* Mich.

Species 2d. Erythronium Albidum.   *Torrey.*

Sp. ch. Leaves elliptical-lanceolate, not punctate; *petals* linear-lanceolate, obtuse; inner ones without dentures, subunguiculate; *style* 3-cleft.

Obs. This plant I have heretofore been accustomed to regard as a mere *variety* of the former, differing from it chiefly in the colour of its flower which is bluish white; nevertheless I follow Dr. Torrey in considering it now as a distinct species,

O

although I have some doubts whether sufficient difference exists between them. The present species is more abundant in this neighbourhood than the yellow-flowered one, but they are found in common, affecting the same localities and blooming at the same time.

12. Genus. CORYDALIS. *Ventenat.*

(*Deriv.* Gr. *Korydalos*, a lark: Larkspur, in reference to the spurred shape of its nectaries.)

Class 16*th.* *DIADELPHIA*—*Order*, *HEXANDRIA.*

Gen. ch. *Calyx* 2-leaved. *Corolla* ringent. *Filaments* 2, membranaceous, each bearing 3 anthers. *Capsule,* siliquose many-seeded.

Species 1*st.* CORYDALIS CUCULLARIA. *Dutchman's breeches.*

Sp. ch. *Scape* naked: *raceme* simple. *Spurs* 2, divaricate, the length of the corolla, style included: *root* bulbous. *Pers.*

This is one of the most delicate and beautiful plants of the country; its finely divided leaves, of a bluish green, are among the earliest vegetation seen in secluded rich situations among decaying logs, &c. Towards the 20th of March its flowers appear gracefully pendent from a naked scape which is generally nodding and 8 or 10 inches high. The flowers are white with a yellowish border, and are surmounted by two spurs. Its leaves are all radical and finely subdivided, two accompanying each flowering stem. The root is a granulated scaly bulb, a bulbous enlargement being produced at the base of the leaf, which is red or pink coloured.

Syn. Fumaria Cucullaria, *Willd. & Mich.*
Bicucullata Canadensis, *Marchant.*
Diclytra Canadensis, *Bosc.*

Species 2*d.* CORYDALIS FORMOSA.

Sp. ch. Spurs 2, slightly curved, obtuse; *scape* naked; *raceme* somewhat compounded; *stigma* 2-angled.

Obs. This is no less interesting than the preceding species, and, indeed, the delightful hyacynthine odour of its flowers gives to the present one an additional charm. The description given by Pursh is apt to mislead the student as he says the flowers are "a lively bright red." As I have seen them they have been universally of a pale purple or bluish white. It is found, in common with the former, on the precipitous banks of water courses, in the rich soil among lime stone rocks, and is readily distinguished from its associate, by its more erect scape, single radical leaf, and by its root, which is a small round, yellow tuber, sometimes aggregated in considerable numbers. The leaves of the two species are very similar, and they flower at the same time.

Syn. Diclytra formosa, *Ell.* Fumaria—*Bot. Mag.*

Species 3d. CORYDALIS AUREA. *Golden-flowered* C.

Sp. ch. Stem branched, diffused; *leaves* bipinnate, leaflets divided, linear-lanceolate, acute; *racemes* leaning one way; *bracteas* oblong acuminate; *pods* linear, 2 to 4 times as long as the peduncle. Spur 1.

Obs. This species differs from either of the preceding in its more diffused and branching character, in the size and colour of its flowers which are small and of a bright yellow, surmounted by a single spur or nectary. It is, moreover, more abundant, and is sometimes found in cultivated situations among the grass &c. in fence corners. Its leaves appear very early in the spring and its flowers towards the 20th of March, continuing in bloom longer than either of the former.

13. GENUS.   SAXIFRAGA.   L.

(*Deriv.* Lat. *Saxum*, a rock, and *frango* to break; from its often growing in the clefts of rocks. *Dar.*)

Class 10th.   DECANDRIA—*Order*, DIGYNIA.

Gen. Ch. Calyx 5-parted, persistent. Petals 5. Capsule 1-celled, many-seeded, opening between the persistent styles.

Species 1st. SAXIFRAGA VERNALIS. *Willd. Early Saxifrage.*

Sp. Ch. Pubescent; *leaves* oval, obtuse, crenate, dentate somewhat petioled; *stem* nearly leafless, paniculated; *flowers* nearly sessile.

Obs. Among the multiplicity of Synonyms by which this common plant is known in books of American Botany, I have been at some difficulty in selecting the most appropriate; but as the plant is by no means restricted in its *habitat* to Virginia, and as it seems to be the earliest flowering species indigenous to the United States, I have chosen to follow Dr. Bigelow in adopting Willdenow's name. The root is perennial; leaves mostly radical. Stem erect fleshy, hairy nearly destitute of leaves, and when fully grown, in good soil, rising to the height of 12 or 18 inches. Flowers often appear by the 20th of March whilst the plant is but an inch or two high: they are small, white, clustered, nearly sessile, and continue unfolding for some weeks. Rocky situations near water courses.

Syn. Saxifraga Nivalis. *Muhl.* S. Virginiensis. *Mx. Ph.* S. Virginica *Bart. Dar.* &c.

14. Genus.   URTICA.   L.   *Nettle.*

(*Deriv.* Latin *uro* to burn or sting, and *tactus* the touch.)

Class 21st.   *MONOECIA—Order, TETRANDRIA.*

Gen. Ch. Male florets. Calyx 4-leaved. *Corolla* none. *Female florets. Calyx* 2-valved. *Corolla* none—seed 1, shining.

Species 1st. Urtica Urens.   *Small stinging nettle.*

Sp. Ch. Leaves opposite, cordate, somewhat 5-nerved, coarsely toothed, decussate: *spikes* by pairs, shorter than the petioles; *flowers* clustered.

Obs. Stem from 12 to 14 inches high, obtusely four-angled, branching from the root and semi-prostrate. Leaves more properly 3, than 5-nerved, sometimes purplish underneath, on petioles an inch long. Flowers small and greenish in axillary racemes, two in each axil, shorter than the petiole. Male and female florets intermixed. The whole plant is densely beset with fine hairs and stiff white prickles, which transmit a poisonous fluid when touched. Frequent in rich moist woods among decaying leaves, flowering in the latter part of March and after.

15. Genus.   DENTARIA, L.   *Toothwort.*

(*Deriv.* Latin. *Dens dentis,* a tooth from the tooth-like appearance of its root.)

Class 15th.   *TETRADYNAMIA—Order, SILIQUOSA.*

Gen. Ch. Pod opening elastically. *Valves* without nerves, revolute. *Partition* somewhat fungous. *Stigma* emarginate. *Calyx* connivent.

Species 1st. Dentaria Laciniata.

Sp. Ch. Leaves ternate, leaflets 3-parted, segments lanceolate, toothed and irregularly notched.

Obs. This is the most showy of our tetradynamous productions, and when growing in good soil not too much shaded, its dense heads of white and purplish flowers, contrasted with the rich green of its verticillate leaves, make it a very pleasing object in early spring. The root is perennial, composed of small tubers, slightly connected together, and emitting numerous fine radicles—these tubers partake of the general properties of the class, being hot and pungent to the taste. Flowers last of March.

16. Genus.   ANEMONE.   L.   *Wind-flower.*

(*Deriv.* Greek *Anemos,* wind from its blooming in boisterous weather.)

Class 12th. *POLYANDRIA*—Order, *POLYGYNIA.*

Gen. ch. Calyx none. Petals 5 to 15. *Involucrum* 3-leaved, distant from the flower. *Seeds* numerous.

Species 1st.   ANEMONE PENNSYLVANICA?   *Tor.*

Sp. ch. Leaves 3-parted; lobes oblong, incisely toothed at the apex; *involucrum* similar, sessile, bearing several pedicels, one of which is naked and 1-flowered, the others involucellate, *fruit* pubescent. *Torrey.*

Obs. I have ventured with some hesitation to affix a specific name to the present plant, since I have reasons to believe that it has been regarded by competent judges, to be the *A. Thalictroides.* From that plant, however, as commonly met with in the Eastern states, it differs essentially in its root, which is less fleshy and more fibrous,—in its leaflets which are not cordate but cuneiform at base, and irregularly 3—5-lobed at the apex—in its flower which is smaller, uniformly of five petals, one only opening at a time. I have questioned whether the present might not be the variety *Uniflora* of *A. Thalic.* of Pursh. It would seem to differ from the *A. Penn.* of Torrey, in the flower which he describes as being large and yellowish white. Found in abundance in woods, flowering from the middle to the last of March.

17.   Genus.   GLECHOMA.   L.

(*Deriv.* an ancient name perhaps from the Greek *Glukus,* sweet or pleasant in reference to its odour. *Dar.*)

Class 14*th*. *DIDYNAMIA*—*Order*, *GYMNOSPERMIA*.

Gen. ch. *Calyx* 5-cleft, subequal. *Anthers* approaching each other in pairs, each pair producing the form of a cross.

Species 1*st*. GLECHOMA HEDERACEA. *Ground ivy*.

Sp. ch. *Stem* procumbent radicating; *leaves* cordate-reniform, crenate.

Obs. A small procumbent plant, abundant on the alluvion bottoms of our creeks and rivers, and in the fence-rows of rich, cultivated fields. Flowers deep blue and strongly scented. Corolla double the length of the calyx, upper lip bifid, lower trifid, middle segment larger, emarginate and bearded internally: peduncles axillary, about 3-flowered, flowers in whorls. Though originally, perhaps, exotic, this plant seems now extensively naturalized in the U. States, being found abundantly in the middle and northern states. Blooms here towards the last of March.

18. GENUS. JEFFERSONIA. *Barton.* (*B. S.*)

(*Deriv.* named by Barton in honor of the late President Jefferson.)

Class 8*th*. *OCTANDRIA*—*Order*, *MONOGYNIA*.

Gen. ch. *Calyx* 5-leaved, coloured, deciduous. *Corolla* of 8 petals, incurvately spreading. *Capsule* obovate, substipitate, 1-celled, opening below the summit by a lunate foramen. *Seeds* many, oblong.

Species 1*st*. JEFFERSONIA DIPHYLLA. *Bart.*

Sp. Ch. *Root* perennial, stemless; *leaves* conjugate or binate; *scapes* naked, 1-flowered; *flowers* caducous, white.

Obs. This is the only species of the genus, and is at this time exceedingly scarce in this locality. A few years since it grew abundantly on the south bank of *Royle's mill pond*, but is now only met with in the more secluded hill-sides bordering the Elkhorn, or on the cliffs of the Kentucky river. It grows in clumps; many leaves issuing together from a fibrous root, and supported on foot-stalks 5 or 8 inches long. The flowers appear about the 30th of March and are somewhat like those of the Puccoon, (*Sanguinaria C,*) though smaller; they are extremely short-lived, and so very caducous as to be preserved with great difficulty in an *Herbarium*.

Syn. Jeffersonia Bartonis. *Mich.*
   Podophyllum diphyllum. *Linn.*

19. Genus. THALICTRUM. L.

(*Deriv.* Supposed to be from the Greek, *thallo*, to be green; from its verdant habit, *Dar.*)

Class 12*th.* POLYANDRIA—*Order*, POLYGYNIA.

Gen. ch. Mostly dioecious. *Calyx* none. *Petals* 4 or 5. *Stamina* very long. *Seeds* without tails, striate.

Species 1*st.* THALICTRUM DIOICUM.   *Meadow rue.*

Sp. ch. Flowers dioecious, *filaments* threadlike: segments of the leaves nearly round, cordate, obtusely lobed, glabrous; *peduncles* axillary, shorter than the leaves.

Obs. The season of its flowering throws some light on this otherwise obscure genus. The present is the first (with the exception of T. Anemonoides, more properly regarded a true Anemone,) to flower in the U. States. Root perennial. Stem herbaceous 12 to 18 inches high; leaves triternate, those from the root embracing the stem by a broad membranaceous expansion; leaflets slightly cordate at base, roundish, divided into from 3 to 7 obtuse lobes. Foot-stalks of the umbels shorter than the leaves, frequently extending and becoming compound and paniculate. Corolla small, dull-white colour; anthers yellow. Grows in rocky bluffs on water courses. Flowers last of March.

20. Genus. TRILLIUM. L.

(*Deriv.* Latin. *Trilix* triple; alluding to the prevalence of the number *three*, in the leaves and other parts. *Dar.*)

Class 6*th.* HEXANDRIA—*Order*, TRIGYNIA.

Gen. ch. Calyx 3-leaved, spreading. *Corolla* 3-petaled. *Stigmas* 3, sessile, recurved. *Berry* 3-celled.

Species 1*st.* TRILLIUM SESSILE.

Sp. ch. Flowers sessile, erect; *petals* lanceolate erect. *Leaves* sessile, wide, oval, acute.

Obs. This species of Trillium is easily distinguished from others of this locality, by its sessile flower. The root consists of a thick tuber, from which descend numerous radicles, Stem from 2 to 8 inches above ground, coloured and spotted, with small decaying sheaths at base. Leaves 3, at the summit of the stem, ovate, acute, entire, strongly marked with 3 veins and curiously spotted. Flower sessile, in the centre of the 3 leaves: petals 3, lanceolate, erect or connivent, dark purple. Calyx 3-leaved, spreading alternately between the stem-leaves. Grows in rich woods or grass grounds. Flowers last of March— April.

21.   Genus.   SANGUINARIA.   L.

(*Deriv.* Latin *Sanguis* blood, from the colour of the juice of the plant.)

Class 12*th.*   POLYANDRIA—*Order,* MONOGYNIA.

Gen. ch. Calyx 2-leaved, deciduous. *Petals* 8 to 12. *Stigma* sessile, 2-grooved. *Capsule* superiour, oblong, 1-celled, 2-valved, apex attenuated. *Receptacles* 2, filiform, marginal. *Nutt.*

Species 1*st.* Sanguinaria Canadensis.   *Puccoon.*

Sp. ch. Leaves sub-reniform, sinuate, lobed: *Scape* 1-flowered.

Obs. No plant is more commonly met with in early spring, in this vicinity, than the puccoon, by which name it is here universally recognised. The flower-stalks appear above ground about the 1st of April, sheathed at base by an accompanying leaf, which unfolds itself after the flower has disappeared. Perhaps no wild plant better deserves cultivation than this, as "with little attention and care a beautiful variety with double flowers might be produced." The whole plant, but particularly the root, emits when wounded, an acrid, blood coloured juice, which is highly medicinal, being emetic, expectorant and escharotic.

It prefers rich, moist, shaded woods, and in such situations it is every where abundant in the spring, disappearing however entirely towards midsummer.

22.   Genus.   RANUNCULUS.   L.

(*Deriv.* Latin diminutive of *Rana* a frog; from some fancied connexion between this plant and that animal.)

Class 12*th.*   POLYANDRIA—*Order,* POLYGYNIA.

Gen. ch. Calyx 5-leaved. *Petals* 5, bearing near the base of their claw, a melliferous pore generally covered with a scale. *Seeds* naked.

Species 1*st.* Ranunculus Abortivus.   *Small flowered crow-foot.*

Sp. ch. *Radical leaves* heart-shaped, crenate; *stem-leaves* ternate, or cleft into 5 or 3 linear lobes; branchlets about 3-flowered.

Obs. This species is easily distinguished from the following, which blooms about the same time, by its small flowers, and undivided radical leaves; these are heart or kidney-shaped, on petioles 2–4 inches long, which embrace the caudex by an expanded base. The stem-leaves vary considerably, the lower ones being irregularly subdivided into 5 lobes which are notched or dentated, and petiolated; the upper are ternate, linear and sessile. The root is fibrous. Stems erect, branching, and ultimately each branch bearing 3–5 flowers, which are small, pale yellow, on peduncles 2 to 1-2 inch long. Grows in woods and meadows. Blooms last of March.

Species 2d. RANUNCULUS FASCICULARIS. *Muhl.*

Sp. ch. Root very much fascicled; *leaves* ternate, subpinnate, glabrous. *Bart.*

Obs. This is the most showy of our Ranunculi; growing to the height of 18 or 24 inches and bearing a profusion of large, shining, yellow flowers: stem erect, much branched, leaves pubescent, ternate deeply incised and dentated: calyx spreading, villous, shorter than the petals and caducous. The root consists of an aggregation of thick fibres. Moist woods and grass lands. Flowers first of April.

Species 3d. RANUNCULUS NITIDUS. *Walt.*

Sp. ch. Very glabrous; *stem* hollow; *radical leaves* rotund-subreniform, obtusely crenate; *stem-leaves* sessile digitate, leaflets irregularly incised, lacinii obtuse; *seed* sub-globose, shining. *Walt. and Lam. by Pursh.*

Obs. I concur with Pursh in regarding this as but a variety of the first, from which it is chiefly distinguishable by its more luxuriant growth and very glossy, varnished appearance.— Flowers small, as in species 1st, of pale yellow colour. Rare; in company with the preceding. 10th of April.

(TO BE CONTINUED.)

ART. VI.—*Florula Lexingtoniensis, secundum florendi œtatem digesta; or a descriptive Catalogue of the Phœnogamous plants indigenous to this portion of Kentucky; arranged in the order of their periods of flowering.* BY CHARLES WILKINS SHORT, M. D. Professor of Materia Medica and Medical Botany in Transylvania University.

CONTINUED FROM PAGE 265. NO. II.

FASCICULUS II.
For April.

23. GENUS.   ACER   L.   *Maple.*

(*Deriv.* Latin; *acer*, sharp; pikes and lances having formerly been made of the wood.)

Class 8th. OCTANDRIA—*Order*, MONOGYNIA.

Gen. Ch. Flowers mostly polygamous. *Calyx* about 5—cleft. *Petals* 5, or none. *Samaras* 2, united at base, 1 seeded, winged.

Species 1st.   ACER SACCHARINUM.   *Sugar Maple.*

Sp. Ch. Leaves palmately 5—lobed, subcordate at base, acuminate, glaucous beneath; *peduncles* corymbose, nodding.

Obs. The Sugar tree, as it is here universally called, is one of the most common of our forest trees, and perhaps in this particular locality, it attains its greatest altitude. As it does not materially interfere with the growth of grasses beneath it, it is often reserved in clearing ground, particularly in situations intended for pasture or meadows. It here forms the densest shade, and in autumn constitutes a prominent feature in the landscape, by the bright orange and red colours assumed by its leaves. Its wood is preferred to almost any other for fuel, and large quantities of sugar are annually made from the sap. Flowers about the first of April: seed ripen in midsummer.

Species 2d.   ACER NEGUNDO.   *Box Elder.*

Sp. Ch. Leaves pinnate and ternate, unequally serrate; *flowers* dioicous.

Obs. Not so common as the preceding, being more restricted to the borders of water courses. It is in every point of view less valuable than the Sugar tree, although the sap is occasionally procured in common with that of the former, in the making of sugar. Flowers at the same time.

Species 3*d.*   Acer Dasycarpum.   *White Maple.*

Sp. Ch. *Leaves* palmate, 5—lobed, acuminate, serrate, pubescent underneath, and almost white; *flowers* in clustered umbels; *germs* tomentose.

Obs. This tree, which in its general habit resembles the Sugar Maple, is however easily distinguished from it by the lighter and smoother colour of the bark, and the singular downy whiteness of the leaves. It attains as large a size and is valuable as fuel and for some of the mechanic arts. Sugar is also made from its sap, but it is now rarely met with in this neighbourhood.

24. Genus.   VERONICA.   L.   *Speedwell.*

(*Deriv.* Probably a corruption of *Vetonica*, or *Betonica*, Betony.)

Class 2*d.*   DIANDRIA—*Order,* MONOGYNIA.

Gen. Ch. Calyx 4—parted. *Corolla* rotate, 4—lobed, unequal, the lower segment narrower. *Capsule* 2-celled, obcordate; *seeds* few.

Species 1*st.*   Veronica Perigrina.   *Neckweed.*

Sp. Ch. Flowers solitary sessile; *leaves* oblong, rather obtuse, toothed and entire; *stem* erect.

Obs. Stem erect or partially procumbent, round, smooth, frequently without branches, 8 inches high. The lowest leaves opposite, sparsely toothed; the upper alternate, linear-lanceolate, nearly entire. Flowers axillary, solitary, nearly sessile. Corolla small, white and, like both the following, very caducous. Capsule inversely heart-shaped and larger than either of the succeeding species.—The plant has had some reputation in scrofula, hence the name of Neckweed. Flowers middle of March and after. Abundant in gardens and cultivated fields.

Species 2*d.*   Veronica Serpyllifolia.   *Speedwell.*

Sp. Ch. Raceme terminal, somewhat spiked; *leaves* ovate glabrous, crenate.

Obs. A small plant common in grass lots, and scarcely distinguishable except when in bloom; stem decumbent, putting forth radicles; lower leaves roundish, ovate, smooth; flowers sky blue with darker stripes, larger than in the preceding species, and borne on the summit of the stem: whole plant does not exceed 6 inches in height, frequently less. Flowers from 1st of April to the last of that month, and occasionally throughout the season.

Species 3d.   VERONICA AGRESTIS.   Germander.

Sp. Ch. Flowers solitary, and with the cordate leaves nearly sessile: *stem* rough, hairy.

Obs. This species is readily distinguished from either of the preceding by its more hispid appearance, and its more diffused and branching habit. The flower is also smaller and of a deeper blue than the preceding. The leaves are mostly opposite, cordate, ovate, notched, strongly veined particularly on the lower surface, and very pubescent. Cultivated fields and pastures common: flowering rather later than the last, 5th—10th of April.

25.   GENUS.   CARPINUS.   L.

(*Deriv.* Celtic, *Car*, wood, and *pin*, head; i. e. wood suitable for making yokes for cattle. *De Theis by Darl.*)

Class 21st.   *MONOECIA.—Order. POLYANDRIA.*

Gen. Ch. MASC. Scales of the *calyx* ciliated. *Stamina* about 10. FEM. *Calyx* scales 2-flowered. *Corolla* trifid. *Nut* ovate, sulcate.

Species 1st.   CARPINUS AMERICANA.   Iron-wood.

Sp. Ch. *Leaves* oblong-ovate, acuminate, unequally serrate; *strobile* with 3—parted scales, the middle segment oblique, toothed on one side.

Obs. The Iron-wood, by which name this tree is here always called, is so well known as to require no description. In other portions of the union it is called Hornbeam. It is found throughout this state among other forest trees and is perhaps especially abundant in the country about Lexington, growing generally to the height of 30 or 40 feet.—The wood is possessed of great hardness and strength, but is not applied to many useful purposes. Flowers beginning of April.

Syn. C. Caroliniana. *Walt.*

26.   GENUS   OSTRYA.   *Micheli.*

(*Deriv.* *Ostreon.* Greek, a shell or scale; from the resemblance of its capsules. *De Theis.*)

Class 21*st.* MONOECIA. *Order,* POLYANDRIA.

Gen. Ch. *Ament* imbricated. Masc. *Calyx* consisting of scales. *Filament* of the stamina ramose, Fem. *Ament* naked. *Capsules* inflated, imbricated at the base, 1-seeded.

Species 1*st.* Ostrya Virginica.   *Hop-hornbeam.*

Sp. Ch. *Leaves* ovate-oblong, cordate at the base, acuminate, unequally serrate; *strobile* oblong-ovate, erect? buds acute.

Obs. This small tree which is also called Ironwood in the Northern and Eastern States, is readily distinguished from the former by its somewhat shaggy bark and differently formed strobiles, or seed vessels: these in the present tree being so similar to those of the garden hop as to have given it the appropriate name of Hop-hornbeam. It is likewise frequent in this locality being found in company with the preceding. Its wood is also hard and strong; but the size of the tree being inconsiderable, it is susceptible of no very useful application. Flowers about the 1st of April.

Syn. Carpinus Ostrya *Mich.*

27. Genus.   PULMONARIA.   L.

(*Deriv.* *Pulmones* the lungs, from its former reputation in diseases of these organs.)

Class 5*th.* PENTANDRIA. *Order,* MONOGYNIA.

Gen. Ch. *Calyx* prismatic 5—angled, 5—toothed: *Corolla* funnel-formed, border 5—lobed; throat pervious.

Species 1*st.* Pulmonaria Virginica.   *American Cowslip.*

Sp. Ch. Smooth; *stem* erect; *calyx* much shorter than the tube of the corolla; *radical leaves* ob-ovate, oblong, obtuse; *stem leaves* narrower.

Obs. This very showy plant, so common in most parts of the Union, is comparatively rare in this immediate vicinity, being only occasionally met with on the alluvion banks of Elkhorn and Kentucky river. Stem 12–15 inches high with numerous broad, smooth, spathulate leaves issuing from the root, and becoming narrower on the stem. Flowers numerous in a terminal, pendulous raceme; their colour varying from pale rose, through violet to blue. April 1st to 15th.

28. Genus. DELPHINIUM. L.

(*Deriv.* Delphinion of the ancient Greeks, from some fancied resemblance of its nectary, to the Dolphin. *Smith.*)

Class 12th. *POLYANDRIA—Order, TRIGYNIA.*

Gen. Ch. Calyx none. Petals 5. *Nectarium* 2—cleft, base extending into a hollow spur. *Capsules* 1—3.

Species 1st. DELPHINIUM TRICORNE. *Wild Larkspur.*

Sp. Ch. Caulis simple. *Leaves* 5—parted many-cleft with the segments linear; *raceme* straight; *nectary* shorter than the corolla; *capsules* 3, arched, expanding from the base.

Obs. The striking similarity of this plant, to the common Larkspur of the gardens at once points it out to the novice. Stem hollow, large at the base, tapering quickly to a point at the summit; rarely more than a foot high. Flowers varying in colour from dark blue to light blue, purple pink and white, are succeeded by three, horn-shaped capsules, whence the specific name. Found on creek sides, particularly preferring rocky precipices. 1st to the 10th of April.

This is one of the plants which are indefinitely called *staggerweed*; to eating which the diseases of cattle are sometimes attributed.

29. Genus. SEDUM. L.

(Deriv. Latin *Sedere* to sit, from its growing or sitting on the surface of rocks.)

Class 10th. *DECANDRIA—Order, PENTAGYNIA.*

Gen. Ch. Calyx 5—cleft. Petals 5. Capsules 5, superior, many seeded, opening internally.

Species 1st. SEDUM TERNATUM. *Stone-crop.*

Sp. Ch. Creeping; *leaves* flat, round spathulate, by threes: *cyme* generally 3-spiked; *flowers* white.

Obs. This handsome little vegetable is apt to mislead beginners in the study of plants, from the circumstance of many of the flowers being *octandrous*, and the calyx, petals and germs being arranged by 4s instead of 5s as laid down in the generic character. The most of the species of this genus, however, are strictly decandrous, and indeed the central flower of the present species is so always. Root perennial; stem procumbent;—lower leaves orbicular; upper lanceolate; all thick and succulent. On the shelving rocks bordering Elkhorn. Flowers beginning of April.

Syn. Sedum Portulacoides, *Muhl.*

Species 2d. SEDUM PULCHELLUM.

Sp. Ch. Glabrous, *stems* assurgent; *leaves* linear, succulent, obtuse; *cyme* many-spiked; flowers sessile.

Obs. Mainly differing from the preceding in the leaves which are linear and cylindrical. Found in company with it on moist rocks and sometimes on the trunks of decaying trees. Owing to this circumstance it is frequently mistaken for a moss by those unacquainted with its character. Flowers a little after the former.

30. GENUS. VIOLA. L. *Violet.*

(*Deriv.* A Latin name of obscure Greek derivation.)

Class 5th. *PENTANDRIA—Order, MONOGYNIA.*

Gen. Ch. *Calyx* 5-leaved, produced at the base. *Corolla* 5-petalled, irregular, the lower petal cornute behind. *Anthers* cohering: *Capsule* superior 3-valved, 1 celled.

Species 1st. VIOLA CUCULLATA. *Hooded Violet.*

Sp. Ch. Stemless; *leaves* cordate, somewhat acute, glabrous, hooded at base; *flowers* inverted; *petals* obliquely bent.

Obs. This is with us the most abundant of the violets, as well as the first to bloom; the whole surface of moist meadows and pastures being covered with them in the fore part of April.—Petals blue and purple, white at base; the base of upper one with violet-coloured veins; of the two lateral bearded; of the lower smooth. Peduncles longer than the leaves with the summit reflexed. Stipules linear—1st to 15th April.

Syn. Viola cordata. *Walt.*

Species 2d. VIOLA OBLIQUA. *Aiton.*

Sp. Ch. Stemless; smooth; *leaves* cordate, acute, flat, crenate, serrate; *flowers* obliquely bent; lateral petals bearded; inferior ones acute, carinate; *stipules* lanceolate.

Obs. This species is by no means easily distinguished from the preceding, with which it is found in common. It is, however, a larger plant, and minute examination will detect specific differences in the leaves, petioles, stipules and flowers. (See

Schweinitz's monograph on the genus Viola in American Journal of Science and Arts, Vol. 5, No. 1.)

Species 3*d*. VIOLA OCHROLEUCA? Schw. *White Violet.*
Sp. Ch. Caulescent. Stem somewhat erect, branched, purplish, smooth; *leaves* cordate, acuminate; *stipules* oblong-lanceolate, dentate-ciliate.

Obs. The present species, about which there seems some obscurity in the books to which I have referred, is easily recognized from its congeners of this locality, by its large, white flowers, with a tinge of yellow. It is found in common with the two preceding, and forms dense patches among the grass in moist situations. As the season advances it rises with a slender flexuose stem to the height of 8—12 inches, and then produces inconspicuous, apetalous flowers.

Syn. V. Striata. *Wild. Pers. Pursh. Nutt.*

Species 4*th*. VIOLA HASTATA. *Yellow Violet.*
Sp. Ch. Caulescent smooth; *stem* simple, leafy above; *leaves* hastate, on very long petioles; *stipules* minute, ciliate denticulate.

Obs. This, although much less frequently met with than either of the preceding, is easily distinguished from them by the deep yellow colour of its flowers. Rare in this neighbourhood, being only occasionally found in shaded woods. Flowers during the fore part of April.

Species 5*th*. VIOLA CONCOLOR. *Muhl.*
Sp. Ch. Caulescent. Stem straight erect; *leaves* cuneate-lanceolate; *stipules* lanceolate entire; *peduncles* very short, axillary, 2-3 flowered; *petals* connivent, emarginate· spur none.

Obs. This anomalous species, which appears to me very unnaturally grouped with the violets, is also very rare in this section of Kentucky. I have only met with it in a solitary, secluded, rocky spot lying to the left of, and near the Woodford road. Several stems issuing from a single root, arise erect and unbranched to the height of 1 or 2 feet, bearing lance-shaped, pointed leaves. The flowers are small and greenish-coloured, produced in 2s and 3s at the axills of the upper leaves about the 10th of April. The whole habit of the plant, however, is so unlike that of the genus, as easily to mislead the student.

Other species of this extensive tribe are no doubt to be found in the neighbourhood of Lexington: as yet however I have detected only the above. In other parts of the state six or eight additional species have been met with.

31. GENUS.   LEONTODON.   L.   *Dandelion.*

(*Deriv.* Greek *Leon* a lion and *odous* a tooth; from a fancied resemblance in the teeth of the leaves.)

Class 19*th.* *SYNGENESIA—Order, ÆQUALIS.*

Gen. Ch. *Calyx* oblong. double; outer one loose. *Receptacle* naked; *pappus* feathered.

Species 1*st.* LEONTODON TARAXACUM.

Sp. Ch. *Outer scales* of the calyx reflexed; *scapes* 1-flowered; *leaves* runcinate.

Obs. No portion of the Union is more completely overrun by this naturalized foreigner than this section, being so abundant as to give a yellowish hue to pastures in early spring (1st of April) from the profusion of its flowers.

(Specific name derived from the Greek *tarasso* to move, or trouble, from its reputed diuretic and laxative properties.)

32. GENUS.   POLEMONIUM.   L.

(*Derir.* According to Pliny derived from Greek, *Polemos*, war: because Kings had contended for the honor of its discovery.)

Class 5*th.* *PENTANDRIA—Order, MONOGYNIA.*

Gen. Ch. *Calyx* 5-cleft. *Corolla* somewhat rotate, 5-lobed, tube short, closed at its base by 5 staminiferous valves or scales. *Stigma* trifid. *Capsule* 3-celled, superior.

Species 1*st.* POLEMONIUM REPTANS.   *Jacob's-ladder.*

Sp. Ch. *Leaves* pinnate, generally by sevens: *flowers* terminal nodding.

Obs. This beautiful native well deserves a place in all flower-gardens; it bears transplantation well and improves by cultivation. It is a hardy plant and, with a little protection, may be made to bloom throughout the winter. Its favorite localities are in rich shaded situations among rocks and decaying logs, where its spikes of sky-blue flowers, with white anthers, appear about the 19th of April. There is a variety with white flowers.

33. Genus. PHLOX. L. *Wild Pink.*

(*Deriv.* Greek *Phlox,* fire or flame, in allusion to the colour of the flowers.)

Class 5th. PENTANDRIA—Order, MONOGYNIA.

Gen. Ch. Calyx deeply 5-cleft, segments connivent. *Corolla* salver-formed; border 5-lobed, flat; tube more or less curved. *Stamina* unequal. *Capsule* subrotund, 3-celled; cells 1-seeded.

Species 1*st.* Phlox Divaricata? *Sweet William.*

Sp. Ch. Stem low, pubescent, decumbent; *leaves* oval-lanceolate; *branches* divaricate, loose, few flowered; segments of the corolla obcordate, teeth of the calyx subulate linear. *Tor.*

Obs. Of this numerous genus, there are but few natives of this locality. The present species is easily distinguished from others, by its earlier period of flowering, its lower growth, rarely rising above 1 foot, and by its partially decumbent habit. The leaves, in the specimens I have met with, have been universally opposite, sessile, and few in number. Flowers in a terminal panicle, pale blue or more frequently rose-coloured. Generally known under the name of Sweet William or May Pink. Abundant in half reclaimed lands and borders of fields, from 10th to 20th April.

34. Genus. CERASTIUM. L.

(*Deriv.* Greek *keration,* a little horn, in allusion to the shape of the capsule. *Sm.*)

Class 10*th. DECANDRIA—Order, PENTAGYNIA.*

Gen. Ch. Calyx 5-leaved. *Petals* 5, bifid or emarginate. *Capsule* 1-celled, bursting at the summit with 10 teeth.

Species 1*st.* Cerastium Hirsutum. *Mouse-ear Chickweed.*

Sp. Ch. Very hairy, diffuse; *leaves* oval obtuse, connate; *flowers* clustered; *petals* 2-cleft a little longer than the acute calyx. *Ell.*

Obs. Mr. Elliott's description suits this plant remarkably well as it obtains with us. Very much branched and villous. Stems rarely rising more than 6–8 inches from the ground. Flowers inconspicuous, rarely fully expanded, small, white. Common in cultivated ground; in grass land frequently assuming a yellowish colour. Flowers middle of April.

Species 2d. CERASTIUM LONGE-PEDUNCULATUM.

Sp. Ch. Viscid-pubescent; *leaves* oblong-linear, acute; *peduncles* long.

Obs. Altogether a larger plant than the preceding, rising sometimes to the height of 12 inches, but more frequently semi-procumbent. The whole plant is remarkably viscid to the touch, and is strongly characterized by the circumstance which affords the specific name, viz. the unusual length of the peduncles. Found in common with the former but much more rare. Flowers a few days later.

Syn. C. Glutinosum. *Nutt.* C. Nutans. *Torrey.*

35. GENUS.   ERIGERON.   *Fleabane.*

(*Deriv.* Greek *Er,* the spring, and *geron,* an old man; because it is hoary in the spring. *Sm.*)

Class 19*th.* SYNGENESIA—*Order,* SUPERFLUA.

Gen. Ch. *Calyx* imbricate. *Florets* of the ray linear, very numerous. *Pappus* double; exterior minute; interior hairy, of few rays. *Receptacle* naked.

Species 1st. ERIGERON BELLIDIFOLIUM.

Sp. Ch. Hairy, gray, *radical leaves* obovate, spathulate, subserrate: *stem leaves* remote, oblong-ovate, amplexicaul, entire; *stems* 3–5-flowered; *rays* nearly twice as long as the hemispherical calyx. *Torrey.*

Obs. The present species, as it occurs in this vicinity, differs from the foregoing description in having the lower *stem-leaves* coarsely though irregularly toothed, while the *upper* ones only are entire or untoothed. The number of flowers also exceed that mentioned in the specific description, being often as numerous as 8–10. The flowers begin to shew themselves about the 10th of April, when the plant is only 3–4 inches high, and continue unfolding, until it has attained the height of 18 or 24 inches. The central flower, as observed by Mr. Elliott, is generally larger than the lateral ones—their colour varying from delicate pink to white—in pastures and meadows abundant.

Species 2d. ERIGERON PHILADELPHICUM.

Sp. Ch. Pubescent; *leaves* cuneate-oblong, cauline semi-amplexicaul; *rays* capillary.

Obs. A much taller species than the preceding, growing 3–4 feet high, very much branched and covered with a profusion of small white or pale purple flowers, with yellow disks. This is one of the greatest pests of the farmer, frequently so completely overrunning meadows as to destroy the hay. Some repute it medicinal, attributing to it tonic and sudorific properties. Flowers later than the last, and continues in bloom much longer.

36. GENUS.   PHACELIA.   *Jussieu.*

(*Deriv.* Greek, *Phakelos,* a bundle, from its cluster'd manner of flowering.)

Class 5th.   *PENTANDRIA—Order, MONOGYNIA.*

Gen. Ch.   *Calyx* 5-cleft.   *Corolla* 5-cleft.   *Stamens* exerted. *Capsule* 2-celled, 2-valved, 4-seeded.   *Ell.*

Species 1st.   PHACELIA FIMBRIATA.

Sp. Ch. *Leaves* pinnatifid, the lobes undivided; segments of the *corolla* fimbriate. *Ell.*

Obs. This plant, abundant throughout the western country, has at first glance the aspect and mode of flowering of an hydrophyllum. The whole part is hispid, the lower leaves somewhat petioled, the upper sessile or amplexicaul; all alternate and pinnatifid. Flowers of a pale blue are borne in a simple terminal raceme, revolute before flowering, become erect afterwards. Calyx persistent. Style 2-cleft. Grows in clumps; outer branches semi-prostrate; central more erect, rising to the height of 10–12 inches. Moist meadows—flowers from the middle of April.

37. GENUS.   CERCIS.   L.

(*Deriv.* Greek *kerkis* of Theophrastus.)

Class 10th.   *DECANDRIA—Order, MONOGYNIA.*

Gen. Ch. *Calyx* 5-toothed, gibbous at base. *Corolla* papilionaceous, with a short vexillum under the wings. *Seed vessel* a legume.

Species 1st.   CERCIS CANADENSIS.   *Red Bud.*

Sp. Ch. *Leaves* nearly round, cordate, acuminate, villous at the axils of the nerves, *legumes* on short foot-stalks.

Obs. The Red-bud, by which name it is universally known in this country, does not occur spontaneously in the level rich lands immediately round Lexington; but as the face of the country becomes more broken on approaching the Kentucky river, it is met with in great abundance; constituting, by the profusion of its pale rose-colour'd flowers, a pleasing object in early spring, before any of the forest trees have put forth their leaves. It never rises, even in the best soil, to any considerable elevation, but when growing singly its branches extend horizontally to a great extent in proportion to its height. The flowers appear generally by the 12th of April and are succeeded by a great number of pods, borne on short peduncles; and the tree becomes clothed, towards the 1st of May, with large heart-shaped leaves of a rich dark green.

38. GENUS. FRAXINUS. L. *Ash Tree.*

(*Deriv.* The Latin name of the Ash Tree: Etymology obscure. *Darl.*)

Class 2d. DECANDRIA—Order, MONOGYNIA.

Gen. Ch. Polygamous: *Calyx* none, or 4-parted. *Corolla* none, or 4-petalled. *Samara* 1-seeded: wing lanceolate.

Species 1st. FRAXINUS AMERICANA. *White Ash.*

Sp. Ch. *Leaflets* petiolate, oval-lanceolate, acuminate, slightly toothed, glaucous beneath.

Obs. This is one of the largest as well as the most useful of our forest trees; growing frequently to the height of 80 feet with a diameter of 3 feet; and applicable to many useful purposes in building, the mechanic arts and rural economy. It is readily distinguished from the *Blue Ash*, with which it is found in common, by its whiter, ash-coloured bark. Flowers about the middle of April, and is abundantly met with on the richer lands throughout the state.

Syn. F. Discolor, *Muhl.* F. Alba. *Marshall.* F. Acuminata. *Pursh.*

Species 2d. FRAXINUS QUADRANGULATA. *Blue Ash.*

Sp. Ch. *Leaflets* subsessile, oval-lanceolate, serrate, pubescent underneath: younger *branches* quadrangular.

Obs. The blue ash is more limited in its geographical range than the preceding species; but in this locality it is equally abundant and attains nearly if not quite to as large a size. Its wood unites strength with durability and elasticity and hence is applicable to a great variety of uses. Flowers about the same time with the former.

Species 3d. FRAXINUS SAMBUCIFOLIA. *Black Ash.*

Sp. Ch. *Leaflets* sessile, oval-lanceolate, serrate, acuminate, base rounded and unequal.

Obs. This is also a large tree, but much less frequent than either of the preceding, in this neighbourhood; in the western part of the State, on the contrary, it becomes more abundant than either, and is made to supply the purposes of both. Its wood, however, being marked with black streaks makes it more unfit for flooring. It is said, moreover, to be less durable than the two species just mentioned.

39. GENUS.   LAURUS.   L.

(*Deriv.* The ancient Latin name of the Bay tree: Origin obscure. *Darl.*)

Class 9th. *ENNEANDRIA—Order, MONOGYNIA.*

Gen. Ch. Calyx none. *Corolla* resembling a calyx, 4–6 parted. *Nectary* with 3 two-awned glands surrounding the germ. *Stamina* variable, 3 to 14. *Drupe* 1-seeded.

Species 1st. LAURUS BENZOIN.   *Spicewood.*
Sp. Ch. *Leaves* obovate, lanceolate, pubescent underneath: *flowers* in clustered umbels: buds and pedicels smooth.

Obs. The Spicewood is a common shrub throughout the Union; and is here met with in all shaded, rich woods where the undergrowth has not been destroyed; preferring mostly situations near small streams of water. Its little, yellow, clustered flowers appear towards the middle of April or earlier, before any appearance of foliage is observed on the branches, and are succeeded by numerous bright red berries. The bark of the wood is pleasantly aromatic and is sometimes used in warm infusion as a diaphoretic.

Species 2d. LAURUS SASSAFRAS.   *Sassafras.*
Sp. Ch. Mostly dioicous; *leaves* some oval and entire, others 2 or 3 lobed.

Obs. This tree, although very abundant in some portions of the state, is not met with any where within a few miles of Lexington. On approaching the Kentucky river, within the bounds of the county of Fayette, it is seen growing in fence corners, having sprung up since the clearing of the land: and on the alluvions and hills bordering that river large trees of 12–18 inches diameter are frequently seen. Flowers generally towards the middle of April, in somewhat the same manner with the Spicewood: its fruit however is larger and of a blue colour. Popular opinion has long since attributed much virtue to the bark of the Sassafras root; and medical countenance is frequently given to the idea of its being a *purifier of the blood.*

By some botanists these two species of Laurus are thrown into a sub-genus called *Euosmus,* from their pleasant aroma.

40. Genus PHALANGIUM. *Tournefort.* *Wild Hyacinth.*

(*Deriv.* A Greek name of a plant, mentioned by Dioscorides, derived perhaps from *phalagx*, a phalanx or legion, in allusion to the number and disposition of its flowers.)

Class 6th. HEXANDRIA—Order, MONOGYNIA.

Gen. Ch. Corolla of six petals, spreading. *Filaments* naked or smooth. *Capsule* ovate. *Seeds* angular.

Species 1st. Phalangium Esculentum. *Nuttall.*

Sp. Ch. Root bulbous, *leaves* all radical, linear, carinate; *stigma* minutely 3-cleft.

Obs. This is decidedly one of the most beautiful of our indigenous plants; throwing up from the centre of a tuft of smooth grass-like leaves, a long solitary stem 1 to 2 feet high, sheathed below by a few convoluted bractes, and clothed at the summit by a number of large purple or pale-blue flowers, 10 or 12 of which are in perfection at a time; these slowly shrivelling, (marcescent,) others are evolved, so as to keep up a succession of bloom for several days. The root, which is bulbous and situated deep in the ground, is eatable and nutritious—Frequent in moist meadows in certain localities, but generally disappearing upon culture—Flowers from the 20th of April.

Syn. Scilla Esculenta. *Bot. Mag.*
Phalangium Quamash. *Pursh.*

41. Genus. ASARUM. L.

(*Deriv.* The Latin name of a plant, spoken of by Pliny.)

Class 11th. DODECANDRIA—Order, MONOGYNIA.

Gen. Ch. Calyx 3—4 cleft, superior, persistent. *Corolla* none. *Anthers* adhering to the sides of the filaments. *Capsule* 6-celled.

Species 1st. Asarum Canadense. *Wild Ginger.*

Sp. Ch. Leaves 2, broad-reniform: *calyx* woolly, deeply 3-parted, reflexed.

Obs. The wild ginger is readily detected, by its two large kidney-shaped leaves, supported on long footstalks, and covered with a velvet softness,—by its solitary and singular flower issuing from the axil of the two leaves; and by the aromatic odour of the root, which has given it its common name. Occasionally abundant in rich shaded woods among rocks: flowering about the 20th of April.

We have followed Michaux, Muhlenberg and Elliott in placing this plant in the class Dodecandria, although by Pursh, Nuttall, Barton and Torrey it is ranked under Gynandria; and by Darlington in Polyandria.

Syn. A. Carolinianum. *Wall.*

42. GENUS.   CAULOPHYLLUM.   *Mx.*

(*Deriv.* Greek *Kaulos*, a stem and *phyllon*, a leaf: from the resemblance of the stem to a leaf-stalk. *Michaux.*)

Class 6*th.*   HEXANDRIA—*Order,* MONOGYNIA.

Gen. Ch. Calyx 3—6 leaved. *Corolla* 6-petalled, with a sub-reniform nectary on each claw. *Berry* stipitate, 1-seeded.

Species 1*st.*   CAULOPHYLLUM THALICTROIDES.   *Pappoose-root.*

Sp. Ch. Glabrous; leaves supradecompound; leaflets oval, terminal one 3-lobed.

Obs. This, the only species of the genus, was once abundant throughout this country, but has now almost disappeared from the more cultivated districts, and is consequently rare about Lexington, being only met with in the more secluded and unfrequented woodlands. It grows to the height of 12 or 18 inches, producing a single triternate compounded leaf; and a panicle of small greenish-yellow flowers, succeeded by dark-blue berries which are covered with a mealy powder.

Under the name of *Pappoose-root* this plant has had some medical virtues ascribed to it.—Flowers towards the latter part of April: berries ripe in June.

Syn. Leontice Thalictroides. *Willd.*

43. GENUS.   ÆSCULUS.   L.

(*Deriv.* Latin *Esca*, food: the fruit of some of the species being esculent.)

Class 7*th.*   HEPTANDRIA—*Order,* MONOGYNIA.

Gen. Ch. Calyx 1-leaved, 4—5 toothed, ventricose. *Corolla*

4—5 petalled. *Petals* unequal inserted upon the calyx. *Capsule* 3-celled. Seeds large, solitary.

Species 1*st.* ÆSCULUS PALLIDA. *Common Buckeye.*

Sp. Ch. *Leaflets* by 5s: *corolla* 4-petalled: *stamina* mostly 7, twice the length of the corolla: *fruit* spinous. Pursh.

Obs. This species is abundant throughout the forests in the rich lands of Kentucky. It is a tree of but ordinary stature, and for the most part of crooked growth, remarkable for the early period of its foliation, being the first of our trees to become green in the spring, and the earliest to cast its leaves in the fall.—The fruit is a large nut of a bright brown colour with a very remarkable hilum or eye, which has given the tree its common name: it is sometimes eaten by cattle, and often with fatal effects: Flowers about the 20th of April, and is then a very beautiful object: fruit ripens in September.

Syn. Pavia Lutea. *Mich. fil.*

Species 2*d.* ÆSCULUS FLAVA. *Sweet Buckeye.*

Sp. Ch. *Leaves* by 5s, pubescent underneath near the midrib, equally serrulate: *corolla* 4-petalled, with the claws of the connivent petals longer than the calyx: *fruit* unarmed.

Obs. A much larger and straighter tree than the preceding, but less abundant than it, being in this locality confined to the alluvion bottoms of the Kentucky river. Unlike the former the wood of the sweet buckeye is susceptible of being applied to many useful purposes.—The flowers are unfolded towards the end of April and are succeeded by smooth capsules containing one or three large seeds.

Syn. Pavia Ohioensis? *Mich. fil.* Sylva. Amer.

STELLARIA. (SEE GENUS 4.)

Species 2*d.* STELLARIA PUBERA. *Starwort.*

Sp. Ch. Pubescent; *leaves* sessile, ovate, ciliate; *pedicels* erect; *petals* longer than the calyx.

Obs. This species differs from the *S. Media*, before mentioned, in its less branching, and more erect habit. A single stem rises to the height of 6–8 inches, bearing a few comparatively large flowers. Rare; in woodlands. Flowers 20th April.

(TO BE CONTINUED.)

ART. VIII.—*Florula Lexingtoniensis, secundum florendi ætatem digesta; or a descriptive Catalogue of the Phænogamous plants indigenous to this portion of Kentucky; arranged in the order of their periods of flowering.* By CHARLES WILKINS SHORT, M. D. Professor of Materia Medica and Medical Botany in Transylvania University.

CONTINUED FROM PAGE 422. NO. III.

FASCICULUS III.

For the last of April and first of May.

---

44. GENUS   CORNUS.   L.

(*Deriv.* Latin; *Cornu,* a horn; in allusion to the horny toughness of its wood. *Smith.*)

Class 4th. *TETRANDRIA,—Order, MONOGYNIA.*

Gen. Ch. Calyx superior 4-toothed. *Petals* 4, small, superior, broader at the base. *Drupe* inferior, containing a 2-celled nut.

Species 1st. CORNUS FLORIDA.   *Dog-wood.*

Sp. Ch. Arborescent; *leaves* ovate, acuminate; *flowers* aggregated in a large 4-leaved involucrum.

Obs. In common with the red-bud, white oak and poplar, (tulip tree,) the dog-wood is confined in this county, to the thinner and more broken soils bordering on the Kentucky river and other water-courses, never being found on the first rate lands. In those situations favourable to its growth it attains considerable size, individuals being occasionally met with whose trunks measure a foot or more in diameter. The large white involucres, which are generally mistaken for its flowers, make a handsome show towards the 20th of April when fully evolved. The bark, dried and pulverized, has been long known as a useful tonic, by some even thought equal in efficacy to that of the Peruvian cinchona; and the durability, firmness and strength of its wood fit it especially for certain mechanical purposes.

This is the only species of Cornel which I have met with in this locality, although in other portions of the state, the cornus sericea and cornus paniculata frequently occur.

45. Genus.　　MALUS.　　L.　　*Apple.*

(*Deriv.* *Malus*, the Latin name for an apple-tree.)
Class 13th. *CALYCANDRIA,*—Order, *PENTAGYNIA.*
Gen. Ch. *Calyx* superior 5-cleft. *Petals* 5. *Styles* connate at base. *Apple* spheroid, umbilicate at each end, fleshy, 5-celled, many-seeded.

Species 1st.　Malus Coronaria.　　　　　*Crab apple.*
Sp. Ch. *Leaves* broad oval, rounded at the base, somewhat angled, serrate, smooth; *peduncles* corymbose.

Obs. The crab-apple tree, which was at one time more abundant than at present, is yet found occasionally in the more secluded woods of this county; and, where in clearing the land it has been allowed to remain, it forms a tree nearly equalling in magnitude the cultivated variety. The flowers of the wild crab are, indeed, more showy than those of the domestic apple-tree: they are white with a slight tinge of red, and are collected into corymbs; when in full bloom they produce a beautiful effect and diffuse a delicious odour to a great distance: The fruit is sometimes preserved with sugar.

Syn. Pyrus Coronaria, *Ell. Pursh, &c.*

46. Genus.　　CRATÆGUS.　　L.　　*Hawthorn.*

(*Deriv.* Greek. *Kratos,* strength: from the strength and firmness of the wood. *De Theis.*)
Class 13th. *CALYCANDRIA,—Order, DI-PENTAGYNIA.*
Gen. Ch. *Calyx* 5-cleft. *Petals* 5. *Styles* 1 to 5. *Fruit* a farinaceous berry, or small apple producing from 2 to 5 bony seeds.

Species 1st.　Cratægus coccinea.　　　　　*Red-haw.*
Sp. Ch. Thorny: *leaves* on long petioles, obovate, subcordate acutely lobed and serrated; *petioles* and pubescent *calyx* glandular: *flowers* pentagynous.

Obs. A small, well known and very common tree, flowering about the 20th of April, and producing an abundance of scarlet haws which are large and pleasantly tasted. They ripen in September.

---

*I here adopt the name proposed for this class by Dr. Darlington in his Florula Cestrica, as being more descriptive of its character, (the insertion of the stamens on the calyx,) than the Linnæan name, Icosandria.

Species 2*d.* CRATÆGUS FLAVA. *Yellow-haw.*

Sp. Ch. Spiny: *leaves* obovate, cuneate, angled, glabrous; *petioles*, *stipules* and *calyx* glandular; *flowers* generally solitary; *berries* turbinated, 4-seeded.

Obs. A small tree, about the size of the red-haw and flowering at the same time, but less common, and differing from it in producing yellow fruit which are larger, and not so numerous: they are acid and also pleasantly tasted, and ripen in October.

Other species of the hawthorn no doubt exist in this locality; but the genus is an obscure one and I have not been able distinctly to define them. Great diversity obtains in the size of the leaves of different individuals; and I have met with one tree whose flowers were all pentandrous!

47. GENUS. ANNONA. *L.* *Pawpaw.*

(*Deriv.* Latin *annona*, provision; from the eatable nature of the fruit.)

Class 12*th.* *POLYANDRIA.—Order*, *POLYGYNIA.*

Gen. Ch. *Calyx* 3-leaved. *Petals* 6. *Stigmas* sessile, obtuse. *Berries* (one or more,) large, cylindrical or ovate, many-seeded.

Species 1*st.* ANNONA TRILOBA. *Pawpaw*, *Custard-apple.*

Sp. Ch. *Leaves* glabrous, long, cuneate-obovate; *exterior petals* four times as long as the calyx, nearly round.

Obs. This portion of Kentucky was once the paradise of pawpaws, where immense orchards of large trees were every where met with; but cultivation and the ravages of cattle have greatly lessened the number. Trees of this species are occasionally met with 25 or 30 feet high, but for the most part they do not attain half that stature; and are often loaded with fruit when not more than 6 or 8 feet high. The flowers, which are large and singular, of a deep black purple, appear about the 20th of April before the leaves are put forth, and are succeeded by fruit of an oblong shape, at first green-coloured, then assuming a yellow and purple hue; when grown they often measure 6 or 8 inches in length, and weigh nearly a pound: they consist of several large seed surrounded by a soft, yellow, pulpy matter and covered by a thin skin. This fruit, when fully ripe, and slightly touched by the frost, is highly esteemed by the most of persons; and although Dr. Smith, the learned president of the Linnæan Society of London, affirms that it is "relished by few except the negroes," yet I have known many persons of cultivated taste declare it equal to any of the tropical luxuries. The bark of the pawpaw tree is so strong and fibrous that ropes are occasionally made of it; the wood is soft and worthless.

Few genera have been more confused by conflicting synonyms than this. Thus the elder Michaux calls the present individual, *Orchidocarpum Arietinum;* Pursh and Nuttall, *Porcelia triloba.* Elliott, *Asimina triloba, &c.* Without stopping to inquire into the expediency of these innovations upon established names, I will barely express my preference for that which is adopted in this catalogue, in which I am sanctioned by Linnæus, Smith and the younger Michaux, whose opportunities of examining all the species were as good as those of any other botanist.

48. Genus. QUERCUS. L. *Oak.*

(*Deriv.* An ancient Latin name of obscure etymology.)

Class 21st. *MONOECIA.—Order, POLYANDRIA.*

Gen. Ch. Masc. *Ament* naked, linear. *Calyx* slightly 5-cleft. *Corolla* none. *Stamens* 5 to 10.

Fem. *Calyx* 1-leaved, entire, scabrous. *Corolla* none. *Styles* 2 to 5. *Nut* coriaceous, surrounded at base by the persistent calyx.

Species 1st. Quercus alba. *White oak.*

Sp. Ch. *Leaves* oblong pinnatifid-sinuate, pale or pubescent beneath; *lobes* oblong, obtuse, mostly entire; *cup* deep, tuberculate; *acorn* ovate.

Obs. The white oak is not often met with in the rich tract of land immediately surrounding Lexington; but is found abundantly in that part of Fayette county bordering the Kentucky river; where the soil becomes thinner and the face of the country more rolling. In these situations it attains its largest size, and is readily distinguished from all other trees of the same family by its whiter bark, which is often, in the younger trees, disposed in alternate bands of a finer and coarser texture, giving to the tree a characteristic appearance. The strength, solidity and durability of its wood fit it for a vast variety of useful purposes.

Michaux, in his elaborate and elegant work on the forest trees of America, hazards the opinion that in process of time, by the gradual deterioration of the soil, the white oak will be spontaneously produced in those sections of the Union which are now too rich to grow it. This tree, in common with the other oaks which follow, blooms about the 25th of April, but their flowers are too inconspicuous to attract attention, and their acorns ripen and fall upon the coming of the first frost.

Species 2d. QUERCUS MACROCARPA. *Over-cup White oak, Bur-oak.*

Sp. Ch. Leaves wooly beneath, deeply lyrato-sinuately lobed; *lobes* obtuse, repand, upper ones dilated; *cup* deep, with the upper scales bristly; *acorn* large, oval.

Obs. This noble species is every where met with in the rich forests of this neighbourhood, towering above the most of other trees and throwing out its large umbrageous branches to a considerable distance around. It is distinguished from all other American oaks by its larger leaves, which are sometimes 12 or 15 inches long by 8 broad: the acorn, which is also of unusual magnitude, is singularly invested by the shaggy scales of the cup, in the form of a fringe. The bark of the trunk and limbs is much rougher and more furrowed than the preceding species, and its wood more porous, and less durable; nevertheless it is valuable for fencing and fuel.

Species 3d. QUERCUS PALUSTRIS. *Pin oak, Swamp Spanish oak.*

Sp. Ch. Leaves on long petioles, deeply sinuate smooth; *lobes* divaricate, dentate, acute; *cup* flat, smooth; *acorn* sub-ovate.

Obs. Next to that just mentioned, the present species is most frequently met with in the woods around Lexington; although, from its specific name, it might not be looked for in the dry upland of this portion of the state; for Michaux affirms that it "grows constantly in moist places, and of preference about swamps enclosed in the forests;" in confirmation of which re mark it may be observed that where such situations occur in this county, the tree will always be found. Like the Q. Macrocarpa, it attains to a great size, and in consequence of its wood splitting well it is often used for rails, shingles, laths &c. although it is not durable. The fine, glossy texture, and beautifully *scolloped* form of the leaves, which are more delicate than those of any other oak, give to this tree a peculiar and softer aspect than is common with the family, whose foliage for the most part is harsh and coarse.—The acorns are middle-sized, seated in shallow cups.

Species 4th. QUERCUS PRINUS ACUMINATA. *Chestnut white oak. Yellow oak.*

Sp. Ch. Leaves on long petioles, obtuse at the base, acuminate, coarsely toothed; teeth subequal; *cup* hemispherical, *nut* ovate.

Obs. This species is not so abundant, nor is it so large a tree as the last, though in common with it, it is found growing on the richest soils. The general appearance is that of the white oak; but they differ essentially in the form of their leaves, the size of their acorns, and still more in the qualities of their wood, the present species being every way inferior to that. The acorn is oval, black, and of a smaller size, and is said by Michaux to be also sweeter than that of any other of the American oaks. Different individuals of this species differ essentially in the size of their leaves, these being generally larger in proportion as the tree is young: a reference, however, to the acorn will always distinguish it.

Syn. Quercus Castanea. *Pursh* and other American botanists.

Species 5*th.*   Quercus imbricaria.   *Laurel oak.*

Sp. Ch. *Leaves* oblong, acute at each end, mucronate, entire, shining above, pubescent underneath; *cup* flat; *acorn* nearly spherical.

Obs. The laurel oak, though a very common tree in some portions of Kentucky, especially in that section called "the barrens," is comparatively rare in this locality; nevertheless it does occur occasionally in company with the last on the richest lands, and is always, when in foliage, a pleasing object, in consequence of the deep glossy green of its leaves, which, unlike any other oak of this country, are oval and entire, without serratures or scollops. This resemblance of the leaf to that of the mountain laurel, (Kalmia latifolia,) has given an appropriate English name to the species. It does not attain any considerable size, nor is its timber valuable.

Species 6*th.*   Quercus tinctoria.   *Black oak.*

Sp. Ch. *Leaves* deeply sinuated, the lobes terminating in sharp points, pulverulent beneath, shining above: *cup* saucer-shaped: *acorn* ovate.

Obs. The black oak derives its common name from the dark colour of its outer bark, by which it may at all seasons be distinguished from its congeners. It is one of the largest trees of the American forest, and highly valuable from the qualities of its wood in the mechanic arts, and of its bark in the processes of dyeing and tanning.—It is comparatively rare in this locality, though abundant in the surrounding country.

Syn. Quercus discolor. *Willd.*

49. Genus. JUGLANS. *L.* Walnut.

(*Deriv.* Contracted from *Jovis glans;* on account of the excellence of the fruit.)

Class 21st. *MONOECIA.—Order, POLYANDRIA.*

Gen. Ch. Masc. *Ament* imbricate. *Calyx* a scale. *Corolla* 5 or 6-parted. *Stamens* 18 to 36.

Fem. *Calyx* superior 4-cleft. *Corolla* 4-parted. *Styles* 1 or 2. *Drupe* coriaceous or spongy. *Nut* rugose, furrowed.

Species 1st. Juglans nigra. Black walnut.

Sp. Ch. Leaflets numerous, oval-lanceolate, serrate, narrowed above: *fruit* globose, scabrous, punctate.

Obs. No tree of the same magnitude is more common throughout the better lands of Kentucky, than the black walnut; but it appears to be particularly obnoxious to lightning and other accidents; hence the older stocks have very generally a mutilated appearance. Next to the elm this tree is the most usual domicil of the parasitic mistletoe. The wood of the black walnut is a good deal used in house-joinery, and in the coarser sort of cabinet work. The kernels of the nuts abound in a mild oil, and when thoroughly dried are palatable to the most of persons; and the spongy envelope of the nut is much used as a domestic brown dye for woolen cloths. Flowers towards the 25th of April. Fruit ripens in September.

Species 2d. Juglans cathartica. White walnut. Butternut.

Sp. Ch. Leaflets lanceolate, serrulate, pubescent: *petioles* villous; *fruit* oblong-ovate; *nut* deeply furrowed.

Obs. This is a smaller tree, and even more abundant than the preceding. It is called white walnut in consequence of the ashy colour of its smooth bark; from which circumstance also one of its botanical synonyms, (J. Cinerea) originates. The wood is soft and light-coloured, little used in mechanicks except for the purpose of making firkins for holding butter, lard and other oily substances, for which it is said to be peculiarly fitted. An extract made from the inner bark by boiling in water and evaporation, has long been a deservedly popular cathartic in the western country. The nut is more oily and less esteemed than that of the preceding walnut.

Florula Lexingtoniensis.

50. GENUS.   CARYA.   *Nuttall.*   Hickory.

(*Deriv. Karya,* the ancient Greek name of the Walnut tree.)

Class 21st.   *MONOECIA—Order, POLYANDRIA.*

Gen. Ch. MASC. *Ament* imbricated. *Calyx* 3-parted scales. *Corolla* none. *Stamina* 4 to 6.
FEM. *Calyx* 4-cleft, superior. *Corolla* none. *Styles* none. *Stigma* partly discoid, 4-lobed. *Pericarp* 4-valved. *Nut* subquadrangular, even.

Species 1st.   CARYA SULCATA.   *Ell. Thick Shell-bark Hickory.*
Sp. Ch. Leaflets about 9, oblanceolate; *fruit* 4-angled; *nut* long, mucronate.

Obs. This is one of the most abundant of the genus in this neighbourhood, rising to a very considerable height, (80 or 90 feet,) with a slender body in proportion to its elevation, and destitute of limbs for more than half its length. The greatest peculiarity, however, of this and the succeeding species is the division of the exterior bark into long narrow plates attached to the tree by inconsiderable holds, and separated from it at each end, giving to the tree a characteristic appearance. The nut is large, invested by a thick covering; its shell is thick, and the kernel well tasted. The wood like that of the most of hickories, is highly prized for fuel, and is much used by mechanics on account of its toughness and elasticity. Flowers towards the last of April; fruit ripens and falls in September.

Syn. Juglans laciniosa. *Michaux.*

Species 2d.   CARYA SQUAMOSA.   *Shell bark hickory, shagbark, scaly bark, &c. &c.*

Sp. Ch. Leaflets about 5, long-petiolate, lance-oblong; *fruit* depressed globose; *nut* small, compressed.

Obs. A large tree very similar in its growth and general appearance to the last, and like it, remarkable for the singular exfoliation of its epidermis, which has given it its common names. The present individual, however, is distinguished from the last by the number of leaflets which are almost uniformly five, and by the size of the nut, which, although enveloped in a thick rind, is much smaller than the preceding. These nuts have thin shells, are easily cracked between the teeth and are more highly esteemed than any other of the hickory nuts, except the pecan. The wood is very similar to that of the preceding, and indeed the trees are often confounded.

Syn. Juglans squamosa. *Mx.*
Carya alba. *Ell.*

Species 3d. CARYA TOMENTOSA. *White heart hickory. Mockernut, &c.*

Sp. Ch. *Leaflets* about 9, oblanceolate; *aments* tomentose; *nut* thick-shelled, hard.

Obs. Less common than either of the preceding in this neighbourhood, and a smaller tree with a less shaggy bark. This is the species so abundant in the barrens of Kentucky where the growth being obstructed by annual fires, whilst the root continues to extend itself, an immense and solid mass is found beneath the soil attached to a bare shrub above it. This species, moreover, is characterized by the large amount of hard, close-grained, white sap-wood which it bears, and which is especially fitted for axe helves and axle-trees. It is thought a superior fuel to all the other hickories.

Syn. Juglans tomentosa. *Mx.*
Juglans alba. *Willd. Muhl. &c.*

Species 4th. CARYA PORCINA. *Pig-Nut Hickory—broom hickory.*

Sp. Ch. *Leaflets* about 7, lanceolate glabrous: *fruit* pyriform, or globose.

Obs. The Pignut is easily distinguished from the other hickories by its smoother bark, its narrower leaves, and smaller fruit; for although the nut itself is about the size of that of the C. Squamosa, or small scaly bark Hickory, yet in the pig-nut the hull is so much thinner as to make the fruit altogether much less. It is in every respect the least valuable of the family, the wood being not fitted for useful application to the arts, less valuable as fuel; and the nut unfit to eat in consequence of its bitterness and astringency. Young trees of this kind are, however, more common around Lexington than any other Hickory.

Syn. Juglans porcina. *Mx.*

51. GENUS.   MORUS.   L.   *Mulberry.*

(*Deriv.* From *Morea*, the Greek name of the tree, which is of obscure derivation.)

Class 21st. *MONOECIA.—Order, TETRANDRIA.*

Gen. Ch. MASC. *Calyx* 4-parted. *Corolla* none. FEM. *Calyx*

4-leaved. *Corolla* none. *Styles* 2. *Calyx* becoming a berry. *Seeds* solitary.

Species 1st. MORUS RUBRA. *Common Mulberry.*

Sp. Ch. *Leaves* cordate, ovate, acuminate, frequently three-lobed, equally serrate, scabrous, pubescent underneath; *fertile aments* cylindrical.

Obs. Owing to the depredations of stock upon this valuable tree, whose bark is a favourite food with horses and sheep, it is becoming rare in this quarter where it once abounded: young trees are never met with in exposed situations, and the old ones have generally a decaying aspect. The sexes are sometimes together on the same plant and again separate, so that trees are occasionally found which never bear fruit. The wood of the mulberry is more durable when exposed to the vicissitudes of weather than any other timber of this region, except the red-cedar and black-locust; hence, in those parts of the country where those trees are not found, this is much used as posts for fencing. It blooms about the last of April, and ripens its fruit in June.

The White Mulberry, lately introduced by seeds from France, seems to thrive well in this climate, so far at least as four or five year's experience can show.

RANUNCULUS. [SEE GENUS 22.] *Crowfoot.*

Species 4th. RANUNCULUS RECURVATUS.

Sp. Ch. Stem erect, and with the petioles clothed with expanding hairs: *Leaves* 3-parted, villous, segments broad-oval, subincised, the lateral ones 2-lobed: *Calyx* reflected: *Petals* lanceolate; *Seeds* with a hooked point.

Obs. This species is easily distinguished from either of the former, by its more villous appearance and its larger leaves; a single stem, or but few, are protruded from each root, which are erect and succulent, and arise to the height of a foot or more, branching towards the summit. The radical leaves are borne on foot-stalks 8 or 9 inches long, those of the stem decreasing as they ascend. The flowers, which are small and of a greenish-yellow colour, appear towards the latter end of April, and are succeeded by globular heads of seed, each one having a hooked point. Rarer than the two first mentioned species. In shaded woods and meadows.

52. Genus. CHELIDONIUM. *L.* *Celandine.*

(*Deriv.* Greek *Kelidon*, a swallow; from the circumstance of its flowering about the time those birds first appear in the spring.)

Class 12*th.* *POLYANDRIA.—Order, MONOGYNIA.*

Gen. Ch. *Calyx* 2-leaved caducous. *Corolla* 4-petalled. *Silique* linear 2-valved, 1-celled. *Seeds* numerous.

Species 1*st.* CHELIDONIUM MAJUS. *Large Celandine.*

Sp. Ch. *Leaves* pinnate, lobed; *Segments* rounded; *Umbels* axillary, pedunculate; *Petals* eliptical, entire.

Obs. This handsome plant, so abundant on the borders of the Ohio river, is comparatively rare in this neighbourhood; its large showy yellow flowers, which would probably double under cultivation, are highly ornamental: in their natural state they are exceedingly fugacious. The whole plant is imbued with a yellow juice of an acrid, bitter, opiate taste. Flowers last of April in rich shaded situations.

53. Genus. PODOPHYLLUM. *L.*

(*Deriv.* Greek, *podos*; a foot and *phyllon*, a leaf. its leaf resembling the web-foot of some animals.)

Class 12*th.* *POLYANDRIA—Order, MONOGYNIA.*

Gen. Ch. *Calyx* 3-leaved. *Petals* 9. *Stigma* plaited, crenate. *Pericarp* a berry, 1-celled, many seeded.

Species 1*st.* PODOPHYLLUM PELTATUM. *May-Apple, Mandrake, Wild Lemon, &c.*

Sp. Ch. *Leaves* peltate-palmate, single, or two on a forked stem, *flowers* solitary, axillary.

Obs. No portion of the Union affords the May-apple in greater abundance than this, where it is found in profusion in all rich shaded woodlands. About the 1st of March its leaves appear above ground, it blooms generally towards the end of April and ripens its fruit in June. The latter is highly grateful to the taste of most persons; its leaves are deleterious and not eaten by any cattle; whilst its root, when properly dried and pulverized, affords an excellent cathartic, but little inferior to jalap.

54. Genus. COLLINSIA. *Nuttall.*

(*Deriv.* Named in honor of *Zaccheus Collins Esq.* of Philadelphia.

a gentleman distinguished for his acquirements in botanical knowledge, and general devotion to the natural sciences.)

Class 14th.   DIDYNAMIA—Order, ANGIOSPERMA.

Gen. Ch.   Calyx 5-cleft. Corolla bilabiate, orifice closed: upper lip bifid; the lower trifid, intermediate segment carinately saccate and closed over the declinate style and stamina. Capsule globose, partly 1-celled, and imperfectly 4-valved. Seeds 2 or 3, umbilicate.

Species 1st.   COLLINSIA VERNA.   Early flowering Collinsia.

Sp. Ch.   Leaves ovate-oblong, sessile, obtuse, the inferior ones attenuated into long petioles.

Obs. This beautiful little plant, which is seen in profuse abundance on many parts of the Dry-ridge road to Cincinnati, is occasionally, though rarely, found in this immediate vicinity. It is characterized by its particoloured flowers, the upper-lip being white, the lower a bright sky blue: they first appear about the last day of April, and continue to bloom during the month of May.

In May 1815, I met with this plant in the neighbourhood of Pittsburgh; but being unable, during a rapid journey to examine it critically, I sent several specimens to my friend, the late lamented Dr. Edward Barton of Philadelphia; he submitted them to the Abbe Correa, who pronounced it a violet. Subsequent more attentive investigations by the accurate Nuttall, who had seen it so early as the year 1810, have proven it to belong to a widely different class.*

55.   GENUS.   MALVA.   L.   Mallow.

(Deriv. Probably from the Greek, Malasso, to soften; in allusion to the mucilaginous and demulcent properties of the tribe.)

Class 16th.   MONADELPHIA—Order, POLYANDRIA.

Gen. Ch.   Calyx double; the exterior mostly 3-leaved. Petals 5.   Capsules many, 1-seeded, disposed orbicularly.

Species 1st.   MALVA ROTUNDIFOLIA.   Round-leaved Mallow.

Sp. Ch.   Stem prostrate; leaves cordate, orbicular, obscurely 5-lobed; peduncles declining when in fruit.

---

*Journal of the Academy of Nat. Sciences of Philadelphia. Vol 1. P. 189.

Obs. An exotic originally, now so thoroughly naturalized as to be met with every where in cultivated grounds and neglected wastes. Its first flowers, of a pale violaceous hue, are sometimes seen in ordinary seasons as early as the last of April; from which time the plant continues to extend itself by trailing on the ground, putting forth flowers and ripening seeds until November; being so hardy as to withstand considerable cold. Children sometimes eat the green fruit which they call ground cheese.

56. Genus.   FRAGARIA.   L.   *Strawberry.*

(*Deriv.* Latin, *fragrans*, smelling sweetly; in reference to its fragrant fruit.)

Class 13*th.* CALYCANDRIA.—*Order*, POLYGYNIA.

Gen. Ch. *Calyx* 10-cleft, *petals* 5. *Receptacles* of the *seed* ovate and deciduous, becoming a berry.

Species 1*st.* Fragaria virginiana.   *Wild strawberry.*

Sp. Ch. *Calyx* of the fruit spreading; *hairs* on the petioles erect, on the peduncles appressed.

Obs. The wild strawberry, which differs by minute distinctions only from the garden species, is not a common plant in this vicinity: it does, however, occasionally occur in old fields and road sides, flowering towards the last of April. In the western part of this state it constitutes a principal feature in the vegetation of the barrens; where, in situations fully exposed to the influence of the sun, its fruit becomes matured to perfection, is darker-coloured and sweeter than the strawberry of the gardens.

57. Genus.   ARUM.   L.

(*Deriv.* Probably from the greek *ara*, injury; in reference to the acrimonious qualities of the root.)

Class 21*st.* MONOECIA.—*Order*, POLYANDRIA.

Gen .Ch. *Spatha* cucullate. *Spadix* naked above; below feminine; in the middle staminiferous. *Calyx* and *corolla* none. *Berry* 1 or many-seeded.

Species 1*st.* Arum triphyllum.   *Indian turnip.*

Sp. Ch. Stemless: *leaves* ternate: leaflets ovate, acuminate, very entire; *spadix* club-shaped; *spatha* ovate, acuminate, convolute below; flat and bent above.

Obs. The singularly formed flower, (spatha) of this plant, its colour, green striped with purple, and the beautiful cluster of scarlet berries, maturing in mid-summer, readily distinguish this from any other plant, except the next following, of this Flora. In rich moist woods it attains the height of 2 feet or upwards. The root weighing an ounce or more, is well known to every body, under the name of Indian turnip, for its acrid properties. Flowers 1st of May.

This plant is said to be sometimes dioecious; more frequently however it is monoecious, the males and females being placed on the same spadix.

Species 2d. ARUM DRACONTIUM. *Green dragon, &c.*

Sp. Ch. Stemless; *leaves* pedate ("rather dichotomous"); leaflets lanceolate, oblong, entire; *spadix* fusiform,* longer than oblong, convolute *spatha.*

Obs. This species is not so common as the preceding, and is easily recognized by its differently formed leaf which is composed of numerous leaflets circularly arranged on a forked petiole; and its spadix which is 6 or 8 inches long, taper-pointed and yellow. The whole plant is generally more luxuriant than the former; bearing a larger cluster of berries which are also scarlet; and having a larger root which is possessed of the like acrimony. Flowers at the same time and is found in similar situations.

53. GENUS.   GERANIUM.   L.

(*Deriv.* Greek *geranos*, a crane; the persistent style resembling the beak of that bird.)

Class 16th. *MONADELPHIA.—Order, DECANDRIA.*

Gen. Ch. Calyx 5-leaved. *Corolla* of 5 petals. *Stigmas* 5. *Arilli* 5-seeded, awned.

Species 1st. GERANIUM MACULATUM. *Spotted crane's-bill, Wild Geranium.*

Sp. Ch. Erect: retrorsely pubescent: *stem* dichotomous: *leaves* opposite, 3-5-parted incised, upper ones sessile: *peduncles* elongated 2-flowered: *petals* twice as long as the calyx.

---

*I have chosen to substitute this term for Subulate, which is used in the description of the spadix, by all the writers. As it obtains with us, this organ has much more resemblance to a large spindle than an awl.

Obs. The pale purple flowers of this pretty plant make a handsome show during May, about the first week of which month they begin to appear. The radical leaves are supported on long foot-stalks, the cauline are sessile, all pubescent, and become spotted with yellow, brown and red, as the plant declines. The root is knotty and tuberous, possessed of considerable astringency, and hence called wild *Tormentil.* It is a good deal used medicinally in some portions of the Union, and is perhaps nowise inferior to the exotic just mentioned. Found in moist, rich situations, about fence-roads &c. rare.

59. GENUS. ROBINIA. L. *Locust.*

(*Deriv.* Named in honor of *M. M. Robin,* French botanists who first introduced the tree into Europe.)

Class 17*th.* DIADELPHIA.—*Order,* DECANDRIA.

Gen. Ch. *Calyx* 4-cleft, the upper segment 2-parted. *Vexillum* nearly round, expanded, reflexed. *Pod* compressed, long, many-seeded.

Species 1*st.* ROBINIA PSEUD-ACACIA. *Black locust.*

Sp. Ch. *Leaves* unequally pinnate: *stipules* spinescent: *racemes* pendulous: *pods* smooth.

Obs. My own observations do not agree with those of M. Michaux in regard to the habits of this tree; for although it does occur in profuse abundance in this and other richest lands of Kentucky; yet I have found the largest and most thrifty stocks on the Ohio river in Boon county, seventy miles north of Lexington, where the soil is greatly inferior to that of this vicinity. Its handsome foliage and deliciously scented flowers have long recommended it here, as elsewhere, as an ornamental tree for plantations, street-walks &c. and the excellence of its wood, in point of durability, hardness and strength, particularly recommends it to the attention of landed proprietors. The forests of the adjoining counties furnish a considerable amount of this timber which is used in the construction of Steam Boats: and there is an immense annual consumption of it in making the posts of fences. Within the last few years, however, this excellent tree has sustained serious injury from the depredations of an insect, which penetrates to the very centre of the wood permeating its whole substance with large hollows; in consequence of which many of the finest trees have become destroyed. Where planted in town the locust tree flowers about the

1st of May, those in the country are observed to be a week or ten days later.

60. GENUS.   PRUNUS.   L.

(*Deriv.* The latin name for plum: etymology obscure.)

Class 13*th.*   *CALYCANDRIA.—Order, MONOGYNIA.*

Gen. Ch. *Calyx* inferior, campanulate 5-cleft, deciduous. *Petals* 5. *Drupe* even. *Nut* with a prominent suture.

Species 1*st.* PRUNUS VIRGINIANA.   *Wild cherry.*

Sp. Ch. *Racemes* erect, elongated; *leaves* deciduous, oval-oblong, acuminate, shining above, serrate, smooth on both sides; *petioles* with 2-4 glands.

Obs. One of the largest trees of our forests, occurring abundantly on the richest soils, and one of the most valuable of the lumber yeilding kind, in consequence of the beauty, hardness, and durability of its wood, which is more extensively used than any North American tree, in cabinet work. When portions of the tree are selected for this purpose, at the bifurcation of the stocks, the plank, when polished, exhibits a rich and varied appearance, nowise inferior to the best mahogany. Flowers about the 8th of May, and cherries ripen in July: these are dark-coloured, of a sweetish bitter taste. The bark has been long used as a domestic medicine in jaundice and debility. It appears to be a vegetable bitter of some activity, modified in its effects, by a notable portion of prussic acid.

Syn. Cerasus Virginiana. *Mich. Darl. &c.*

Species 2*d.* PRUNUS CHICASA.   *Chickasaw plum.*

Sp. Ch. *Flowers* fasciculate, lateral fascicles sessile; *leaves* narrow lanceolate, serrulate; *branches* spiny, glabrous.

Obs. A small tree ten or fifteen feet high, thickly studded with limbs which are garnished with small shining leaves, persistent to a late season in the fall, and giving to the tree an evergreen appearance. Flowers from 1st to 15th of May: fruit, of a yellowish red colour, ripens in August: it is pleasantly tasted when thoroughly ripe and is frequently preserved with sugar. Frequent in shrubberies occasionally occurring wild.

Syn. Prunus angustifolia. *Marshall.*

(TO BE CONTINUED.)

ART. IX.—*Florula Lexingtoniensis, secundum florendi œtatem digesta; or a descriptive Catalogue of the Phænogamous plants indigenous to this portion of Kentucky; arranged in the order of their periods of flowering.* By CHARLES W. SHORT, M. D. &c.

FASCICULUS IV.

From the first to the middle of May.

---

61. GENUS   AQUILEGIA.   *L.*

(*Deriv.* Latin, *aquila*, an eagle; the nectaries being fancied to resemble an eagle's claws.)

Class 12*th.* POLYANDRIA—*Order,* DI-PENTAGYNIA.

Gen. Ch. Calyx none. *Petals* 5. *Nectaries* 5, bearing spurs between the petals. *Capsules* 5, distinct.

Species 1*st.* AQUILEGIA CANADENSIS.   *Wild Columbine.*

Sp. ch. Spurs straight; *styles* and *stamens* exserted; *flowers* pendulous; *leaves* ternate and bi-ternate, their segments 3-parted, obtuse at the summit, notched and toothed.

Obs. This, the only native species of the genus, is among the most beautiful and common of the North American plants, surpassing, in the delicacy of its leaves and brilliancy of its flowers, the common cultivated species, (*A. vulgaris*). The wild columbine is found throughout the Union, always preferring the rocky, moist banks of creeks and rivers, but thriving well when removed to different situations. It is readily recognized by its drooping flowers, of bright red and yellow colours, in which the alternate arrangement of 5 petals, and 5 hollow, spurred nectaries, constitute the characteristic of the genus. These, after remaining for a considerable length of time, fall off and leave 5 distinct capsules, terminated by long styles and filled with numerous seed.

Flowers usually about the 1st of May: in favourable seasons somewhat earlier.

62. GENUS.   DODECATHEON.   L.

(*Deriv.* Greek, *dodeka theoi*, twelve Gods; an old name of heathenish origin, taken from the twelve flowers, or thereabouts, comprising the umbel of the plant.)

Class 5th.   PENTANDRIA—*Order*, MONOGYNIA.

Gen. ch. *Calyx* 5–cleft. *Corolla* rotate, reflected, 5-parted. *Filaments* very short; anthers connivent. *Capsule* 1-celled, oblong, opening at the apex.

Species 1st.   DODECATHEON MEADIA.   *American Cowslip.*

Sp. ch. *Leaves* oblong, oval, (repandly toothed?) *umbel* many-flowered lax: *bractes* oval.

Obs. I have been disposed to question the accuracy of those who have made two species of this genus; viz. *D. Meadia* and *D. integrifolium*; the characteristics of the latter being, according to Michaux, who is followed by Pursh, Nuttall and Torrey, "leaves oblong-oval, subspathulate, entire; umbel few flowered, straight; bractes linear,"—"a much smaller plant than the preceding;" and Dr. Torrey gives 4 inches as the ordinary length of the leaves of *D. Meadia*. A plant before me, selected as a medium specimen from many others found on the Kentucky river, has leaves 10 inches long, and more than 2 inches broad, which are perfectly entire on the edges; the scape being about 1 foot in height, and from 12 to 14-flowered. The leaves of this specimen would consequently point it out as a luxuriant growth of *D. integrifolium*, whilst its very size, the number of flowers, and their drooping habit would designate it as *D. Meadia*. I conclude consequently that they are but varieties of the same species, differing in appearance from soil, situation and exposure.

The plant in question is among the most interesting of our Flora. Like the Columbine, in whose company it is often found, it prefers the moist and shaded hill-sides bordering water-courses; and is strikingly characterized by its tuft of smooth radical leaves; its naked stem, bearing at the summit, on long pendent peduncles an umbel of white flowers, sometimes tinged with delicate purple, their petals reflected and twisted, marked in the centre with a brown areola, which is tinged exteriorly with yellow. These successively evolving, make a beautiful show, and continue for some time in bloom. Flowers about the 1st of May.

PHACELIA. (See Genus 36.)

Species 2nd. PHACELIA BIPINNATIFIDA.

Sp. ch. Stem erect; *leaves* pinnatifid; segments incisely lobed; *racemes* mostly bifid, oblong, many-flowered; divisions of the *corolla* entire.

Obs. This plant is also an inhabitant of the cliffs and precipitous, rocky banks of the Kentucky river and other water-courses in this neighbourhood. It is distinguished from the first mentioned species (*P. fimbriata,*) by its more luxuriant growth, deeper blue flowers, which are not fringed, and by a peculiar, strong, resinous odour emitted by the plant, particularly when the seeds are maturing. At this stage of its growth, from the elongation of the racemes, which are thickly beset with capsules, it assumes a diffuse, procumbent habit. Flowers 1st of May.

The genus *Phacelia* seems to have been unnecessarily severed from *Hydrophyllum*; and the present individual approximates still nearer to that genus in the bearded character of its stamens.

63. Genus. HYDROPHYLLUM. *L.*

(*Deriv.* Greek, *hydor,* water, and *phyllon* a leaf—water-leaf.)

Class 5th. PENTANDRIA.—*Order,* MONOGYNIA.

Gen. ch. Corolla campanulate 5-cleft, with five internal, longitudinal, nectariferous grooves; *stamens* exserted, filaments bearded in the middle, *capsule* 1-celled, 2-valved, 4-seeded, with 3 of the seed abortive.

Species 1st. HYDROPHYLLUM CANADENSE. *Shawnee salad.*

Sp. ch. Leaves simple, lobed, angular; *flowers* in crowded fascicles.

Obs. Root leaves on long petioles, large and broad, somewhat palmate, 5-7 lobed, cut and toothed. Stem leaves smaller and on shorter petioles; flowers white, pale blue, or purple, less densely crowded together than in the succeeding species. The plant is about 18 inches high when fully grown, and every where covered with an hairy pubescence, particularly on the calyx. The leaves are said to be eaten by the Indians as a salad. Common in half cultivated lands, about fence corners &c. Flowers about 5th of May.

Species 2nd. HYDROPHYLLUM APPENDICULATUM.

Sp. ch. Very hairy; *radical leaves* sub-pinnatifid; *cauline* ones angularly lobed; sinuses of the *calyx* with minute oval appendages.

Obs. This species of water-leaf is more commonly confined to the rocky banks of creeks and rivers, being distinguished, even when not in flower, by its large sub-pinnate, coarsely toothed, deep green leaves, which are marked with maculæ of paler green. From the tuft of root-leaves arise one or more stalks to the height of 12 or 13 inches, sparsely supplied with leaves, and garnished at the summit with one or more dense, globose heads of flowers: these like the preceding are of various shades of colour, from white to pale blue and purple. The whole plant is hairy, and especially the calyx. Flowers usually during the first week of May.

PHLOX. (SEE GENUS 33.)

Species 2nd. PHLOX SETACEA? *Ground Pink.*

Sp. ch. Cespitose, (pubescent?) *leaves* fasciculate, subulate, rigid, ciliate; *flowers* few, terminal, somewhat umbelled; segments of the *corolla* cuneate, emarginate; teeth of the *calyx* much shorter than the tube of the corolla.

Obs. I have ventured with doubt to affix this name (*setacea*) to the present species, although it agrees nearer with the description given above, than any other specific character to which I have access, and I can scarcely suppose it a new species. I have met with the plant but in a single locality, on the Kentucky river at the mouth of Hickman creek, where on the precipitous cliffs which over-hang the river, it forms a beautiful object during the month of May. Its root being fixed in the soil collected in the fissures of perpendicular cliffs, the main branches hang down to the length of 10 or 12 inches but are not stoloniferous, and from them arise numerous secondary branches about 4 inches long; these are thickly beset at their origin with stiff, narrow, smooth leaves of about 1 inch in length, which are shorter on the ramuli and become somewhat oval and ciliate. Each small stem supports from 1 to 8 flowers, which are white or pale blue throughout. These flowers, thus produced in immense numbers, form dense circular tufts on the surface of the rocks quite concealing the foliage of the plant. The whole plant is destitute of pubescence except the ciliæ of the smaller stem leaves. Flowers about the first week of May.

64. GENUS.　　SILENE.　　L.　　*Catchfly.*

(*Deriv.* Probably from the Greek *sialon* saliva; in allusion to the frothy, viscid moisture on the stalks.)

Class 10*th.*　DECANDRIA.—*Order,* TRIGYNIA.

Gen. ch. *Calyx* cylindrical. *Petals* 5, clawed, crowned at the throat. *Capsule* 3-celled.

Species 1*st.*　SILENE PENNSYLVANICA.　　*Wild pink.*

Sp. ch. Viscidly pubescent; *radical leaves* cuneate; *stem leaves* lanceolate; *panicle* mostly trichotomous; *petals very obtuse.*

Obs. "A small semi-procumbent plant with large rose-coloured flowers." Several stems arise from a common root to the length of 6 or 9 inches, each bearing at the top, about three flowers which are quite handsome. The lower leaves, when the plant is in bloom, are for the most part yellow and decaying, those on the stem generally petiolated, sometimes almost connate. On the poorer, exposed hill-sides bordering the Kentucky river. Flowers about the 5th of May.

Species 2*nd.*　SILENE VIRGINICA.　　*Crimson Catchfly.*

Sp. ch. Erect or partially decumbent, vicidly pubescent; *leaves* oblong lanceolate, scabrous on the margin; *panicle* dicotomous; *petals* bifid; *stamens* exserted.

Obs. A much taller plant than the preceding, more viscidly pubescent on the leaves and stems, and especially the calyx; it is moreover strikingly distinguished by its bright scarlet flowers, the petals of which are deeply bifid at their ends. The plant when fully grown is 1 or 2 feet high, branching towards the summit, each branch bearing from 1 to 3 flowers. Leaves opposite and of a dark green. Less common than the preceding, but found in similar situations; blooming somewhat later.

TRILLIUM.　　(SEE GENUS 20.)

Species 2*nd.*　TRILLIUM ERECTUM.　　*Upright Trillium.*

Sp. ch. *Peduncle* inclined; *flower* nodding; *petals* ovate, acuminate, flat, spreading, broader and a little longer than the calyx; *leaves* broad rhomboid, acuminate, sessile.

Obs. A much larger plant than the first mentioned species, (*T. sessile.*) stem 12 or 18 inches high. Peduncle inclining to one side nearly at right angles from the stem, 1 to 3 inches long. Flower large, drooping, dark purple or white. Leaves 4 or 5

inches long and of the same breadth. Found during the forepart of May in rich secluded woodlands.
Syn. T. rhomboideum. *Mich.*

65. GENUS.   MITELLA.   *L.*

(*Deriv.* Latin, diminutive of *Mitra;* the ripe capsule resembling a cap, or little mitre.)

Class 10th.   *DECANDRIA.—Order, DIGYNIA.*

Gen. ch. Calyx 5-cleft, persistent. *Petals* 5, pinnatifid, inserted into the calyx. *Capsule* 1-celled, 2-valved, valves equal.

Species 1st.   MITELLA DIPHYLLA.   *Two-leaved Mitella.*
Sp. ch. Leaves somewhat lobed, with the lobes acute and dentate; *stem* erect with two opposite leaves about the middle.

Obs. This delicate little plant is readily distinguished by its cordate root-leaves on long petioles; its single stem, about one foot high, having, in the middle two opposite sessile leaves, and bearing at the top a spike of small white flowers, delicately fringed on the edges. It is rare in this locality, being only found occasionally on the moist and shaded borders of watercourses. Flowers early in May.

66. GENUS.   IRIS.   *L.*   *Flag.*

(*Deriv.* From the hues of the flower resembling in variety those of the rainbow.)

Class 3d.   *TRIANDRIA.—Order, MONOGYNIA.*

Gen. ch. Corolla 6-parted, alternate segments reflected. *Stigmas* resembling petals.

Species 1st.   IRIS CRISTATA.   *Small crested Flag.*
Sp. ch. Bearded, *beard* crested; *scape* generally 1-flowered, as long as the leaves; *petals* nearly equal.

Obs. This tribe is readily recognized by the student from their near resemblance to the cultivated species of the gardens. The present is the only one native of this section, and is found on the rocky or gravelly margins of the larger water-courses. The flowering stems are generally about 6 inches high, bearing one or two handsome mottled flowers. The larger leaves are about the same length. The roots are fibrous and creeping, and when chewed impart a pungent sweetness to the taste. Kentucky river. Fore part of May.

67. GENUS. VIBURNUM. *L.*

(*Deriv.* Probably from the Latin, *rieo*, to bind; from the use formerly made of some of the species.)

   Class 5*th.* PENTANDRIA.—*Order*, TRIGYNIA.

Gen. ch. *Calyx* small, 5-parted, superior. *Corolla* campanulate, 5-cleft. *Berry* or drupe 1-seeded.

Species 1*st.* VIBURNUM PRUNIFOLIUM. *Black-haw.*
Sp. ch. *Leaves* obovate, nearly round and oval, glabrous, sharply serrate; *petioles* winged.

   Obs. The Black-haw is a common shrub or small tree on the more broken and rocky lands bordering the Elk-horn and Kentucky river. Its small white flowers collected into dense heads are quite ornamental, in contrast with the deep glossy green of the leaves; and the fruit, which ripens in September, is sweet and palatable. Blooms about the 10th of May.

68. GENUS. CELTIS. *L.*

(*Deriv.* An old name for an Asiatic tree; Etymology obscure.)

   Class 5*th.* PENTANDRIA.—*Order*, DIGYNIA.

Gen. ch. Polygamous. *Calyx* 5-parted. *Corolla* none. *Styles* thick, divaricate. *Drupe* 1-seeded. *Masculine* flowers (inferior.) *Calyx* 6-parted, with 6 stamina.

Species 1*st.* CELTIS OCCIDENTALIS. *Hackberry.*
Sp. ch. *Leaves* ovate, acuminate, equally serrate, unequal at the base, scabrous above, pubescent beneath; *flowers* solitary.

   Obs. The Hackberry is a very common tree throughout the best lands of this state, attaining in such situations a very great height. The wood splits well but is not durable, nor does it make good fuel. Its small inconspicuous flowers are unfolded during the first part of May, and are succeeded by berries about the size of small garden peas, the kernels of which are surrounded by a thin pulp, of very sweet taste, which has given to the tree, in some parts of the country, the name of sugar-berry-tree. These berries are eagerly sought after by birds, and the coarse harsh leaf of the tree is the favourite food of many insects.

   In the western part of Kentucky a dwarfish species of this tree (*C. pumila,*) is met with, bearing fruit when not more than 2 feet high.

69. GENUS. GYMNOCLADUS. *Lamark.*

(*Deriv.* Greek, *gymnos*, naked, and *klados* a branch; in allusion to the naked and seemingly dead appearance of the branches in winter.)
Class 22nd. *DIOECIA.—Order, DECANDRIA.*
Gen ch. MASC. *Calyx* tubular, 5-cleft. *Corolla* of 5 petals. FEM. Flower as the male. *Style* 1. *Legume* 1-celled, internally somewhat pulpy. *Seeds* roundish, large and indurated.

Species 1st. GYMNOCLADUS CANADENSIS. *Coffee-nut-tree.*
Sp. ch. *Leaves* bipinnate; *leaflets* oval, acuminate, pubescent. *Pursh.*

Obs. The coffee nut, tree, as it is here universally called, is the only species of the genus, and is peculiar to the forests of Canada and the western states of North America, in no portion of which is it more commonly met with, or seen in greater perfection than in the immediate neighbourhood of Lexington. It is strikingly characterized by its naked trunk, covered with a rough contorted bark, lofty in proportion to its size; its thick obtusely pointed branches; its large compound leaves, formed of a great number of small leaflets, arranged by double pairs; and more particularly by its large brown pods, which remaining on long after the leaves have fallen, give a peculiar effect. The wood is porous and of a reddish hue, not unlike the coarse kind of mahogany: it splits well but is little used in mechanicks. The seed, of which 6 or 8 are found in each pod, are large and hard; the kernel, extracted by roasting in the fire, ground and boiled in water forms a drink not unlike coffee.

Although this tree is usually ranked among the dioecious vegetables, (in which the male and female flowers are borne on different plants,) I have been induced to believe that it was frequently polygamous or hermaphrodite, from observing that a barren tree is very rarely met with, and that individuals bear fruit abundantly although solitary and distant from all others of the kind. Pursh even places it in the class Decandria. Flowers generally from the 10th to 15th of May. Fruit ripens in October.

Syn. Guilandina dioica. *Linn.*

70. GENUS. PTELEA. *L.*

(*Deriv.* Greek, *ptelea*, the elm; from the resemblance of the fruit of this shrub to that of the elm.)

Class 4th. *TETRANDRIA.—Order, MONOGYNIA.*

Gen. ch. *Corolla* 4-petalled. *Calyx* 4-parted, inferior. *Stigmas* 2. *Samara* compressed, nearly round, 1-seeded in the centre.

Species 1st. PTELEA TRIFOLIATA.   *Shrubby trefoil.*

Sp. ch. *Leaves* ternate; *flowers* in panicles, polygamous.

Obs. A shrub of 8 or 10 feet in height with a smooth greyish bark. The leaves are trifoliate, or arranged in threes, of a bright glossy green on their upper surface but paler underneath. The flowers are not showy, but the seed being large and collected into clusters are quite ornamental. The whole plant has a strong unpleasant odour, not unlike that of the common buckeye (*Æsculus pallida*). Grows on stony lands bordering water courses. Rare in this neighbourhood. Flowers from 10th to 15th May.

71. GENUS.   EUONYMUS.   *L.*

(*Deriv.* So called by antiphrasis from *euonymos*, Greek, good name, because the plant was deemed infamous for its properties.)

Class 5th. *PENTANDRIA.—Order, MONOGYNIA.*

Gen. ch. *Calyx* 4 or 5-cleft, with a flat peltate disk at base, within; *Corolla* 4 or 5-petalled. *Capsule* 3 to 5-angled, 3 to 5-valved, coloured.

Species 1st. EUONYMUS ATROPURPUREUS. *Burning-bush. Spindletree. Indian arrow-wood. Wahoo.*

Sp. ch. *Leaves* petiolate, oblong-lanceolate; *peduncles* divaricate, *fruit* smooth. *Darl.*

Obs. The Indian arrow-wood or Wahoo, by which names this shrub is here universally known, is found in rich moist forests, not too much frequented by cattle. Its small flowers of a dark purple appear about the 10th of May, and are succeeded by numerous flesh-coloured, angular capsules, which bursting disclose its bright red seed attached by slender filaments: these continuing on the bushes throughout the fall, and even until mid-winter, give to the plant a highly ornamental appearance. The bark of the root is actively cathartic, and a decoction in water exhibited in small and frequently repeated doses, has proved highly beneficial in asthmatic cases.

Species 2nd. EUONYMUS AMERICANUS.   *Small burning-bush.*

Sp. ch. Branches smooth quadrangular: *leaves* subsessile, smooth, acute, serrate: *peduncles* 3-flowered: *flowers* 5-cleft: *fruit* warty.

Obs. Much less abundant in this locality than the preceding, being confined to the rocky banks of water courses, and even there, not often met with: in the western part of the state it is frequently found in such situations. The flowers are less darkly coloured; the leaves smaller and persistent until late in the fall; the fruit exteriorly warty, but interiorly of the same bright colour. The whole plant is of humbler growth but equally ornamental. Flowers about the same time.

RANUNCULUS.   (SEE GENUS 22.)

Species 5th. RANUNCULUS FLUVIATILIS.   *River crow-foot.*

Sp. ch. Stem swimming; *leaves* all capillary, many-cleft; *petals* obovate, larger than the calyx; *seeds* glabrous.

Obs. A small aquatic plant found in shallow-running waters. Numerous stems arise in common from one spot and subsequently branching take root at each bifurcation; the leaves, which arise from the same points, are alternate, and finely dissected, giving the plant, before it blossoms, the appearance of a moss. The flowers are small, of a yellowish white colour, and arise about an inch above the surface of the water. Found in Elkhorn on the George-town road: rare: blooms about the 10th of May.

Syn. R. pantothrix. *Elliott.*

72. GENUS.   STAPHYLEA.   *L.*

(*Deriv.* Greek, *staphyle,* a bunch, or cluster; alluding to the manner of its fructification.)

Class 5th. *PENTANDRIA.—Order, TRIGYNIA.*

Gen. ch. Calyx inferior, 5-parted, coloured. *Corolla* 5-petalled. *Capsules* 2 or 3, inflated, connate. *Nuts* mostly 2, globose.

Species 1st. STAPHYLEA TRIFOLIA.   *Bladder-nut.*

Sp. ch. Leaves trifoliate; *racemes* pendulous; *petals* ciliate below.

Obs. This shrub, attaining the stature of a small tree in favourable situations, is most generally found growing on the

rich declivities of hills and among rocks bordering water-courses. The pale, yellow flowers, produced abundantly in lax racemes, make a handsome show about the middle of May; and in the fall the shrub is conspicuous among all others by its large inflated capsules not unlike those of the ground cherry. (*Physalis.*) The wood is soft and valueless.
Syn. S. trifoliata. *Marshall.*

73. GENUS.   ORCHIS.   L.

(*Deriv.* An ancient Greek name, alluding to the testicular shape so common in the roots of this genus.)

Class 18*th.*   *GYNANDRIA—Order,* *MONANDRIA.*

Gen. ch. Corolla ringent, upper leaflet vaulted. *Lip* dilated, base spurred beneath. *Pollinia* 2, terminal, adnate.

Species 1*st.*   ORCHIS SPECTABILIS.   *Showy Orchis.*
Sp. ch. *Lip* obovate, crenate; *spur* clavate, shorter than the germ; *bractes* large.

Obs. Of this extensive genus, the present subject is the only species I have met with in this neighbourhood, where, indeed, gynandrous plants of any kind are rare. A few years since this occurred frequently in moist rich woods; it has now, however, almost disappeared before cultivation and the ravages of cattle. When met with it is readily recognized by its particoloured flowers, the upper lip being purple, the under one and spur a pure white; by its two radical leaves sheathing the stem below; by its angular scape, and large bractes. Flowers about the middle of May.

In other parts of the state the *Orchis ciliaris* and *O. fimbriata* are abundant.

74. GENUS.   BIGNONIA.   L.

(*Deriv.* Named by Tournefort in honour of the *Abbe Bignon*, a learned Frenchman of the 17th century.)

Class 14*th.*   *DIDYNAMIA.—Order,* *ANGIOSPERMIA.*

Gen. ch. *Calyx* 5-toothed, cup-shaped, coriaceous. *Corolla* campanulate, 5-lobed, ventricose on the under surface. *Pod* 2-celled. *Seeds* winged with a membrane.

Species 1*st.*   BIGNONIA CAPRIOLATA.   *Yellow creeper.*   *Cross vine.*
Sp. ch. *Leaves* conjugate, bearing tendrils on the petioles, leaflets ovate, acuminate, sub-cordate, at base; *racemes* axillary.

Obs. This handsome climber occurs frequently among the mural cliffs of the Kentucky river, sometimes covering the face of the rock to a considerable extent; attaching itself by tendrils which arise from the foot-stalks of the leaves. The leaves are in pairs, two arising in common, and opposite to two others; they retain their verdure partially throughout the winter. The flowers are numerously produced at the axils of the leaves; they are of a reddish colour exteriorly and yellow within, appearing about the middle of May, but so transient in duration as not often to be met with in bloom.

Syn. B. crucigera. *Walter.*

Species 2nd. BIGNONIA RADICANS. *Trumpet flower.*

Sp. ch. Leaves pinnate, leaflets ovate, dentate, acuminate; *corymb* terminal; *tube* of the *corolla* twice as long as the calyx; *stem* radicant.

Obs. No vine is more common in the forests of this country, or more commonly planted for ornament, than the trumpet flower; climbing over buildings and the loftiest trees, throwing out radicles all along the stem by which it attaches itself firmly to walls, fences, or the bark of trees. Its large red flowers, produced in clusters, are highly ornamental; they appear somewhat later than those of the preceding species, and are succeeded by long pods filled with membranaceous seed. Some circumstances have occurred within my knowledge which induce me to think this plant is always injurious and sometimes fatal to the tree supporting it.

75. GENUS. RHUS. *L.*

(*Deriv.* Probably ftom the Celtic *rhudd*, red; in reference to the colour of the fruit.)

Class 5th. PENTANDRIA.—*Order.* TRIGYNIA.

Gen. ch. Calyx 5-parted. *Petals* 5. *Berry* small, sub-globose, with one bony seed.

Species 1st. RHUS RADICANS. *Poison oak. Poison vine.*

Sp. ch. Leaves ternate, leaflets petiolate, ovate, glabrous, generally entire; *stem* radicant; *flowers* dioicous.

Obs. This vine is generally known from all others by its poisonous properties, producing swelling, inflammation and a peculiar eruption on the skin of most persons touching it; some constitutions, however, are much more liable to its deleterious impression than others. It is extremely common in this section of the Union, covering almost every dead tree, and climbing to the tops of the loftiest branches, attaching itself by radicles from the stem in the same manner with Bignonia radicans. Its clusters of small greenish coloured flowers, appear towards the middle of May, and are succeeded by dark berries not unlike the small winter-grape.

Syn. R. toxicodendron, (*Michaux*,) which is regarded by some as a mere dwarfish variety of the present plant.

Species 2nd.   RHUS GLABRUM.   *Common Sumach.*

Sp. ch. Leaves pinnate, leaflets lanceolate, acuminate, acutely serrate, villous underneath.

Obs. This, the only other species of Rhus found in this neighbourhood, is universally known by the name of Sumach. It is frequently introduced into shrubberies and forms a pleasing object in ornamental gardening; its rich drooping foliage having somewhat a tropical appearance. The flowers appear considerably later than those of the preceding species, and are produced in dense conical clusters, succeeded by clumps of red berries, which are covered with a mealy efflorescence of very acid properties. In autumn the leaves assume a scarlet colour which adds much to the beauty of its appearance, and the berries hang on during the winter. The berries and leaves are used in tanning morocco.

The *Rhus copalinum* is common in the *barrens* of Kentucky.

76. GENUS.   HYDRANGIA.   *L.*

(*Deriv.* Greek, *hydor*, water, and *aggos*, a vessel; in allusion to the pitcher-like shape of the seed-vessels.)

Class 10*th.*   *DECANDRIA.—Order. DIGYNIA.*

Gen. ch. Calyx superior, 5-toothed. Petals 5. Capsule 2-beaked, opening by a foramen between the horns.

Species 1*st.*   HYDRANGIA CORDATA.—*Pursh.*

Sp. ch. Leaves broad ovate, slightly cordate at base, acuminate, coarsely toothed, glabrous underneath; *cymes* generally radiate.

Obs. This Hydrangia occurs frequently on rocky situations near water throughout the Western country. The leaves are large, opposite and heart-shaped. The flowers produced in cymous clusters are composed of small central fertile florets, whilst those of the circumference are larger, more showy and

barren. On the Kentucky river: growing to the height of 4 or 6 feet: flowers middle of May.
Syn. H. vulgaris.—*Mich.*

77. GENUS.   CYNOGLOSSUM.   *L.*

(*Deriv.* Greek; *kyon, a dog,* and *glossa,* a tongue, from a fancied resemblance in its leaves.)

Class 5th.   *PENTANDRIA.—Order, MONOGYNIA.*

Gen. ch. Calyx 5-parted. • *Corolla* short, funnel-formed, the the orifice closed with connivent scales. *Seeds* depressed, fixed to a central column.

Species 1st. CYNOGLOSSUM OFFICINALE. *Common hounds-tongue.*
Sp. ch. Leaves broad-lanceolate, attenuate at the base, sessile, downy; *stamens* shorter than the corolla.

Obs. This plant, originally exotic, has been gradually dispersed over the greater part of the Union. The whole plant is of a dull green and downy; lower leaves broad and lanceolate, not unaptly giving name to the genus from their similitude in form to a dog's tongue: upper leaves narrower, more pointed and sessile. The stems arise to the height of about 2 feet, branching towards the top; each branch bearing a spike of small, dark purple flowers, which are succeeded by large seed covered with prickles, by which they adhere to fleeces or clothes. Common in pastures and waste grounds. Flowers about middle of May.

Species 2nd. CYNOGLOSSUM VIRGINICUM. *Virginian hounds-tongue.*
Sp. ch. Leaves oval-oblong, acute, hairy, upper ones cordate and amplexicaul at base; *corymb* on a long naked peduncle.

Obs. Differs from the preceding in the colour of the flowers which is a bluish white, it is moreover less branched and more hirsute. Found in oak woods, though less abundantly than the former species. Flowers about the same time.
Syn. C. amplexicaule. *Mich.*

78. GENUS.   VERBASCUM.   *L.*

(*Deriv.* A corruption of *Barbascum,* from *barba* a beard, on account of the hairy or woolly leaves of some of the species.)

Class 5th.   *PENTANDRIA.—Order, MONOGYNIA.*

Gen. ch. Calyx 5-parted. *Corolla* rotate, 5-lobed, unequal.

Stamina declined, bearded. *Stigma* simple. *Capsule* 2-celled, valves inflected, many seeded.

Species 1st. VERBASCUM THAPSUS. *Common Mullein.*
Sp. ch. Leaves decurrent, woolly on both sides; *raceme* spiked, dense, two of the *stamens* glabrous.

Obs. Every one is familiar with this very common plant, which though originally introduced is now but too thoroughly naturalized among us. Popular opinion has long pronounced it possessed of considerable medical virtue; and Dr. Smith, of London, says "the whole herb is mucilaginous, emollient, and sometimes narcotic." Abundant in old fields, stony grounds, and washed hill-sides. Begins to bloom towards the middle of May and continues flowering until fall.

Species 2nd. VERBASCUM BLATTARIA. *Moth mullein.*
Sp. ch. Leaves amplexicaul, oblong, smooth, serrate; *peduncles* 1-flowered, solitary.

Obs. A less luxuriant plant than the former, and although a foreigner also, equally abundant. It is found in similar situations with the common mullein, and is frequently seen growing between the bricks of pavements and moist walls. The stem is ordinarily about 2 feet high, densely clothed at the bottom by smooth serrate leaves, and bearing on the summit a spike of white flowers tinged internally with purple; the anthers being a bright orange colour. These appear ordinarily towards the 15th of May, continue evolving for some weeks and are succeeded by dry, roundish capsules filled with small seed. The variety of this species with yellow flowers I have not seen in this country.

79. GENUS.   OXALIS.   *L.*

(*Deriv.* Greek, *oxys*, acid: in reference to the quality of the plants.)

Class 10th. DECANDRIA,—*Order,* PENTAGYNIA.

Gen. ch. Calyx 5-leaved. Petals 5, connected by claws. *Stamina* alternately shorter. *Capsule* 5-celled, 5-angled.

Species 1st. OXALIS STRICTA.   *Sheep-sorrel. Wood-sorrel.*
Sp. ch. Caulescent; *stem* erect, branched, hairy; *leaves* ternate, obcordate; *umbels* longer than the petioles; *petals* obovate, entire; *styles* as long as the interior stamens.

Obs. Although considerable diversity obtains, according to the season, in the time of the sorrels' flowering, yet the middle of this month may be regarded as the medium period: however it is occasionally found in bloom much earlier. This species is distinguished by its upright hairy stem, branching towards the top, and bearing several umbels of small yellow flowers. It is common in gardens and other cultivated grounds.

Species 2nd. OXALIS VIOLACEA. *Violet wood-sorrel.*

Sp. ch. Stemless; *scape* umbelliferous, *flowers* nodding: *leaves* ternate, obcordate, glabrous; *styles* shorter than the stamens, recurved.

Obs. Easily distinguished from the preceding by its lower growth, for having no proper stem the leaf and flower-stalks arise from the root, which is tuberous. The leaves are moreover larger than those of *O. stricta*, and are marked with purplish stains: the flowers are also larger and of a handsome violet hue. Grows in shaded woods or damp soils, blooming first about the middle of May; Mr. Nuttall remarks that it appears often to flower again late in the Autumn, and is then destitute of leaves.

30. GENUS. ANTHEMIS. L.

Deriv. Greek, *anthemon*, a flower; from the profusion it bears.)

Class 19*th.* SYNGENESIA.—*Order,* SUPERFLUA.

Gen. ch. Calyx hemispherical, scales nearly equal. *Corolla*, rays more than 5. *Pappus* none or marginal.

Species 1st. ANTHEMIS COTULA. *May-weed. Dog-fennell.*

Sp. ch. Receptacle conic, chaff setaceous; *seed* naked; leaves bipinnate, leaflets subulate, 3-parted.

Obs. The road sides and waste grounds are every where covered with this obtrusive weed, which, originally introduced, has become quite too well known among us. It commences flowering about the middle of May and continues from that time till the coming of frost, to put forth blossoms, and ripen its seed. The whole plant has strong sensible properties and is reputed medicinal; it is however entirely destitute of the aroma of the cultivated chamomile, *A. nobilis.*

[TO BE CONTINUED.]

NOTICES OF WESTERN BOTANY AND CONCHOLOGY

C[harles] W[ilkins] Short and H. Hulbert Eaton

Art. IV.—*Notices of Western Botany and Conchology.* By C. W. Short M. D. and H. Hulbert Eaton A. M. (r. s.)

HAVING made during the last fall, in company together, an excursion from this place to the Ohio river, a distance of about eighty miles due north from Lexington, sometimes travelling by stages, and sometimes on foot; we had a fair opportunity and abundant leisure for examining the vegetable productions of the intervening country; and also the shells of the Ohio, and the contiguous portion of the great Miami river. Of these, as we have thought it might not be uninteresting to naturalists in other portions of the country, we subjoin a catalogue of each, restricting it to those which were found on this excursion; with a few desultory remarks. It may not be amiss to observe, as accounting for the paucity of plants found in bloom, that the summer and fall had been unusually hot and dry, and that, in many portions of the western country, the grasses and other small herbaceous vegetation were literally burnt up by the drought. The catalogue may, nevertheless, be regarded as a tolerably fair specimen of the latest autumnal Flora of this section of the Union—no plant being mentioned which was not found in flower, and none having bloomed subsequently, in consequence of the occurrence of severe frosts, before our return from the excursion, which commenced on the 16th of September, and terminated on the 1st of October.

The aridity of the season, if it lessened the number of botanical acquisitions, proved, on the contrary, eminently favorable to conchological researches; as the waters of the Ohio and Miami rivers were much lower than they had been for many years preceding, and consequently afforded an opportunity of examining their shores some distance into these streams. The particular localities which were especially and very carefully examined, for shells, were those portions of the Ohio river, on the northern side, lying a mile or two above and below the mouth of Muddy-creek, (a small stream which empties into that river about fifteen miles below Cincinnati,) and the eastern borders of the great Miami, contiguous to the village of Cleves, in Hamilton county, Ohio.

I. PLANTS.

Lycopus Europæus.
Lycopus Virginicus. } Both met with occasionally on the moist rocky banks of creeks, &c.

Collinsonia Canadensis. (Var. ovata.) Found in the flat moist woods of Ohio, above the North Bend.

Commellina communis. In abundance on the alluvion borders of Eagle creek at the crossings; and on Muddy-creek, Ohio.

Schollera graminifolia, W. In the low waters of the Miami, at the Cleves ford; rare.

Ceresia fluitans. Moist woods, Ohio.

Isnardia palustris, W? (Ludwigia apetala Walt. L. nitida, Ph. and Mx. L. palustris, Ell.) On the marshy borders of the

Ohio river, at the mouth of Muddy-creek. Although this plant is placed by the most of botanists among the apetalous species of Ludwigia, the specimens here found had distinct petals of some size, and a purple colour.

Chenepodium botrys. Abundant on the sandy banks of the Ohio every where: its odour highly fragrant.

Chenepodium anthelminticum. (Wormseed.) Equally abundant in some situations on the river, with the former.

Gentiana quinqueflora. (G. amarelloides, Mx.) In the woods around Big-bone lick—not frequent.

Gentiana saponaria. Found in a single locality on Muddy-creek.

Impatiens pallida, N.
Impatiens fulva, N. } Both of these species of Touch-me-not occur abundantly, and in equal profusion, in all damp shaded and rich soils throughout the western country, especially among the drift-wood and debris of creeks; and they continue to flower and ripen seed from an early period in the summer, until the frosts destroy them.

Lobelia syphilitica. Occurs abundantly in neglected pastures around Lexington.

Lobelia inflata. In equal profusion and in similar situations.

Lobelia cardinalis. A solitary specimen of this beautiful species was found in bloom, at this late season, on a branch of Big-bone creek.

Onosmodium hispidum. On a clayey hill-side near the tavern at the Big-bone lick: rare and nearly out of bloom.

Elodea petiolata. Ell. (Hypericum petiolatum, Walt.) Ohio bank.

Mimulus ringens.
Mimulus alatus. } Both in abundance on the moist alluvion of Muddy-creek and other similar situations.

Mentha borealis.
Mentha tenuis? } On the rocky beds of Eagle and Big-bone creeks:—the former species much most common.

Gerardia tenuifolia, W. (G. erecta, Vahl.) On the summit of the Dry-ridge near Jones's:—the only locality in which we have met with it in the western country.

Verbena hastata. Banks of the Ohio river, common.

Zapania nodiflora. First met with on the dry gravelly beds of small streams, and afterwards, in much greater luxuriance, on the banks of Muddy-creek.

Capraria multifida. Big-bone creek, and the sandy borders of the Ohio river.

Lindernia attenuata. Mouth of Muddy-creek.

Chelone glabra. (Var. *purpurea*) In a marsh on Muddy-creek, in company with Gentiana saponaria.

Hyssopus nepetoides. Frequent in pastures and meadows on the Ohio river.

Scrophularia marilandica. Abundant in the corners of fences and waste grounds, throughout the Western country.

Erysimum palustre. Mouth of Muddy-creek.

Cleome dodecandra, W. (*Polanisia graveolens*, T.) Abundant on the gravelly margin of the Ohio river; nearly out of bloom at this time.

Strophostyles angulosa. Abundant among the sand and gravel of the Ohio borders, growing quite to the water's edge.

Rudbeckia triloba. In the oak-woods about Gaine's—rather rare.

Rudbeckia fulgida. A common yellow-flowering weed; abundant in fence corners throughout the fall.

Coreopsis tricosperma. A very rare and pretty plant,—a single specimen only was found, on Muddy-creek.

Bidens bipinnata. A small kind of Spanish-needle; common.

Bidens chrysanthemoides. This pretty species of an unsightly genus is abundantly met with throughout the western country, in all moist situations; its large, showy, yellow flowers making a very handsome appearance at this late season of the year.

Actinomeris squarrosa. A tall weed, common in the fence rows of cultivated fields.

Conyza camphorata. Quite common on the ridge road. The specific name is surely a very inappropriate one, its smell being much more similar to the peculiar odour of the negro than to that of camphor.

Eupatoreum perfoliatum. (Thoroughwort &c.) Exceedingly common in all marshy situations.

Eupatoreum cælestinum. This beautiful plant first occurred to us on the head-waters of Big-bone creek; and afterwards in profuse abundance on the higher banks of the Ohio river.

Aster conyzoides. And several other Asters not accurately determined.

Prenanthes ————? Ohio bottoms.

Gnaphalium uliginosum. Big-bone Lick.

Helenium autumnale. (Sneeze-weed.) Every where abundant, especially about water-courses.

Eclipta procumbens. Frequent on water-courses, sometimes being strictly procumbent in its growth, and again entirely erect.

Acnida cannabina. (Water hemp.) Common on approaching the Ohio river.

Ambrosia trifida. (Horse-weed.) Very common every where in waste grounds.

Asplenium angustifolium. On the high table lands between the Ohio and Miami rivers: rare.

II. SHELLS.

As already observed, our principal examinations for shells were made near the mouth of Muddy-creek in the Ohio river, and near Cleves in the great Miami river; in this list we shall refer to these two localities as Ohio and Miami. A fact well worth relating, is, that the shells from the Miami are almost invariably much larger than those of the same species from the Ohio; and what is very remarkable, are rarely or never in the least degree decorticated even on the beaks; and several species are found there, free from erosion, which are commonly described as possessing decorticated beaks. The shells from the Miami are generally covered with a greyish, granulated, calcareous crust, deposited from the water—which, running over Geodiferous Limerock, always contains more or less carbonate of lime in solution.

In the few remarks which we shall make in relation to the Naiades, we shall follow Cuvier in considering that margin of the shell anterior which contains the mouth, and which always moves foremost when the animal is in a progressive state—it being the margin towards which the beaks of the shell incline. In stating the dimensions of the shells, the figures always refer to inches and decimals of inches.

At the commencement of the list of the species of each genus, enough of the generic characters are given to distinguish our four genera from each other, and no more.

UNIO. *Valves free, having one or more cardinal and lateral teeth in each.*

Unio plicatus, LE SUEUR. (U. costata of Raf., is probably a variety of this species. See Raf., p. 49, pl. 82, fig. 13 and 14.*) Ohio and Miami: rather common. The undulating surface and the thickness of the different specimens of this species vary so much as to offer some apology for Barnes's subdivision of it into three species, (plicatus, crassus and undulatus.) The folds are nearly wanting in some specimens, while in others they are very profound. This shell was observed from half an inch to five inches in breadth. We have one specimen from the Miami with beaks perfectly entire and white; its dimensions are as follows:—Diameter 2. 0, Length 3. 2, Breadth 4. 2, while a young one from the Ohio is eroded, and measures—Diameter . 6, Length . 8, Breadth 1. See Am. Jour. Sc., Vol. 6, pages 118—120, pl. 1, 2 and 3.

Unio mytiloides, RAFINESQUE. (U. undatus, Banes.) Ohio and Miami: most abundant species in the Ohio. This shell varies much with regard to several particulars: sometimes there is a deep sulcus running from the beaks to the posterior basal margin, while other shells have no sign of a furrow. The nacre varies from white to perfect pink: the lateral tooth of the right valve of the pink variety is sometimes *treble*, and in some of the white ones it is hardly double. Very young shells are often marked with brown rays, particularly on the beaks and over the umbo. See Am. Jour. Sc., vol. 6, p. 121, pl. 4, fig. 4.

Unio scalenius, RAF. Ohio and Miami: common. The spe-

---

* We refer to a work "on the bivalve fluviatile shells of the Ohio river" by S. C. Rafinesque; published in 1820.

cimens from the Ohio are very much decorticated on their beaks, but those from the Miami are always perfectly entire. The beaks of the Ohio shells are terminal and projecting, while those from the Miami are not terminal; yet there is no doubt of their identity. See Raf., p. 43, pl. 81, fig. 24 and 25.

Unio ellipsis, LEA. Ohio: great abundance. Sometimes beautifully radiated with green. See Lea's Naiades, p. 10, pl. 4, fig. 4.

Unio sulcatus, LEA. Ohio: rather rare. Our specimens are all more or less purple within, none of them being as represented by Mr. Say, "pearlaceous-white." See Lea's Naiades. p. 44, pl. 8, fig. 12; and Am. Con., vol. 1, No. 1, pl. 5, lower figures.

Unio ridibundus, SAY. Ohio and Miami: rare. This beautiful little shell, first described, with his usual minuteness and accuracy, by Mr. Lea, as a variation of his *U. sulcatus*, has since been made a new species by Mr Say, and described and figured by him in the first number of his "American Conchology," plate 5, upper fig. All of our specimens are more or less purple within—some very much so.

Unio torulosus, RAF. (U. cornutus Barnes; U. foliatus, Hildreth.) Ohio and Miami. All possible varieties of this heteramorphous shell were found in the Ohio: the *U. foliatus* of Hildreth, which Mr. Lea thinks nothing more than a variety of the *U. cornutus* of Barnes was found, and among our numerous specimens of this variety, not one had hardly the rudiment of a horn. In the variety described and figured by Rafinesque. the tubers begin to appear, so as to render the shell *torulose*. Neither *torulosus* nor *cornutus* will apply to every variety; but since Mr. Rafinesque's name was given first, it must be adopted. and that of Mr. Barnes, although generally used, laid aside. See Raf., p. 88, pl. 82, fig. 11 and 12; and Amer. Jour. Sc., vol. 6, p. 122, pl. 4, fig. 5; and Lea's Naiades, page 32, note.

Unio verrucosus, BARNES. Both varieties, *purpureus* and *albus*, occur plentifully in the Ohio. The warts are more or less numerous, and in some instances almost entirely wanting. See Am. Jour. Sc., vol. 6, p. 123, pl. 5, fig. 6.

Unio metanever, RAF. (U. nodosus, and rugosus, Barnes.) Ohio: rare. See Raf., p. 39, pl. 81, fig. 15 and 16; and Am. Jour. Sc., vol. 6, pp. 124 and 126, pl. 6 and 7.

Unio lachrymosus, LEA. Ohio and Miami: very rare, we only finding three specimens. A very large specimen from the Miami measures—Diameter 2. 8, Length 3. 3, Breadth 4. 1. The epidermis in this remarkably large specimen is brownish-yellow with a very slight tinge of olive in some places: the beaks are perfectly entire: the anterior, inferior, and posterior-inferior portions of the disk of the shell are smooth and free from tubercles. See Lea's work, page 8, pl. 6, fig. 8.

Unio tuberculatus, BARNES. Ohio and Miami: rather rare. One from the Miami with the beaks free from decortication, measures—Diameter 1. 35, Length 2. 65, Breadth 4. 7.

Unio cylindricus, SAY. Ohio: rather rare. See Nich. Enc., vol. 4, pl. 4, fig. 3; and Am. Jour. Sc., vol 14, page 282, pl. 2, fig. 13.

Unio cariosus, SAY. (U. crassus, Say; U. carinatus and ellipticus, Barnes.) Ohio and Miami: very abundant. Some of the specimens of this species were more ponderous than any other found during this excursion. This is also a polymorphous shell; some are nearly circular, some quadrangular, some ovate, and some almost perfectly elliptical. The color of the nacre varies from perfect salmon to pure white: the epidermis is of all shades from dark brown to light yellowish. All the shells from the Miami have perfectly entire white beaks, and not being in the least degree *carious* are not entitled to the specific appellation it bears. From this it appears evident that the *decortication* of the beaks of shells ought not to be mentioned as an *essential* character. The dimensions of three of the Miami shells follow:

Diameter 1. 9, Length 3. 3, Breadth 5. 2.
do. 2. 1, do. 3. 3, do. 4. 7.
do. 1. 7, do. 2. 5, do. 2. 3.

See Nich. Encyc., vol. 4, pl. 2, fig. 7, and pl. 1, fig. 8; and Am. Jour. Sc., vol. 6, p. 259 and 271, pl. 11, fig 10, and pl. 13, fig. 19.

Notices *of Western Botany and Conchology.*

Unio phaseolus, HILDRETH. (U. planulatus, Lea.) Ohio and Miami: rather rare. This shell was first accurately figured by Mr. Lea, and described by him under the name of *U. planulatus*, but, (as very justly observed by Mr. Peter of Pittsburgh,) as Dr. Hildreth's name has the priority it must be adopted. Some specimens are arcuated on the basal margin as represented by Dr. Hildreth, but more commonly slightly curved or straight. The dimensions of one of our shells is, Diameter 1. 1, Length 1. 7, Breadth 2. 9. See Lea's work, page 45, pl. 19, fig. 13; and Am. Jour. Sc., vol. 14, p. 283.

Unio securis. LEA. (U. depressa, Raf.) Ohio and Miami: not very abundant. A specimen from the Miami measures— Diameter 1. 5, Length 2. 8, Breadth 3. 7. The posterior basal margin of this large specimen is slightly arcuated, and in several specimens it is straight.

Unio torsus, RAFINESQUE. Ohio: in great profusion. Some specimens are rendered emarginate posteriorly by a broad furrow running from near the beaks to the posterior margin. Lateral teeth generally double in both valves. See Raf., p. 45, pl. 82, fig. 1, 2 and 3.

Unio circulus, LEA. Ohio: common. It was suggested to us by Mr. Peter that this shell was the *U. orbiculatus* of Dr. Hildreth, but we are unable to say whether the suggestion be correct; and if it is, it is highly probable that his name will not be retained, for Rafinesque has probably described it before him under the name of *U. subrotundus*; if so, this latter name is the one to be appropriated to the shell. The color of the nacre varies from perfect white to beautiful flesh color or pink. Some of our specimens are emarginate, on account of sulci running from the beaks to the posterior basal margins. See Lea's work, page 47, pl. 9, fig. 14; Amer. Jour. Sc., vol. 14, p. 284; and Raf., p. 42, pl. 81, fig. 21, 22 and 23.

Unio irroratus. LEA. Ohio and Miami: rather common. See Lea's work, p. 11, pl. 5, fig. 5.

Unio rectus, LAMARCK. (U. prælongus, Barnes.) Ohio and Miami: common. This species occurs of all sizes, with the nacre either clear and white, or (in young specimens) beautifully colored, either entirely or only in the centre of the cavity of the umbo, of a lively purple, pink or salmon. In some instances the cardinal teeth are very small, while in other shells they are thick and prominent, and often beautifully serrated. A large one measures—Diameter 1. 5, Length 2. 3; Breadth 5. 5. See Am. Jour. Sc., vol. 6, p. 261, pl. 13, fig. 11; and vol. 14, p. 286.

Unio gibbosus, BARNES. Ohio: common. Some of our specimens are rather long, with the basal margin arcuated; others are shorter, and with a straight basal margin. See Am. Jour. Sc., vol. 6, p. 262, pl. 11, fig. 12.

Unio cuneatus, BARNES. Ohio and Miami. A specimen from the Miami, with entire white beaks, measures—Diameter 1. 6, Length 2. 5, Breadth 3. 6. See Am. Jour. Sc., vol. 6, page 263; and vol. 14, p. 279, pl. 1, fig. 3.

Unio ovatus, SAY. Ohio, but far more abundant and of a larger size, in the Miami; one measures—Diameter 2. 5, Length 3. 8, Breadth 5. 4. A few small specimens were found in the Ohio beautifully radiated, thin and exceedingly fragile: one of these measures—Diameter 1. 1, Length 1. 6, Breadth 2. 1. The posterior slope of the large specimens is far less flattened than that of the smaller ones. See Nich. Encyc., vol. 4, pl. 2, fig. 7; and Am. Jour. Sc., vol. 14, p. 287, pl. 2, fig. 21.

Unio occidens, LEA. Ohio and Miami: not very abundant. See Lea's work, page 49, pl. 10, fig. 16.

Unio triangularis, BARNES. Ohio and Miami: common. We found two varieties of this shell; one figured by Barnes, measuring—Diameter 1. 2, Length 1. 0, Breadth 1. 8; in this the cavity of the beaks and umbo are very deep: the other figured by Say, measures—Diameter 1. 1, Length 1. 8, Breadth 2. 4; the cavity of the umbo and beaks of this variety are not much over half as deep as in the first. The latter variety occurs more frequently in the Miami, and in that locality the beaks are never eroded. See Am. Jour. Sc., vol. 6, p. 272, pl. 13, fig. 17; and Am. Con., vol. 1, No. 1, pl. 4.

Unio parvus, BARNES. Ohio: rare. The smallest American species. Shell thick. Diameter . 4, length . 6, breadth 1. 0.

Old specimens are generally very much eroded, while young ones are nearly entire on the beaks. See Am. Jour. Sc., vol. 6, p. 174, pl. 13, fig. 18.

Unio zig-zag, LEA. Ohio and Miami: common. A beautiful little shell; when full grown larger and thinner than the U. parvus. See Lea's work, page 54, pl. 12, fig. 19 and 22, a.

Unio triqueter, RAFINESQUE. (Unio calceolus, Lea.) Miami: rare. Mr. Rafinesque having described and figured this shell under this name first, is entitled to it. Mr. Lea's specimens were very young, yet there is no doubt that his shell and ours are the same. The beaks are entirely free from decortication, and invariably present two or three deep transverse folds: the substance of the shell is thin and fragile until it attains to nearly its full size, when it becomes near one eighth of an inch in thickness. The *posterior dorsal* portion presents slight longitudinal folds, which, going to the margin of the shell, in some instances cause it to be crenulated: basal margin is either slightly curved, straight or arcuated on its posterior half. The posterior slope is much more flattened than represented by Lea, a prominent ridge passing from the beaks to the posterior angle of the shell. In our specimens the epidermis is olive-yellow, either light or dark, with numerous dark green diverging rays nearly covering the whole disks; in old specimens the rays are so far interrupted by the wrinkles as to appear in the form of radiating square spots. None of our specimens have any appearance of a lateral tooth, except the smallest, in which it is but rudimentary, and is far less prominent than in an *Alasmodonta*, so that there would be some propriety in removing this shell to that genus. The nacre is bluish-white, and in the youngest, the dark exterior rays are visible through it. The dimensions of the largest and smallest of our shells—

Diameter 1. 6, Length 2. 2, Breadth 3. 5,
do. 1. 1, do. 1. 5, do. 2. 7.

See Raf., p. 34, pl. 81, fig. 1, 2 and 3; and Lea's work, p. 7, pl. 1, fig. 1.

Unio monodonta, SAY. (Alasmodonta costata, Rafinesque.) Ohio: rather rare. This shell is evidently intermediate between the Unio and Alasmodonta, and argues something in favor of Lea's proposed division of our Naiades into two genera. Diameter 1. 0, Length 1. 6, Breadth 4. 5. See American Conchology, vol. 1, No. 1, pl. 6, and description; also Raf., p. 52, pl. 82, fig. 15 and 16.

SYMPHYNOTA.* *Valves connate.*

Symphynota alata, LEA. (Unio alatus, Say.) Ohio and Miami: great abundance, particularly in the latter river; some of which were of enormous size—measuring eight inches in breadth, with entire beaks. Nacre always purple. See Nich. Encyc., vol. 4, pl. 4, fig. 2; Am. Jour. Sc., vol. 6, p. 260; and vol. 14, p. 285, pl. 1, fig. 17; and Lea's work, p. 62.

Symphynota complanata, LEA. (Alasmodonta complanata, Barnes.) Ohio and Miami: rare. Valves more compressed than the S. alata: nacre white. See Am. Jour. Sc., vol. 6, p. 278, pl. 13, fig. 22; and Lea's Naiades, p. 62.

Symphynota lævissima, LEA. Ohio: rather rare. A very delicate highly polished shell, connate before and behind the beaks. See Lea's Naiades, p. 58, pl. 13, fig. 23.

Symphynota gracilis, LEA. (Unio gracilis and planus, Barnes.) Ohio and Miami: rather common. Some specimens from the Miami were rayed with green, and some with brown. See Am. Jour. Sc., vol. 6, pp. 274 and 272, pl. 13, fig. 16; and Lea's work, p. 66.

Symphynota tenuissima, LEA. (Anodonta lata, Raf.?) Ohio and Miami: rather rare. An exceedingly thin fragile shell. One

---

* Whether Mr. Lea is to be followed in his division of the Naiades is a question to be decided by other Naturalists; and it is not now our province to criticise particularly the advantages and disadvantages resulting from the division, yet a few remarks may not be improper. Objections can be raised against either arrangement: we find some shells which seem to connect the Unio with the Alasmodonta, for example the U. monodonta of Say (A. costata, Raf.) is intermediate, and in some specimens there is no appearance of lateral teeth, and sometimes it even approaches the Anodonta: and the U. triqueter of Rafinesque (U. calceolus, Lea) in old specimens is certainly a true Alasmodonta, it having no lateral teeth, while young specimens shew it to be a real Unio. Nor would the difficulty be entirely done away by following Mr. Lea; for some of his connate shells are often found free, when they would appear to be perfect. There is some doubt respecting the *U. monodonta* of Say, for we have some young specimens that appear to have been slightly connate.

specimen measures—Diameter . 9, Length 1. 8, Breadth 3. 4. See Lea's Naiades, p. 67, pl. 11, fig. 21; and Raf., p. 51, pl. 82, fig. 17 and 18.

ALASMODONTA. *Valves free, with one or more cardinal and no lateral teeth.*

Alasmodonta rugosa, BARNES. Found in great abundance and of enormous size in the Miami, and sparingly in the Ohio. The Miami shells have entire white beaks, while the Ohio shells are decorticated. Some specimens are rayed: nacre from pale salmon to bluish-white. A large specimen measures Diameter 1. 8, Length 2. 9, Breadth 5. 1: and a young specimen from the Ohio measures—Diameter . 4, Length . 9, Breadth 1. 8. It is possible that this may prove to be a symphynota, for in some specimens the ligament is almost concealed by the projecting edges of the dorsal margin which appear as though they might have been united. See Am. Jour. Sc., vol. 6, p. 278. pl. 13, fig. 21.

ANODONTA. *Valves free, without teeth.*

Anodonta undulata, SAY? Ohio and Miami: rare. Those from the Miami have entire beaks, but those from the Ohio have them eroded. Our specimens are so much larger than the one figured and described by Say, as to leave us a little in doubt as to the certainty of our having his shell. Our specimens have a brown epidermis, but agree in all other particulars with Mr. Say's description, especially when he says "in the left valve, immediately under the beak, the margin is curved inwards for the reception of a corresponding marginal projection of the opposite valve." Two specimens measure as follows:

Diameter 1. Length 1. 7, Breadth 2. 9,
    do. .75, do. 1. 2, do 2.

See Nich. Encyc., vol. 4, pl. 3, fig. 6, (a young one?)

In Lamarck's family—"*Conques*"—we only found an individual species.

Cyclas similis, SAY. Ohio: common. About the size of a cherry stone, though sometimes even half an inch broad. See Nich. Encyc., vol. 4, pl. 1. fig. 9.

As we paid but little attention to the collection of univalve shells, our list will be small.

Melania Sayii, Wood. Ohio: very abundant. We have seen no description of this shell, but it is readily distinguished by a broad deep furrow passing around the centre of the whorls, with a ridge bounding each side: the lower ridge and a portion of the furrow are successively concealed by new volutions, the *body whorl* alone showing the entire furrow. It is figured by Mr. Wood in his "Supplement to the Index Testaceologicus," pl. 4, fig. 24, (under Stronbus;) and named on page 42 of the same work.

Melania Virgimca, (Lymnæa Virginica, Say.) Ohio and Miami: very common. A smaller and smoother shell than the last. See Nich. Enc., vol. 4, pl. 2, fig. 4, and Say's description, article Conchology.

Paludina decisa, Say. Ohio and Miami: common. Some very large ones were found—more than an inch and a half in length. Epidermis varies from dark brown to light greenish-yellow. See Am. Con., vol. 1, No. 1, pl. 10, upper and lower figures.

Paludina? (Perhaps poor specimens of P. vivipara.) Ohio: rather common. Our specimens appear intermediate between Melania and Paludina, yet they are so much eroded that we cannot say to which our shell belongs. See Am. Con., vol. 1, No. 1, pl. 19, middle figures.

SUMMARY OF THE SHELLS.

We collected of the *Unio*	28	species.
Symphynota	5	—
Alasmodonta	1	—
Anodonta	1	—
Cyclas	1	—
Bivalves		36,
Melania	2	—
Paludina	2	—
Univalves		4,
Total number of Species collected		40.

A CATALOGUE OF THE NATIVE PHAENOGAMOUS PLANTS AND FERNS OF KENTUCKY

[Charles Wilkins Short,
Robert Peter and Henry A. Griswold]

Art. III.—*A Catalogue of the Native Phænogamous Plants, and Ferns of Kentucky.*

(*Note.*—The following Catalogue is doubtless very incomplete, since it includes only those species which have fallen under the actual observation of three of our botanical friends, Prof. SHORT, and Messrs. PETER and GRISWOLD, who are still diligently extending their researches and daily adding to the number. It is, therefore, offered at the present, as an outline, faithful so far as it goes, of the Botany of Kentucky. The arrangement and the names are those adopted in the 6th Edition of Eaton's Manual.—ED.)

Abies Canadensis,
Acalypha Virginiana,
Acer rubrum,
  " dasycarpum,
  " saccharinum,
  " negundo,
Acerates viridiflora,
Achillea millifolium,
Acnida cannabina,
Acorus calamus,
Actæa alba,
Actinomeris squarrosa,
Adiantum pedatum,
Æsculus Ohiensis,
  " pallida,
Agave virginica,
Agrimonia eupatoria,
  " parviflora,
Agrostemma githago,
Agrostis vulgaris,
  " lateriflora,
  " clandestina?
  " dispar?
Alisma plantago,

Allium tricoccum,
  " cernuum,
  " canadense,
Alnus serrulata,
Alyssum dentatum, (*Nutt.*)
Amaranthus, 2 or 3 species,
Ambrosia trifida,
  " elatior,
Ammannia humilis,
Amorpha fruticosa,
Ampelopsis quinquefolia,
Amphicarpa monoica,
Amsonia latifolia,
Andromeda arborea,
Andropogon scoparium,
  " Virginicum,
  " furcatum,
  " ciliatum,
Anemone Virginiana,
  " aconitifolia,
  " nemorosa,
  " thalyctroides,
Anthemis arvensis,
  " cotula,

Antirrhinum linaria,
Apios tuberosa,
Aplectrum hyemalis,
Apocynum cannabinum,
" hypericifolium,
Aquilegia canadensis,
Arabis thaliana,
" falcata,
" rhomboidea,
Aralia spinosa,
" racemosa,
Arctium lappa,
Arenaria serpyllifolia,
" stricta,
Aristolochia serpentaria,
Aronia botryapium,
" melanocarpa,
Arum dracontium,
" triphyllum,
Asarum canadense,
Asclepias syriaca,
" phytolaccoides,
" amæna,
" incarnata,
" quadrifolia,
" verticillata,
" tuberosa,
" nivea,
Ascyrum crux-andreæ,
Aspidium acrostichoides,
" marginale,
" felixmas,
" bulbiferum,
" tenue,
Aplenium rhyzophyllum,
" angustifolium,
" ebenum,
" thelypteroides,

Aplenium ruta-muraria,
" montanum,
" melanocaulon,
Aster linarifolius,
" ericoides,
" multiflorus,
" flexuosus,
" cornifolius,
" humilis,
" amygdalinus,
" novæ-angliæ,
" phlogifolius,
" diversifolius,
" cordifolius,
" amplexicaulis,
" prenanthoides,
" lævis,
" conyzoides,
" fragilis,
" Shortii, (*Boott.*)
Astragalus canadensis,
Atriplex, 1 or 2 species.
Atropa physaloides,
Azalea nudiflora,
Baptisia cærulea,
" alba,
" tinctoria,
Barbarea vulgaris,
Batschia canescens,
Bellis integrifolia,
Betula, 2 or 3 species,
Bidens cernua,
" chrysanthemoides,
" frondosa,
" bipinnata,
Bignonia radicans,
" crucigera,
Bœhmeria lateriflora,

Botrychium obliquum,
" virginicum,
Bromus secalinus,
Cacalia atriplicifolia,
" suaveolens,
Cactus opuntia,
Callitriche verna,
Caltha palustris,
Campanula amplexicaulis,
" accuminata,
Capraria multifida,
Cardamine rotundifolia,
" pennsylvanica,
" uniflora,
Carex multiflora,
" lupulina,
" digitalis,
" retrorsa,
with several other species,
Carpinus americana,
Carya alba,
" sulcata,
" amara,
" porcina,
" olivæformis,
Cassia marylandica,
" chamæcrista,
" nictitans,
" tora,
" aspera,
Castanea vesca,
" pumila,
Catalpa cordifolia,
Caulophyllum thalyctroides,
Ceanothus americana,
Celastrus scandens,
Celtis crassifolia,
" pumila,

Cephalanthus occidentalis,
Cerastium hirsutum,
" vulgatum,
" glutinosum, (*Nutt.*)
" arvense,
Cercis canadensis,
Cerosia fluitans,
Chelone glabra,
Chenopodium hybridum,
" album &v. viride,
" botrys,
" anthelminticum,
Chimaphila maculata,
" umbellata,
Chionanthus virginica,
Chrysopsis mariana,
Cicuta maculata,
Cinna arundinacea,
Circæa lutetiana,
Claytonia virginica, (2 vars.)
Clematis virginica,
" reticulata,
Cleome dodecandra,
Cnicus lanceolatus,
" altissimus,
" discolor,
" virginianus,
Collinsia verna,
Collinsonia canadensis,
Commelina communis,
" virginica,
Conium maculatum,
Convallaria racemosa,
" multiflora,
Convolvulus repens,
" arvensis,
" panduratus,
" spithameus,

Convolvulus machrorhizus,
Conyza camphorata,
Corallorhiza odontorhiza,
Coreopsis trichosperma,
" tripteris,
" auriculata,
" senifolia,
Cornus florida,
" sericea,
" alba,
Corydalis aurea,
Corylus americana,
Cratægus coccinea,
" crus-galli,
" populifolia,
" several other species,
Croton capitatum,
Cucubalus stellatus,
Cunila mariana,
Cuphea viscosissima,
Cupressus disticha,
Cuscuta americana,
Calopogon pulchellum,
Cynoglossum officinale,
" amplexicaule,
Cyperus flavescens,
" inflexus,
" phymatodes,
" strigosus,
" others undetermined,
Cypripedium pubescens,
" parviflorum,
" spectabile,
" acaule,
Dactylis glomerata,
Danthonia spicata,
Datura stramonium,
" tatula,

Decodon verticillatum,
Delphinium tricorne,
" exaltatum?
Dentaria diphylla,
" laciniata,
" heterophylla,
Diclytra cucullaria,
" canadensis,
Digitaria sanguinalis,
Dioscorea villosa,
Dyospyros virginiana,
Dypsacus sylvestris,
Dirca palustris,
Dodecatheon meadia,
Dracocephalum virginianum,
" denticulatum,
" cordatum,
Drosera longifolia,
" rotundifolia,
Dulichium spathaceum,
Eclipta procumbens,
Elephantopus carolinianus.
Eleusine indica,
" mucronata?
Elymus canadensis,
" villosus,
" hystrix,
Elodea petiolata,
Enslenia albida,
Epigæa repens,
Epilobium coloratum,
Epiphegus virginianus,
Equisetum arvense,
" hyemale,
Erigeron bellidifolium,
" purpureum,
" philadelphicum,
" strigosum,

Erigeron canadense,
Erigenia bulbosa,
Erysimum palustre,
Erythronium americanum,
" albidum,
Euchroma coccinea,
Euonymus atropurpureus,
" americanus,
" obovatus,
Eupatorium sessilifolium,
" purpureum,
" verticillatum,
" perfoliatum,
" cælestinum,
" ageratoides,
" glaucescens?
Euphorbia corollata,
" peplus,
" hypericifolia,
" maculata,
" thymifolia,
Fagus sylvatica,
Fedia radiata,
Festuca elatior,
" pratensis,
Flœrkea uliginosa,
Fragaria virginiana,
" canadensis,
Frasera verticillata,
Fraxinus quadrangulata,
" acuminata,
" sambucifolia,
Galardia bicolor,
Galega virginiana,
" hispidula?
Galium trifidum,
" tinctorium,
" asprellum,

Galium aparine,
" circæzans,
" boreale,
Gaultheria procumbens,
Guara biennis,
Gentiana saponaria,
" ocroleuca,
" quinqueflora,
Geranium maculatum,
Gerardia flava,
" pedicularia,
" purpurea,
" tenuifolia,
" quercifolia,
Geum virginianum,
Gillenia stipulacea,
Glechoma hederacea,
Gleditschia triacanthos,
Gnaphalium polycephalum,
" plantagineum,
" purpureum,
" uliginosum,
Gonolobus hirsutus,
Goodyera pubescens,
Gratiola virginica,
Gymnocladus canadensis,
Gyromia virginica,
Habenaria ciliaris,
" fimbriata,
Hamamelis virginica,
Hedyoma pulegioides,
Hedyotis glomerata?
Hedysarum canadense,
" viridiflorum,
" Aikinii?
" rotundifolium,
" nudiflorum,
" glutinosum,

Hedysarum acuminatum,
" pauciflorum,
others undetermined.
Helenium autumnale,
Helianthus trachelifolius,
" decapetalus,
" altissimus?
" pubescens,
" frondosus,
others, undetermined.
Heliopsis laevis,
Heliotropium indicum,
Helonias diocia,
Hepatica acutiloba,
Heracleum lanatum,
Hesperis pinnatifida,
Heteranthera reniformis,
Heuchera americana,
" pubescens,
" caulescens,
" acerifolia, (Raf.)
Hibiscus moscheutos,
" militaris,
Hieracium venosum,
" gronovii,
" paniculatum,
Hippuris vulgaris,
Hottonia inflata,
Houstonia caerulea,
" longifolia,
" purpurea,
Humulus lupulus,
Hydrangea cordata,
" vulgaris,
Hydrastis canadensis,
Hydropeltis purpurea,
Hydrophyllum appendiculatum
" canadense,

Hydrophyllum virginicum,
Hypericum prolificum,
" perforatum,
" corymbosum,
" parviflorum,
others, undetermined.
Hypopithys lanuginosa,
Hypoxis erecta,
Hyssopus nepetoides,
" scrophularifolius,
Ilex opaca,
Impatiens pallida,
" fulva,
Inula helenium,
Ionidium concolor,
Ipomaea, several species,
Iresine celosioides?
Iris versicolor,
" cristata,
" verna,
Isopyrum thalyctroides,
Isanthus coeruleus,
Isnardia palustris,
Jeffersonia diphylla,
Juglans nigra,
" cinerea,
Juncus effusus,
" tenuis,
" others, undetermined,
Juniperus virginiana,
Justicia pedunculosa,
Kalmia latifolia,
Krigia amplexicaulis,
Kyllingia pumila,
Lactuca elongata,
Lamium amplexicaule,
Laurus benzoin,
" sassafras,

Lechea major,
" minor,
" racemulosa,
Leersia virginica,
" oryzoides.
Lemna minor,
" trisulca,
Leontodon taraxacum,
Leonurus cardiaca,
Lepidium virginicum,
Leptandra virginica,
Lespedeza capitata,
" violacea,
" procumbens,
" prostrata,
Liatris squarrosa,
" spicata,
" graminifolia,
Lilium canadense,
" superbum,
" Catesbei,
Lindernia dilatata,
" attenuata,
Linum virginianum,
Liquidambar styraciflua,
Liriodendron tulipifera,
Lithospermum arvense,
" latifolium,
Lobelia cardinalis,
" syphilitica,
" inflata,
" Claytoniana,
" puberula,
Lonicera parviflora,
Ludwigia alternifolia,
Luzula ?
Lycopodium complanatum,
and others.

Lycopus europeus,
" virginicus,
Lysimachia quadrifolia,
" ciliata,
" hybrida,
" quadriflora?
Lythrum hyssopifolium,
Macrotrys racemosa,
Magnolia tripetala,
" macrophylla,
" cordata,
" ariculata,
Malaxis liliifolia,
Malva rotundifolia,
Marrubium vulgare,
Martynia proboscidea,
Meconopsis petcolata,
Melica speciosa,
Menispermum canadense,
" smilacinum?
Mentha tenuis,
" borealis,
" viridis,
Miegia macrosperma,
Mikania scandens,
Mimulus alatus,
" ringens,
Mitchella repens,
Mitella diphylla,
Mollugo verticillata,
Monarda oblongata,
" fistulosa,
" hirsuta,
" ciliata,
Monotropa uniflora,
Morus rubra,
Muhlenbergia diffusa,
" erecta,

Catalogue of Plants of Kentucky. 497

Myosotis arvensis,
Myosurus Shortii, (*Raff.*)
Nelumbium luteum,
Neottia tortilis,
Nepeta cataria,
Nuphar advena,
Nyssa aquatica,
" tomentosa,
Obolaria virginica,
Œnothera biennis,
" muricata,
" grandiflora,
" tetragona?
    others, undetermined.
Onoclea sensibilis,
Onosmodium hispidum,
" molle,
Ophioglossum vulgatum,
" bulbosum,
Orchis spectabilis,
" tridentata,
Orobanche uniflora,
" americana,
Osmunda regalis,
Ostrya virginica,
Oxalis violacea,
" stricta,
" corniculata?
Pachysandra procumbens,
Panax quinquefolia,
Pancratium rotatum,
Panicum crus-galli,
" clandestinum,
" latifolium,
" dichotomum,
" nitidum,
" capillare,
" virgatum,

Parietaria pennsylvanica,
Paspalum ciliatifolium,
" plicatulum,
Passiflora, lutea,
" incarnata,
Pedicularis canadensis,
" pallida,
Penthorum sedoides,
Penstemon pubescens,
" lævigatum,
Petalostemon candidum,
" violaceum,
Phacelia bipinnatifida,
" fimbriata,
" heterophylla,
Phalangium esculentum,
Phaseolus perennis,
Phlox paniculata,
" pyramidalis,
" maculata,
" aristata,
" pilosa,
" divaricata,
" reptans,
" subulata,
" setacea,
" cordata,
Phryma leptostachya,
Physalis viscosa,
" obscura,
" pennsylvanica,
Phytolacca decandra
Pinus inops,
" alba,
Piptatherum nigrum,
Plantago major,
" lanceolata,
" virginica,

Plantago cordata,
Platanus occidentalis,
Poa pratensis,
" annua,
" trivialis,
" compressa,
" nervata,
" capillaris?
" reptans,
" eragrostis,
Podophyllum peltatum,
Podostemum ceratophyllum,
Podostigma viridis,
Pogonia ophioglossoides,
" verticillata,
Polemonium reptans,
Polygala incarnata,
" senega,
" purpurea,
" verticillata,
" setacea,
Polygonum aviculare,
" erectum,
" punctatum,
" virginianum,
" persicaria,
" pennsylvanicum,
" amphibium,
" sagittatum,
" hastatum,
" arifolium,
" scandens,
Polymnia canadensis,
" uvedalia,
Polypodium vulgare,
" hexagonopterum,
" incanum,
Pontederia cordata,

Pontederia angustifolia,
Populus tremuloides,
" candicans,
" lævigata,
Porcelia triloba,
Portulacca oleracea,
Potamogeton natans,
" lucens,
" acutifolium,
" gramineum,
Potentilla canadensis,
Prenanthes alba,
" serpentaria,
" crepidinea,
" deltoidea,
Proserpinaca palustris,
Prunella vulgaris,
Prunus pennsylvanica,
" virginiana,
" serotina,
" chicasa,
" depressa,
Psoralea eglandulosa,
Ptelea trifoliata,
Pteris aquilina,
" atropurpurea,
Pulmonaria virginica,
Pycnanthemum incanum,
" linifolium,
" lanceolatum,
Pyrus coronaria,
Quercus phellos,
" imbricaria,
" ferruginea,
" tinctoria,
" falcata,
" palustris,
" obtusiloba,

Quercus macrocarpa,
" alba,
" castanea,
" pumila,
Queria canadensis,
Ranunculus flammulus,
" abortivus,
" sceleratus,
" fascicularis,
" recurvatus,
" fluviatilis,
" lacustris,
" nitidus,
Rhamnus carolinianus,
" lanceolatus,
Rhexia mariana,
" virginica,
Rhododendron maximum,
Rhus glabrum,
" copallinum,
" toxicodendron,
" aromaticum,
Rhyncospora, 1 or 2 species,
Ribes conosbati,
" floridum,
Robinia pseudo-acacia,
Rochelia virginica,
Rosa parviflora,
" rubiginosa,
" others undetermined,
Rubus ideus,
" villosus,
" occidentalis,
" trivialis,
" odoratus,
Rudbeckia purpurea,
" hirta,
" triloba,

Rudbeckia laciniata,
" pinnata,
Ruellia stepens,
Rumex crispus,
" acetosellus,
" persicarioides,
" others undetermined,
Sabbatia angularis,
" gracilis,
Sagittaria sagittifolia,
" pusilla,
Salix, several species not deter.
Salvia lyrata,
Sambucus canadensis,
Samolus valerandi,
Sanguinaria canadensis,
Sanicula marylandica.
Saponaria officinalis,
Sarothra gentianoides,
Saururus cernuus,
Saxifraga virginiensis,
Schollera graminifolia,
Scirpus tenuis,
" autumnalis,
" palustris,
" capitatus,
" americanus,
" atrovirens,
" brunneus,
" eriophorum,
Scrophularia marylandica,
Scutellaria lateriflora,
" galericulata,
" parvula,
" canescens,
" cordifolia,
" ovalifolia,
" gracilis,

500   *Catalogue of Plants of Kentucky.*

Scutellaria ambigua,
Sedum ternatum,
" pulchellum,
Senecio obovatus,
" balsamitæ,
Seymeria pectinata,
Sicyos angulata,
Sida spinosa,
" abutilon,
Silene pennsylvanica,
" virginica,
" regia,
" rotundifolia,
Silphium perfoliatum,
" terebinthinaceum,
Sison trifoliatus,
Sisyrinchium anceps,
" mucronatum,
Smilax rotundifolia,
" peduncularis,
" herbacea,
" bona nox,
" others undetermined,
Solanum dulcamara,
" nigrum,
" carolinense,
Solidago canadensis,
" nemoralis,
" odora,
" bicolor,
" graminifolia,
" cæsia,
" flexicaulis,
" latifolia,
" axillaris,
Sonchus oleraceus,
" spinulosus,
" ludovicianus,

Sparganum americanum,
Spermacoce diodina,
" glabra?
Spigelia marylandica,
Spiræa salicifolia,
" tomentosa,
" corymbosa,
" opulifolia,
" aruncus,
" betulifolia,
Stachys aspera,
Staphylea trifolia,
Stellaria media,
" pubera,
Streptopus lanuginosus,
Stylosanthes elatior,
Symphoria racemosa,
" glomerata,
Synandra grandiflora,
Teucrium canadense,
Thalictrum doicum,
" corynellum,
" ranunculinum,
Thesium umbellatum,
Thlaspi bursa-pastoris,
Thuya occidentalis,
Tiarella cordifolia,
Tilia pubescens,
" americana,
Tipularia discolor,
Tradescantia virginica,
" rosea,
Tricodium laxiflorum,
" scabrum,
Trichostema dichotoma,
Trifolium reflexum,
" repens,
" pratense,

Catalogue of Plants of Kentucky. 501

Trifolium procumbens,
" stoloniferum,
Trillium sessile,
" pendulum,
" erectum,
" grandiflorum,
" cernuum,
" pictum,
Triosteum perfoliatum,
Triphora pendula,
Troximon virginicum,
Turritis glabra,
Typha latifolia,
Ulmus americana,
" fulva,
" alata,
Uniola latifolia,
Uraspermum claytoni,
" hirsutum,
Urtica pumila,
" urens,
" dioica,
" canadensis,
Utricularia macrorhiza,
Uvularia perfoliata,
" sessilifolia,
" grandiflora,
Vaccinium stamineum,
" resinosum,
" corymbosum,
" frondosum,
Valeriana pauciflora,
Vallisneria spiralis,
Verbascum thapsus,
" blattaria,
Verbena hastata,
" urticifolia,
" augustifolia,

Verbesina siegesbeckia,
Vernonia noveboracensis,
Veronica serpyllifolia,
" anagallis,
" arvensis,
" agrestis,
" peregrina,
Vexillaria virginiana,
Viburnum prunifolum,
" lentago,
" dentatum,
" pubescens,
" acerifolium,
Vicia cracca,
Viola cucullata,
" affinis,
" palmata,
" sororia,
" sagittata,
" amœna,
" blanda,
" primulifolia,
" lanceolata,
" pedata,
" canadensis,
" rostrata,
" Muhlenbergiana,
" striata,
" pubescens,
" heterophylla?
Virgilia lutea,
Viscum verticillatum,
Vitis lubrusca,
" cordifolia,
Windsoria seslerioides,
Xanthium strumarium,
Xyris flexuosa,
Zanthoxylum fraxineum.

A SUPPLEMENTARY CATALOGUE OF THE PLANTS OF KENTUCKY

[Charles Wilkins] Short and [Robert] Peter

ART. VIII.—*A Supplementary Catalogue of the Plants of Kentucky.* By PROFESSORS SHORT and PETER.

[NOTE.—In the "Catalogue of the Plants of Kentucky" published in the 6th vol. of the Transylvania Journal of Medicine, &c., it was suggested that the number of species therein contained fell far short of the entire amount embraced by the Flora of Kentucky. We now append to that list the following additions and corrections made during the past season; still inserting none which have not fallen under our own observation.]

I. ADDITIONS.

Actæa palmata,
Acer nigrum,
Andromeda paniculata,
Archemora rigida,
Agrimonia suaveolens,
Agrostis tenuiflora.
Arrenatherum Kentuckiensis,
Aristida
Asclepias variegata,
Aster Carolinianus,
" Novi Belgii,
" diffusus,
" divergens,
" multiflorus,
" miser,
Bidens comosa, *Hooker*,
Bletia aphylla.
Boehmeria cylindrica,
Bromus Canadensis,
" pubescens,
" mollis?
Botrychium dissectum,
Carex alba,
" anceps,
" Willdenovii,
" varia,
" Muhlenbergii,
" folliculata,
" acuta,
" hirsuta,
" pubescens?
" setacea?
" pellita?
" granularis?
" multiflora?
" stipata?
" hystericina?
" gracillima?
" stellulata?
Cardamine Ludoviciana, *Hook*,
Coculus Carolinianus,
Cunila glabella,
Cyperus Nuttallii,
Digitaria filiformis,
Echium vulgare,
Eupatorium ovatum, *Bw.*
" rupestre, *Rafn*.
Festuca nutans,
" tenella,
Gentiana Catesbœi,
Gonolobus macrophyllus?
Glyceria fluitans,
Hedysarum paniculatum,
" scaberrimum,
" cuspidatum,
" bracteosum,
" Marylandicum,
" obtusum?
Houstonia ciliolata,
Hordeum pusillum,
Hypopeltis obtusa,
Kæleria truncata,
" Pennsylvanica,
Lemania fluviatilis,
Leptanthus ovalis,
Lycopodium dendroideum,
Malaxis ophioglossoides,
Melica diffusa,
Œnothera Frazeri,
" fruticosa,
Oxydenia attenuata,
Panax trifolia,
Panicum proliferum,
" agrostoides,
Phlox glaberrima,
Poa multicaulis, *Torrey*,
" pectinacea,
" parviflora,

Poa pungens,
Polygonum lapathifolium,
Potamogeton compressum,
Polypodium connectile,
Prunus obovatus,
Psoralea onobrychis,
Quercus chinquapin,
Rosa corymbosa,
" rubifolia,
Ranunculus pusillus,
Rhyncospora glomerata,
" lata,
Sagina *fontinalis,
Sagittaria obtusa,
Scirpus triqueter,
" lacustris.
Senecio hieracifolius,
" aureus,
Seymeria macrophylla,
Sisymbrium canescens,

Spartina cynosuroides,
Stachys sylvatica,
Strophostyles angulosa,
" peduncularis,
Stylipus verna, *Rafin.*
Solidago *cordata,
" serotina,
" rupestris, *Rafin.*
Tragia macrocarpa,
Triosteum angustifolium,
Uniola gracilis,
Uraspermum procumbens,
" Canadense,
Udora Canadensis,
Veratrum angustifolium,
Viola tenella,
Veronica scutellata,
Zizia cordata,
" integerrima.

II. CORRECTIONS.

Alyssum dentatum, *Nutt.* of the former Catalogue, is the Draba dentata,
Asclepias nivea,   is the   Asclepias variegata, [*Hook.*
Agrimonia parviflora,   " "   Agrimonia suaveoleus,
Aster fragilis,   " "   Aster Carolinianus,
Clematis reticulata,   " "   Clematis viorna,
Dracocephalum denticulatum,   " "   Dracocephalum variegatum,
Eupatorium glaucescens?   " "   Eupatorium rupestre, *Rafin.*
Hedyotis glomerata?   " "   Spermacoce glabra,
Luzula ————?   " "   Luzula campestris,
Menispermum smilacinum?   " "   Coculus Carolinianus,
Thalictrum ranunculinum,   " "   Actæa palmata.

III. DESCRIPTIONS AND OBSERVATIONS.

*Solidago *cordata.* Stem striated, pubescent; lower leaves petiolate, cordate, sharply and irregularly serrate, acute, upper ones ovate, gradually becoming sessile and entire, radical leaves, broad cordate and serrate; spikes axillary and terminal, densely flowered; folioles of the perianth lanceolate, obtuse, adpressed.

Stem erect, generally purple, often branching at the summit with a few lax, divaricate branches; leaves scabrous beneath; flowers small, of a bright golden yellow colour; ligules about half the length of the cylindrical light-green perianth. Perennial; flowers from August to October, grows from two to four feet in height.

Hab. On the steep, wooded, hill-sides, on the banks of the Kentucky river; where large patches of its broad cordate radical leaves are very conspicuous at most seasons. This species has some agreements with the description of *S. sphacelata* (Raf.), but it differs in having no sphacelations on the folioles of the perianth, as well as in the colour of the flowers, those of *S. spacciata* being "of a dirty brownish yellow," and in its broad cordate, serrate leaves, which are from two to four inches long. Even should the present species be the one intended by that author, we consider the name now proposed decidedly preferable to his, since it has reference to a somewhat peculiar character always present, instead of "a desperate microscopical one," not to be met with in healthy perfect specimens.

Sagina *fontinalis. Stem procumbent, branching, dichotomous above; leaves opposite, linear-spatulate, entire; pedicels solitary, alternate, longer than the leaves. Annual.

Glabrous, apetalous; calyx 4–5 leaved; sepals ovate, obtuse; stamens 4 to 6; capsule somewhat 4-sided, one-celled, many-seeded.

Hab. On the cliffs of the Kentucky river and Elkhorn creek; forming mats in wet places where the water of springs flows over. Flowers in April and May; stems 8–15 inches long.

Cunila glabella. This is undoubtedly the original plant of Michaux; and it agrees much better with his description than do specimens which under the synonymous name of *Hedeoma glabra* we have received from the Niagara falls. Our plant is usually from 1 to 2 feet high; its larger leaves 2 inches long by ¾ broad, coarsely serrate towards the apex, attenuated at base, and distinctly petioled; whorls from 3 to 15 flowered.

Hab. We have only found this plant in one locality, on the borders of a rivulet emptying into Elkhorn, at the Forks near Frankfort, Ky. At this point in rich soil among fragments of limestone, (a locality altogether analogous to Michaux's original one,) it occurs in great abundance, flowering in June. From an accurate comparison of the two plants we are compelled to believe that the New York species is distinct from the present—and we prefer for our plant the name given by Michaux, although our specimens were all distinctly didynamous.

A SECOND SUPPLEMENTARY CATALOGUE
OF THE PLANTS OF KENTUCKY

[Charles Wilkins Short and Robert Peter]

Art. IX.—*A Second Supplementary Catalogue of the Plants of Kentucky.*

During the past season of 1835 our attention has still been directed to an examination of the plants of Kentucky, and we are now enabled to add nearly two hundred species to the number contained in our preceding catalogues, published in the XXIV and XXVIII numbers of this Journal. To this addition many species have been contributed by our friend Mr. Griswold, from the immediate neighbourhood of Louisville, his present residence—a locality especially rich in paludal and aquatic plants; and a few have been added from the borders of the Ohio river, opposite the mouth of the Scioto, where they were observed by Mr. Riddell, of Cincinnati. For accurately determining a number of the Carices contained in this supplement, we are indebted to Professor Dewey, of Pittsfield, Mass. who has made this difficult genus the object of his particular study.

Those species marked with the asterisk (*) are either new or have not been introduced into any of the systems of American Botany.

CATALOGUE, &c.

Anagallis arvensis,
Actinomeris helianthoides,
Agrostis Virginica?
" vaginæflora,
" trichopodes,
Aletris farinosa,
Alopecurus geniculatus,
Amaranthus spinosus,

Amaranthus hybridus,
Arabis lævigata,
" hastata,
" hirsuta,
" lyrata,
Ammi costatum,
Aristida purpurascens,
" gracilis,

Aristida dichotoma,
Artemisia Canadensis,
Arum Virginicum,
Aspidium Noveboracense,
" Goldianum,
" angustum?
Asclepias purpurascens,
" variegata,
Aster *amethystinus, *Nutt.*
Astragalus Carolinianus,
Atheropogon apludoides,
Boltonia asterioides?
Buchnera Americana,
Cannabis sativa,†
Carex oligocarpa,
" muricata, var. cephaloi-
dea,
" festucacea,
" straminea,
" squarrosa,
" Hitchcockiana,
" sparganoides,
" milliacea,
" retroflexa,
" virescens,
" pubescens,
" rosea, large and small
varieties,
" intumescens,
" paleacea,
" crinita,
" laxiflora,
" Davisii
" *Shortiana, *Dew. & Tor.*
" conoidea,
" *Stenolepsis, *Torrey.*
" cephalophora,

Carex tentaculata,
Ceratophyllum demersum,
Convallaria angustifolia,
" bifolia,
Coreopsis verticillata,
Croton ellipticum,
Cyperus erythrorhizos,
Cornus paniculata,
" asperifolia,
" alternifolia,
Convolvulus *micrantha, (1)
Riddell,
Crataegus punctata,
Delphinium azureum,
Diarrhena Americana,
Dicksonia pilosiuscula,
Digitaria glabra,
Draba hispidula,
Dracaena umbellata,
Elymus striatus,
" Virginicus,
Erigeron *amplexicaule, *Tor.*
Eryngium aquaticum,
" gracile,
Eupatoreum serotinum,
" album,
" pubescens,
" ceanothifolium,
" *Torreyanum, (2)
Short.
" maculatum,
Euphorbia obtusata,
" depressa,
" dentata?
Ferula villosa,
Festuca duriuscula,
Galium lanceolatum,

Catalogue of Plants of Kentucky.

Galium tinctorium,
" pilosum,
" trifidum,
Gaura angustifolia,
Gentiana rubricaulis,
Gerardia glauca,
Geranium pusillum,
" Carolinianum,
Hedysarum obtusum,
" canescens?
Habenaria fissa,
Helianthus angustifolius,
" divaricatus,
Helonias erythrorhizos,
Hieracium marianum,
Hydrophyllum *macrophyllum,
   (3) *Nutt.*
Hypericum angulosum?
" nudiflorum,
Houstonia ? (4)
Ixia Chinensis, (5)
Iris hexagona,
Jeffersonia *lobata, (6) *Nutt.*
Juncus polycephalus,
" bulbosus,
" acuminatus,
Krigia Caroliniana,
Kuhnia eupatorioides,
Lathyrus palustris,
Lespedeza polystachya,
" repens,
" angustifolia,
Liatris scariosa,
Lilium Philadelphicum.
Ludwigia Jussieuoides,
" *polycarpa, (7)
Lysimachia revoluta,

Mentha piperita,
" arvensis,
Mariscus echinatus,
Melanthium Virginicum,
Melissa officinalis
Monarda mollis,
Myosotis palustris,
Myriophyllum scabratum,
Neottia cernua,
Panicum hispidum,
Paspalum læve,
Parthenium integrifolium,
Pennisetum glaucum,
" verticillatum,
Penstemon latifolium,
Phlox acuminata,
Phyllanthus obovatus,
Pontederia cordata, var.
  *albiflora, (8)
Poa nemoralis,
" dentata,
" rigida,
Polygala ambigua,
" cruciata,
Polygonum mite,
" tenue,
Potamogeton heterophyllum
" crispum?
" fluitans,
Polypodium dryopteris,
Prinos verticillatus,
Pinus variabilis, (9)
Potentilla Norwegica,
Prenanthes altissima,
" aspera,
Pycnanthemum pilosum,
" muticum,

Physalis angulata,
" lanceolata?
Rhododendron callendulaceum,
Rhus typhinum, (9)
Rhyncospora longirostris,
Rosa Carolina,
" gemella, (9)
Rumex verticillatus,
Rubus obovalis, (9)
Salix Muhlenbergiana,
Sagittaria graminifolia,
Scirpus quadrangulatus,
" lineatus,
" subsquarrosus,
Scutellaria integrifolia,
" pilosa,
" serrata,
" *hirsuta,(10)
Silene antirrhina,
Silphium laciniatum,
" trifoliatum,
Sium latifolium,
Solidago *hirsuta, *Nuttall*,
" elliptica,
" rigida,
" gigantea,
" altissima,

Solidago tortifolia,
" glomerata,
" ulmifolia,
" arguta,
" recurvata,
" procera?
" squarrosa,
" others undetermined.
Sonchus acuminatus,
" macrophyllus,
Sparganum ramosum,
Stellaria palustris,
Symphitum officinale, (11)
Tanacetum vulgare, (11)
Thalictrum revolutum,
Thaspium barbinode,
" actæifolium,
Trichodium alatum,
" scabrum,
Trifolium arvense,
Trisetum purpurascens,
Urtica gracilis, *Raf.*
" procera,
Veronica beccabunga,
Vicia parviflora,
Villarsia lacunosa,
Zizania aquatica.

Notes to the Preceding Catalogue.

(†) *Cannabis sativa.* The hemp has long been extensively cultivated in the "Elkhorn country" around Lexington, and the exuberant fertility of the soil of this district is admirably adapted to its culture. Owing to these circumstances it has become partially naturalized, and we have met with it in secluded situations, miles distant from any scene of cultivation.

(1) *Convolvulus micranthus.* For a description of this species, see "A synopsis of the Flora of the Western States. By John L. Riddell, A. M." (Cincinnati, O. 1835.) p. 70. "Closely allied to *C. lacunosus, Spreng?* perhaps only a variety of it."

(2) *Eupatoreum *Torreyanum.* Leaves ternate and opposite, sub-sessile, narrow-lanceolate, coarsely serrate, three nerved, punctate beneath, glabrous above.

Description: Stem solid, erect, striate, purplish, slightly pubescent below, becoming more so above, about two feet high; lower leaves by threes, narrow lanceolate on short petioles or mostly subsessile, with a few coarse serratures, and scabrous on the margin, three nerved and thickly sprinkled beneath with glandular dots; upper leaves opposite, or by threes, narrower and less serrate. At the axil of each leaf is a small branch with numerous small narrow entire leaves, all glandular-punctate. Flowering branches by threes and twos. Corymb nearly fastigiate. Involucrum 5-flowered, 8-10 leaved, exterior leaves small, acute, interior long, strap-shaped, pubescent and fringed at the summit. Seeds 5-angled smooth; pappus slighty scarious, pistil deeply cleft, the divisions revolute.

Found on dry sandstone knobs in the barrens of Kentucky, near the Mammoth Cave; flowering September 20th.

This species has some agreements with *E. parviflorum,* and perhaps still more with *E. amœnum,* but seems in some particulars to differ from both; from the last especially in not having the "coloured" leaves of the involucrum, nor the "purple or flesh-coloured flowers"—ours are a pure white. The name *trifoliatum,* or *ternifolium,* would be peculiarly appropriate for this plant, inasmuch as all its leaves are constantly by threes, except occasionally one or two sets of opposite ones near the summit; these names, however, seem applied to very different species from the present; and we, therefore, venture to dedicate this handsomest of the genus to one who is deservedly placed at the head of American Botanists.

(3) *Hydrophyllum *macrophyllum*, Nutt. See Jour. Acad. Nat. Sciences, Phila. vol. vii. p. 111, 1834. Mr. Riddell, in the Synopsis above alluded to, has introduced this species under the name *H. hispidum*, which is entirely in consonance with its character; but as Mr. Nuttall's name is prior, it must be adopted.

(4) *Houstonia* ? This plant has always been considered by us the *H. longifolia*, Willd. and numerous correspondents to whom we have sent it under that name, have received and acknowledged it as such. Among these, Professor Hooker, in remarking on it as *H. longifolia*, says "it is exactly what I have so called in the Botanical Magazine, No. 3099." That figure, however, plainly refers to *H. ciliolata*—a plant profusely abundant on the denuded hills around the Blue-licks, in this state, and the knobs back of New-Albany, Indiana; whereas our present species has occurred to us only among the rich debris of the limestone cliffs bordering the Kentucky river; where, rooting deeply in the fissures of the rock, it forms dense clumps of considerable magnitude, with numerous semo-prostrate stems a foot long.

Unless, therefore, luxuriance of growth has given to it an aspect very different from that of specimens which we have received from other portions of the Union, as *H. longifolia*, we are inclined to consider our species distinct, but without more thorough investigation we do not pronounce it so.

(5) *Ixia Chinensis*. This pretty exotic now so generally met with in our gardens under the name of "black-berry lilly," is becoming abundantly naturalized in this state. In the western part of it, we observed, last autumn, one locality especially, where it had spread from a garden to a considerable distance both into the adjoining barrens and timbered land.

(6) *Jeffersonia* *lobata, Nutt. Acad. Nat. Sc: Phila. vol. vii. p. 99. This is assuredly only a variety of *J. diphylla*. We have met with them both growing in the same spot, and passing into each other by insensible gradations.

(7) *Ludwigia* *polycarpa. Erect, much branched; leaves narrow-lanceolate, acute at each end, alternate, glabrous; flowers apetalous? closely sessile, axillary and congregated; capsules spherical, two-leaved.

Description: Stem erect, 1 to 3 feet high, angled and very branching, branches of irregular length and irregularly disposed. Leaves narrow-lanceolate and very acute, alternate, sub-sessile, glabrous on both surfaces and scabrous on the margin; the lower ones 4 inches long by ¼ inch wide, diminishing upwards. Flowers apetalous? axillary and closely sessile, generally solitary, but frequently collected in confused heads on the main stem, or smaller branches; capsules spherical, slightly angled, with two small, narrow, lanceolate, serrulate leaves seated on it, near the base; leaves of the calyx shorter than the capsule.

Discovered by Mr. H. A. Griswold in the wet lands around Louisville, where it occurs in greatabundance, flowering from ———— to October. This species certainly bears considerable affinity to the *L. mollis* as described by Elliott, but it differs from that in being altogether destitute of the characteristic villosity, and in having an angled stem. We have therefore given it a name from the profusion of its capsules—a greater profusion by far than is borne by any other species within our knowledge.

(8) *Pontederia cordata*, var. *albiflora. Our friend and fellow-labourer, Mr. Griswold, pointed out this variety to us in a pond near Louisville. It there occurred in company with the common blue or purple flowered species, from which it seems to differ only in the colour of its flowers, which is a pure white, with a slight tinge of pink.

(9) *Pinus variabilis, Rhus typhinum, Rosa gemella, &c.* These species have not been met with by ourselves, within the limits of this state: they are introduced into this Catalogue on the au-

thority of Mr. Riddell, who reports to us his having found them on the Kentucky side of the Ohio river, opposite to the mouth of the Scioto river.

(10) *Scutellaria *hirsuta.* Stem erect, simple, sparingly branched, hirsute; leaves petioled broad-ovate, crenate, obtuse, hirsute; bractes ovate, ciliate; calyx hairy.

Description: Stem erect, stout from 1 to 2 feet high, quadrangular and grooved between the angles, with a few opposite branches towards the summit, the whole thickly beset with a hirsute pubescence standing out at right-angles from the stem: leaves few and large; the lower ones sub-cordate, on petioles of some length; the upper broad-ovate attenuated into petioles which become shorter upward, all obtuse and coarsely crenate, covered on the upper surface and the veins beneath with stiff hairs. Floral leaves entire, broad-oval, nearly round, pubescent, ciliate, longer than the calyx which is very hairy, especially the upper lip. Flowers not seen.

This species approaches nearest to the *S. pilosa* but is altogether a more stout and hirsute plant. They differ also in the form of their leaves and bractes.

Discovered by Mr. H.A. Griswold on the borders of marshes around Louisville, Ky. Unfortunately the flowers had passed before it was met with.

(11) *Symphitum officinale—Tanacetum vulgare.* These two exotics having passed the confines of cultivation, are becoming naturalized. We have met with them both in situations remote from settlements.

A THIRD SUPPLEMENTARY CATALOGUE
OF THE PLANTS OF KENTUCKY

ART. VI.—*A Third Supplementary Catalogue of the Plants of Kentucky.* By C. W. SHORT, M. D. &c. &c.

Since the publication of our second supplementary list, in the 32nd No. of this Journal, the following species have fallen under our observation, within the limits of this State. For the determination of the *mosses* contained in this supplement, we are indebted to Sir William Hooker, Regius Professor of Botany in the University of Glasgow, whose accurate and elegant works on this department of the science, have justly placed him at the head of the muscologists of the age.

Agrostis Canadensis,
Aster concolor,
" corymbosus,
" patens,
" squarrosus?
Azalea viscosa,
" callendulacea, (1)
Betula excelsa,
Calamagrostis Canadensis,
Carex pseudo-cyperus,
" polytrichoides,
" scirpoides,

Carex lupulina, var. polystachya,
Eupatoreum aromaticum,
Helianthus heterophyllus, *Nutt.* (2.)
Hypericum procumbens,
" sphærocarpum,
Lespedeza reticulata,
" Stuvei
Lithospermum arvense, (3)
Nasturtium natans,
Neottia æstivalis,

Nyssa multiflora,
Osmunda cinnamonea, (4)
" interrupta, (5.)
Panicum pedunculosum,
" multiflorum,
" nervosum,
" strictum,
Poa autumnalis?
Potentilla simplex,
Quercus illicifolia,
Sagittaria heterophylla,
Salix conifera, (6)

Salix nigra,
" tristis,
" cordata,
Scutellaria laevigata,
" saxatilis, *Riddell*, (7)
" versicolor, *Benth*,
Senecio lobatus, (8)
Sisymbrium officinale, (10)
" dentatum, *Torr.* (9)
" brachycarpum, *Hooker.*
Solidago speciosa, (11)
Vesicaria Shortii, *Tor.* (12)
Xanthoriza apiifolia, (13.)

Mosses.

Bryum aureum,
" argenteum,
" cæspititium,
" cuspidatum,
Climacium dendroides,
Dicranum zanthodon,
" purpureum,
Fontinalis capillacea,
" antipyretica,
Fumaria hygrometrica,
Grimmia apocarpa,
Gymnostomum pyriforme,
Hypnum salebrosum,
" serpens,
" curvifolium,
" proliferum,
" minutulum,

Hypum serrulatum,
" orthocladum, with }
other undetermined species,}
Leskea gracilescens,
" rostrata,
Leucodon brachyssus?
Neckera cladorhizans,
" seductrix.
" ———?
Pterogonium tricomitrion,
Polytrichium commune, }
" var. formosum, }
" angustatum,
Timmia megapolitana,
Weissa contraversa,
" microdus.

NOTES TO THIS SUPPLEMENT.

(1.) *Azalea callendulacea.*—This very beautiful and somewhat rare species occurs in those mountainous portions of Kentucky, especially, bordering on Licking and Rockcastle rivers. It appears, however, to be destitute of the delightful mignionette odour of the *A. viscosa*, with which it is found in common.

(2.) *Helianthus heterophyllus*—This species, first detected by Mr. Nuttall in Alabama, is met with in the Barrens of Western Kentucky, bordering on the Ohio river. It is one of the few well-characterized species of this extensive and difficult genus.

(3.) *Lithospermum arvense.* An introduced plant which within the last year or two has first made its appearance in this neighborhood, where it is rapidly over-running the lots and commons around Lexington and is likely soon to become a pestiferous weed.

(4.) *Osmunda Cinnamonea.* Through inadvertence this fern, which is abundant in many portions of the State, has been omitted in our previous catalogues. Its favourite localities are moist vallies in mountainous regions, where the barren fronds frequently attain the height of from 4 to 6 feet, far exceeding the size of any other of our filicoid plants.

(5.) *Osmunda interrupta.* This species seems as rare, as the preceding is abundant in this State; we have never met with it until the present season, and then but in a single locality, on the "Big-Hill," in Madison county.

It is somewhat remarkable, as we are informed by our esteemed correspondent, Mr. Oakes, of Massachusetts, that all the species of Fern yet found in Kentucky occur also in New England, except *Polypodium incanum* and *Ophioglossum bulbosum;* and that nearly half of the Ferns of Kentucky are also common to Europe, as will appear by the following synopsis.

FERNS OF KENTUCKY,

Common to Europe.	Not common to Europe.
1. Polypodium vulgare,	13. Polypodium incanum,
2. " phlegopteris, (hexagon-opterum—connectile.)	14. Hypopeltis obtusa,
	15. Aspidium acrostichoides,
3. " dryopteris,	16. " marginale,
4. Aspidium thelypteris, (thelypteroides—noveboracense.	17. " bulbiferum,
	18. Dicksonia pilosiuscula,
5. " Filix-mas (A. Goldianum.)	19. Asplenium rhyzophyllum,

Common to Europe.
6. " fragile.(dentatum—tenue.)
7. Asplenium trichomanes, (melanocaulon, *Mx.*]
8. " Ruta muraria,
9. " Filix fœm'na, (asplenioides—angustum.)
10. Pteris aquilina,
11. Osmunda regalis?
12. Ophioglossum vulgatum.

Not common to Europe.
20. Asplenium angustifolium,
21. " ebenum,
22. " thelypetroides,
23. Pteris atropurpurea,
24. Osmunda cinnamonea,
35. " interrupta,
26. Adiantum pedatum,
27. Onoclea sensibilis,
28. Ophioglossum bulbosum,
29. Botrychium Virginicum,
30. " lunarioides (obliquum—dissectum.)

30 species as yet discovered in Kentucky;
39 " in New England, which probably are nearly all that will be found there.
12 Kentucky species are common to Europe,
18 " " are not common to Europe.

(6.) *Salix conifera, S. longirostris, Mx.*—A little willow which forms a conspicuous feature in the Barrens of Kentucky in early spring, putting forth its large catkins before any appearance of leaves. The cone-like bodies, so frequently seen on it, are the productions of insects.

(7.) *Scutellaria saxatilis,* described by Dr. Riddell in a supplementary catalogue of Ohio Plants, (West. Med. & Phys. Jour. 1836.] Several years ago, we met with this plant in a marshy flat at the Olympian Springs—a locality of a totally different kind from that assigned to it by Dr. R.; and although then convinced that it was a nondescript, we omitted making it known. Whilst, therefore, we cheerfully concede to our friend the honor of its discovery, we regret that the name given it is by no means characteristic.

(8.) *Senecio lobatus.* This species, which seems to be abundant on the lower Mississippi, has been found by Mr. Griswold at Louisville; but we believe has not been seen higher on the Ohio.

(9.) *Sisymbrium dentatum, Tor. Mss.* This plant was noticed in our first catalogue under the name *Arabis hirsuta,* in accordance with the views of a scientific friend to whom it was submitted, although it had but few agreements with specimens so labelled in our Herbarium. Dr. Torrey has since satisfactorily determined that it is totally distinct—even belonging to a different genus. It occurs abundantly on the sandy banks of the Ohio river, flowering very early in the spring.

(10.) *Sisymbrium officinale*. A troublesome weed, occurring every where in neglected and uncultivated grounds. It has strangely escaped mention in our preceding lists.

(11.) *Solidago speciosa, S. sempervirens, Mx*. This, decidedly the most beautiful of an extensive and beautiful genus, occurs in profuse abundance throughout the Barrens of Kentucky. Its tall purplish stem—large, smooth, entire leaves, and long erect raceme of large florets, sufficiently distinguish it from its numerous associates.

(12.) *Vesicaria Shortii, Tor. Fl. Am. ined*. This very rare plant, of which we have only met with two imperfect specimens, on Elkhorn creek between Lexington and Frankfort, is considered by Dr. Torrey a new species.

(13.) *Xanthoriza apiifolia*. Although Mr. Nuttall (Gen. Am. Pl.) states that this is found plentifully on the Ohio river, yet in our frequent explorations of the borders of that stream at various points, we have not met with it thereon; and indeed never until this summer, on the borders of Rockcastle river, in the southern portion of Kentucky, where it is found in the greatest profusion.

Nelumbium luteum, Linn.—Cyamus luteus, Salisbury.— "Wancopin"—"Water chinquepin"—"Egyptian Bean"—"Sacred Bean of India," &c. &c. This splendid aquatic, confessedly the most magnificent of American plants, and one to which the title of *Queen of American Flowers* has been with much propriety given, was mentioned in our first catalogue; having, then however, only seen it in one locality—a pond in the Barrens of Western Kentucky. Since that we have heard of its occurrence in various portions of the State; and but a few days ago we had the pleasure of seeing it, in all its glory, in a pond on the borders of Jesssamine county, within six miles of Lexington. The account of its introduction there, is somewhat curious, and shows how easily this elegant ornament of the water may be introduced, and how rapidly it is propagated. Two year ago, in the summer of 1835, one plant was for the first time observed in this locality, where it was ascribed to the agency of some water-fowl. It was undisturbed, and suffered to mature its seeds. The next summer showed a great increase from this parent stock; and this year (1837,) it has spread over half an acre, and threatens the entire occupancy of a large pond, in the course of a year or two more. This rapidity of propagation is effected, not only by its numerous seeds, but also, by its running roots, one of which, as we were assured by the proprietor of the pond in question, had been pulled out thirty feet in length, the production apparently of one season!

Another curious circumstance connected with the history of this plant, occurred to our notice a few days ago, and was communicated to Professor Hooker, of Glasgow, who inserted it in the *Journal of Botany for* 1834, from which notice we here extract the following:—"On the Ohio river, a hundred miles north of Lexington, my brother owns a considerable tract of land, a piece of which adjoining the river was subject to inundation, and in a shallow basin of 50 acres or more, the water remained throughout the year. Twenty years ago this basin was drained, sown in grass and is now a productive meadow,—the upper stratum being a tough, whitish clay. In ploughing this piece of ground lately, immense quantities of the seeds of the *Cyamus* were turned up from among the clay, in which they were embedded to a considerable depth; they are perfectly sound and hard, requiring much effort break them open, and exhibiting within, the cotyledons and embryo, full, plump and apparently fresh;—none of them. however, manifest the slightest disposition to vegetate. The plant has certainly not grown there for twenty years, and the oldest resident of the neighborhood has no recollection of having ever seen it."

Lexington, Ky. July 17th, 1837.

A FOURTH SUPPLEMENTARY CATALOGUE
OF THE PLANTS OF KENTUCKY

ART. II.—*A Fourth Supplementary Catalogue of the Plants of Kentucky.* By C. W. SHORT, M. D., Professor of Materia Medica and Medical Botany in the Medical Institute of Louisville.

Having several years ago, published in the Transylvania Journal of Medicine, a catalogue of the phenogamous and filicoid plants, native to and naturalized in this state, so far as they had then been observed by me, I afterwards published, in three subsequent numbers of the same Journal, supplementary catalogues of other species, as they became known to me, either by personal observation, or the reports of others competent to determine them. I now offer a *fourth* supplement to the preceding lists, embracing merely the names of, and a few remarks on, some other plants, which have occurred to my notice in different parts of Kentucky, since the publication of the last. Like the others, this list is arranged alphabetically, without reference to systematic classification.

Ampelopsis cordata, on the banks of the Ohio River.

Aspidium dilatatum.

Aspidium asplenoides.

Acerates angustifolia.

Arabis lyrata, found by Dr. Riddell among the knobs of Greenup county, Ky.

Aronia latifolia, from the same locality, detected by the same botanist.

Anthoxanthum odoratum, (Sweet-scented Vernal grass.) This grass, which imparts such delightful odor to new-mown hay, is becoming gradually naturalized in our meadows.

Adonis autumnalis, (Pheasant's eye.) A showy exotic flower, found in the barrens of Kentucky, where it was introduced from a neighbouring garden.

Allium striatum.

Arenaria serpyllifolia.

Angelica triquinata, barrens of Ky.

Angelica atropurpurea, borders of Rock-Castle River, and other mountainous situations.

Asclepias parviflora. This species, so common in the southern States, has only been observed by me in the wet lands bordering on Green River.

Azalea nudiflora. (Bush Honey-suckle.)

Bumelia tenax, on the rocky banks of Little River, a branch of the Cumberland.

Boltonia glastifolia, swamps around Louisville.

Cyperus filiculmis, Islands of the Ohio.

Cyperus erythrorizos, (Grass nut.) The tubers attached to the roots have very much the taste of the cocoa nut.

Cypripedium candidum, (small white lady-slipper.) This interesting species was first pointed out to me in the barrens of Christian county, by the Rev. Mr. Jones, of Hopkinsville, Kentucky.

Chrysanthemum leucanthemum, (Ox-eye daisy.) A troublesome weed in the Eastern States, which will soon be extensively introduced into the West.

Carex bromoides.

Convolvulus sepium, (Bind-weed.)

Convallaria stellata. I have met with this pretty species only on Corn Island, opposite to Louisville.

Clethra tomentosa. I know this plant, as a native of Kentucky, only through a solitary imperfect specimen gathered by my pupil, the late Dr. Clarendon Peck, among the hills of Licking River.

Desmodium strictum.

Eupatoreum rotundifolium.

Epilobium palustre.

Euchroma pallida, barrens of Kentucky; much less abundant than E. coccinea.

Gaura angustifolia.

Gerardia auriculata, wet lands in the barrens.

Hypericum Virginicum, knobs among the barrens.

Hypericum angulosum, " "

Hypericum nudiflorum, " "

Hieracium Kalmii. This plant, in common with many others, is reputed to possess curative properties in snake bites.

Itea Virginica. This pretty shrub was observed by me for the first time this spring, (1840) among the wet timbered lands bordering on Green River, near Rumsey.

4 *

Ilex Canadensis, wet lands of Henderson county.
Ilex prinoides,   "   "   "
Juncus marginatus.
Jussieua grandiflora. This plant, to which so much interest attaches, in consequence of the publication of Dr. Cartwright, in the July number of this Journal, was observed by me in the spring of 1838, in a marsh of Henderson county, Kentucky, ten miles south of the Ohio River. It was rare; but its existence there proved its adaptation to the climate; and if the views lately promulgated as to its health-preserving influences be sustained, it would doubtless be desirable to propagate it extensively in malarious and miasmatic districts.

Lythrum alatum.
Liatris cylindracea.
Leavenworthia aurea.
Leavenworthia uniflora, *Torrey.* Cardamine uniflora, *Mich.* These two little plants occur in common on wet rocks among the barrens. The genus, separated by Torrey from Cardamine, has been very justly dedicated to Dr. Leavenworth, of the United States Army, who has done much towards the elucidation of the botany of Louisiana, Arkansas and Florida, whilst stationed at different posts of the South and West.

Mariscus ovularis.
Plantago pusilla. A diminutive species of plantain, frequent in the pastures of Christian county.

Peplis Americana, common in the poor lands and pastures of Muhlenburg county.

Phlox pilosa. This is distinct from the plant, published under the same name, in a previous catalogue. That is most probably P. aristata, and the present is undoubtedly the genuine P. pilosa of Michaux. It occurs in great abundance in early spring among the barrens; and is a very handsome, low species, with dark purple flowers.

Psoralea congesta,—a new species lately discovered by Dr. Clapp and Mr. Jones, of New Albany, on the Islands of the Ohio River, near that place.

Psoralea latifolia. In thickets among the barrens; rather rare.

Prenanthes Illinoensis, abundant in the barrens of Kentucky, as well as the prairies of Illinois.

Quercus triloba. Observed by Dr. Riddell on the knobs of Greenup county, Ky.

Quercus ilicifolia.

Salix petiolaris, } Two dwarf willows detected by Dr. Clapp
Salix longifolia, } on the Islands of the Ohio River.

Sagittaria lanceolata,

Sisymbrium palustre.

Salvia urticifolia, in the thin oak lands of the barrens.

Styllingia sylvatica, rare—barrens of Kentucky.

Stellaria graminea.

Smyrnium atropurpureum.

Sedum telephoides, first pointed out to us by Dr. Clapp, on the lime-stone cliffs above Utica, on the Indiana shore. It no doubt occurs also in similar situations, on the Kentucky side of the Ohio.

Trillium petiolatum. A species having considerable resemblance to the common T. sessile, but totally distinct; barrens of Ky.

Trichostema brachiata, barrens.

Tripsacum dactyloides, (Gama grass.) A luxuriant grass to which public attention was called a few years since, as an excellent article of provender; a character which further experience has proved it not to deserve. It occurs, as a native, among the grasses of the barrens; and has been introduced into different parts of the state.

Taxodium distichum, (Cypress tree.) This truly valuable timber tree is met with abundantly in the lakes and lagoons of all the counties bordering on the Ohio river, in the West of Kentucky; where the peculiar excrescences called "Cypress Knees" form obstacles in the way of crossing the water-courses.

Verbena spuria, roadsides in the barrens, in common with V. angustifolia

Wistaria frutescens. A flowering pea-vine, now common in gardens and shrubberies; abundant on the banks of Little River in the West of Kentucky.

Xanthium spinosum. A pestiferous species of cockle-bur, which, it is to be feared, will become extensively naturalized. As yet, I have only met with it on the commons of Portland, below the falls of the Ohio.

Yucca filamentosa, (Adam's thread, Bear-grass, &c.) A showy and ornamental plant, frequent in gardens; and which I am informed by the Rev. Mr. Jones, of Hopkinsville, grows abundantly on the Cumberland mountains, in the S. E. corner of Kentucky. An opinion is entertained by some, that the stream which enters the Ohio River at Louisville, derives its its name from this plant, which is supposed to have once grown on its banks. This is most probably erroneous; and it is more likely that the name of the creek was taken from some of those rank and luxuriant grasses, so common in similar alluvions, as Panicum crus-galli, and others.

August, 1840.

REVIEW
OF WILLIAM DARLINGTON'S *FLORA CESTRICA*

REVIEWS.

ART. XIV.—*Flora Cestrica.*—An attempt to enumerate and describe the Flowering and Filicoid Plants of Chester cty., in the State of Pennsylvania, with brief notices of their properties and uses, in Medicine, Domestic and Rural Economy, and the arts. By WILLIAM DARLINGTON, M. D. &c. &c., West Chester, Pa., printed for the author, by S. Siegfried and for sale by Kimber and Sharpless, Philadelphia. 1 vol. 12 mo. pp. 640.

The Botany of that portion of America lying adjacent to Philadelphia may be considered as more thoroughly explored and better known, than that of any other district of similar magnitude in our country. This has no doubt resulted in a main degree from the greater attention paid, and the importance attached to the study of this science by the university of Pennsylvania, and in an especial manner to the labours of the Bartons (Professor Benjamin Smith, and Dr. William P. C.) who for many years in succession have delivered courses of lectures on this favourite and popular branch of science, not only to the large classes of medical students, yearly in attendance on the institutions of that city, but to general and popular audiences. Indeed, to the same source we do not hesitate to ascribe, in a considerable degree, whatever of devotion to, or taste for this fascinating study we have seen developed in any portion of the continent. But certainly no portion of the favored district alluded to has been so patiently, diligently and thoroughly explored as that which is embraced in the work before us. Its amiable and excellent author, an elève of the University of Pennsylvania, and a pupil of the elder Barton, from whom doubtless he derived his predilections for the study of Nature, has been so fortunate as to be located in a highly intellectual community; and although his residence is an inconsiderable village, yet he has managed to draw around him a cohort of its most influential citizens; and to diffuse, both through town and country, a very general fondness for the natural sciences. The fruits of their labours have been already manifested in the establishment of a very flourishing Cabinet of natural sciences, the Library and collections of which in the various departments, would do credit to a much older institution; an institute in which several popular and highly instructive courses of lectures have been delivered; and the work before us; in the collection of the materials of which our author acknowledges himself greatly indebted to the aid of numerous friends residing in Chester county, *twenty-five* of whom are named in the course of the work, as having kindly and liberally contributed specimens, and a knowledge of localities to the author—a larger number of botanists, we venture to assert, than is to be found in any other county in the Union. With one of these gentlemen, David Townsend, Esq. to whom our author's acknowledgments are repeatedly expressed, we have had ourselves the pleasure of some correspondence and exchange; and we can, therefore, readily appreciate the value of such liberal, accurate and industrious colaborators in the publication of such a work as that before us.

Besides the advantages to be derived from such able assistance as well as from a reference to all printed authorities, the author has fully availed himself of the aids obtained from an extensive correspondence and exchange of specimens with many fellow laborers in other portions of the United States; among whom he mentions Drs. TORREY, PICKERING, GRAY and SHORT, with Messrs. NUTTALL and CURTIS. Nor are his efforts at the attainment of accuracy limited to information sought on this side the Atlantic, but he has drawn freely on foreign aid, and that aid has been as freely rendered by Dr. BOOTT, formerly of Boston, now resident in London, who besides his intimate acquaintance with American Botany, enjoys, as secretary of the Linnæan Society, the rare privileges of comparing specimens with the originals in the Linnæan and other authentic herbaria. SIR WILLIAM J. HOOKER, too, has kindly communicated to our author the results of his laborious investigation of American Plants; and Professor DE CANDOLLE's authority is frequently adduced. With all these facilities and aids, backed by much persevering industry, accuracy, discernment and *ardor botanicus* on the part of the author himself, it would have been surprising if he had not produced the most comprehensive, minutely accurate and satisfactory treatise which has ever appeared on the local botany of any portion of America. But it is time to let the work speak for itself; and in the first place, on the subject of the arrangement or classification the author makes the following remarks.

> An apology will doubtless be expected from me, for still adhering to the Linnæan arrangement, when the modern botanical world have so generally abandoned it for the *Natural method*. I am fully conscious of the old-fashioned garb in which this work is arrayed, and have a thorough conviction of the value and importance of studying plants according to their natural affinities: But, observing that the Natural method is yet kept, as it were, in a continual state of fermentation, by the labors and researches of the great Masters in the Science,—and feeling my inability to co-operate, or aid in adjusting its details,—I thought it most advisable, in the present attempt, to adhere mainly to the Linnæan classification. Whilst I freely admit that the true science of vegetables can only be attained by a well-disciplined and philosophical investigation of their structure, functions, and natural affinities, I cannot help thinking that even the superficial knowledge of genera and species, which is so readily acquired by the Linnæan system, may be advantageous to the cause, by exciting an early interest in learners, and facilitating the first steps of the uninitiated. When the young recruits are once securely *enlisted*, we may venture to exact a more rigid *discipline*. In the meantime, a good foundation may be laid for a scientific knowledge of plants, by the study of such admirable elementary works as those of DE CANDOLLE, or RICHARD,—and that recently published in our own language, by Dr. A. GRAY, of New York.

In all this we are free to confess that we are old-fashioned enough to agree entirely with the author; nor can we hesitate for a moment to believe that to the uninitiated—the new beginner, the study of Plants by the Linnæan classes is a much easier and less repulsive process than by their natural affinities; indeed a knowledge of those affinities presented by the Linnæan arrangement seems a necessary prerequisite to the commencement of the study of the natural orders. Our author has even gone upon this principle so far as to attempt something like a compromise; and, in our opinion, the success of the attempt has fully warranted the innovation; but yet we apprehend that with the exclusive advocates of the modern method, our author will find his sentence of condemnation but little mitigated in consequence of the *middle course* he has pursued; for, as he has very appropriately observed elsewhere; "The Poet's dogma—"*in medio tutissimus*"—may be true enough in conducting the chariot of the sun; but it will not hold good in politics, religion or science. Partizans in either of these pursuits will not tolerate a middle course." His reasons for the arrangement followed are briefly set forth in the following paragraph.

Notwithstanding the arrangement according to the Sexual System is confessedly *artificial*, the reader cannot fail to remark how many of those great families of plants which are obviously *natural*, are yet preserved under it, nearly or quite entire. By doing a slight violence to the Linnæan method (as I have ventured to do, in this work, at the suggestion of my friend, Dr. Pickering,) it will be seen the genera belonging to the following eminently Natural Orders, may be all kept together—viz: *Cyperaceæ Gramineæ, Boragineæ, Umbelliferæ, Rosaceæ, Pomaceæ, Amygdaleæ, Labiatæ, Cruciferæ, Leguminosæ, Compositæ, Orchideæ, Filices*, and *Lycopodiaceæ.* These orders comprise nearly half the genera, and more than half the species, enumerated in the present work. In addition to the foregoing, it will be found that the genera (84 in number) belonging to 20 additional Natural Orders, and comprising about 180 species, are all grouped together under the Linnæan arrangement; and a large proportion of the genera belonging to several other natural orders, will also be found in company. In short, upwards of 800 plants out of 1073, enumerated in the Flora, will be found congregated together, by a slight modification of the Sexual System, almost as completely as under the Natural method. Having them thus grouped, their affinities and true character may be studied as thoroughly, and nearly with the same convenience, as under any natural arrangement.

Adopting the Linnæan class and orders, thus modified, the following is the plan pursued in the description of the genera and species:

1. The *name of the Genus* with reference to its original projector, modern authorities for its continuance, are given.

2. The *derivation* of the generic name so far as it is known.

3. The *description* of the genus, in which the amended characters of the best modern authors, and especially of De Candolle are given.

4. A few general remarks on the Plants of the genus, with

reference to the number and name of the *natural order*, according to LINDLEY, under which it is placed.

5. Next follows the *species* belonging to each genus; under each of which are given, the *name* with its authority—a short *specific description*, with reference to the source where obtained. These descriptions instead of being blindly copied from other writers, are rigidly examined, and when necessary altered and improved by the author.

6. All the *synonyms* are next given, with particular reference to the works in they are found; and to *plates*, when such have been published.

7. The *specific name Anglecised*—an item of much gratification to those who are not versed in the Latin language, as it makes them familiar with the *meaning of the specific*, as they had been previously made acquainted with the *derivation of the generic name*.

8. The *common English name* of the Plant, where it has such; together with those of the German, Spanish, Italian, &c. when they are known to the author.

9. Next follows a *detailed description* of the species under consideration, drawn up by the author from his own personal analysis; or the trust-worthy authority of others. This we esteem the most valuable, as it certainly has been the most labored and tedious portion of the work; and those who have occasion to refer to these descriptions, in the examination of Plants, will have abundant reason for thankfulness to the author for this patient labour, and the minute accuracy of its results.

10. The *Habitat* is next given, or a reference to the soil and situation in which the species is most generally met with, with particular directions to some locality in Chester county, where it may be or has been found—the time of flowering, and ripening its fruit, &c. &c.

11. and lastly, some *general observations* in relation to the properties, uses, peculiarities, culture, &c. &c. of the Plant under consideration. This is a highly interesting and useful portion of the work, and one in which the farmer, physician,

housewife, and general reader, even those who make no pretensions to Botany, will find much to instruct and amuse them. These several particulars will best appear by an extract from the work itself and we select the generic and specific descriptions of a familiar plant.

117. LOBELIA. *L. Nutt. Gen.* 568.

[Named in honor of *Matthias de Lobel*; a Flemish Botanist.]

Calyx 5 parted. *Corolla* tubular, irregular, somewhat labiate, cleft on the upper side nearly to the base. *Stamens* more or less united; *anthers* coalescent into a tube, which is curved, perforate, and bearded at summit. *Stigma* 2-lobed. *Capsules* sometimes half superior, 2 or 3-celled, opening at summit. *Seeds* numerous, minute, oblong, scabrous.

Herbaceous, or rarely *fruticose*: leaves alternate; flowers solitary, axillary, or in terminal bracteate recemes. *Nat. Ord.* 175. *Lindl.* LOBELIACEÆ.

L. INFLATA. *L.* Stem erect, somewhat paniculately branched, hirsute; leaves sessile, lance-ovate, crenate-dentate, racemes leafy; capsules inflated. *Beck, Bot. p.* 215.

INFLATED LOBELIA. *Vulgo*—Eye-bright. Indian Tobacco.

Lactescent. *Root* biennial. *Muhl. Eat.* (perennial, *Ell.* annual, *Willd. Torr. Bigel.*) *Stem* 9 to 18 inches high, sometimes alate-angular by the decurrence of the leaves, often very hairy; branches axillary. *Leaves* to 1 to 2 and 3 inches, and half an inch to an inch and half wide, more or less ovate, rather acute, unequally crenate or sinuate-dentate, pilose. *Peduncles* axillary, one fourth to half an inch long, roughish pubescent. *Corolla* pale blue, small. *Capsule* ovoid, or oval, thin and membranaceous, 10-nerved, reticulately veined, smoothish. *Seeds* numerous, minute, eliptic-oblong, subdiaphanous, rough, with ferruginous, reticulated ridges, under a lens.

Hab. Pastures; roadsides, &c. frequent. *Fl.* July—Sept. *Fr.* Aug.—Oct.

Obs. This is an acrid plant, posssessing active emetic, cathartic and narcotic properties; and may be used for good or for evil, according to the degree of skill and discretion with which it is employed. It is said to be a prominent article in the Materia Medica of a modern race of Empirics, who, in some districts of our country, have attained a notoriety, and consequence, which is not very creditable to the discernment of the communities in which they flourish. The indiscriminate use of *any* active medicine, is as dangerous as it is preposterous."

We have alluded to the general and popular *observations* made at the close of the scientific descriptions of the different plants, as containing a mass of useful, curious, and entertaining matter—of this we will take the liberty of citing a few instances. Under the head of *Plantago major*, greater plantain, we find the following.

Obs. A naturalized foreigner;—remarkable for accompanying civilized man,—growing along his foot-paths, and flourishing around his settlements. It is said our Aborigines call it "*the white man's foot*," from this circumstance. The leaves have long been known and used as a popular dressing for blisters and other sores, a practice sportively noticed by Shakespeare:—

"*Rom.* Your *Plantain leaf* is excellent for that.
Ben. For what, I pray thee?
Rom. For your broken shin."
ROMEO AND JULIET, *Act.* 1. *Sc.* 2.

Under *Ribes uva-crispa*, Gooseberry, a hint of much practical importance to the gardener is found.

Obs. There appear to be several varieties of this plant, —which is cultivated for its fine fruit. It rarely succeeds well, with us;—partly, no doubt, owing to the climate, and partly, perhaps, for want of skill and care in the management. The young fruit is apt to become covered with a russet kind of mould, which causes it to blight; and the bushes generally are prone to send up too many suckers from the root. My friend, Mr. S. R. GRUMMERE, of Burlington, N. J. who is a Botanist and a very successful Horticulturist, informs me that this last mentioned evil may be prevented, by carefully removing the buds from that portion of the cuttings (when they are planted,) which is inserted in the ground. Seventeen or eighteen additional species are enumerated as natives of the United States; of which the R. aureum, or Missouri Currant, is much cultivated, and greatly admired, for the beauty and spicy fragrance of its flowers.

After *Valisneria spiralis*, Eel grass, we find the following:

Obs. I have not yet observed the staminate plant. The pistillate ones are numerous, and obvious enough at the season of flowering, in the waters of the Brandywine, and other considerable streams. *Wilson,* in his Ornithology, says the *roots* of this plant are the favorite food of the *Canvass-back Duck*; to which the peculiarly delicate flavor of the flesh of that bird has been ascribed. The *leaves* which are usually procumbently floating, afford a hiding place for Eels, whence one of its common names. It is the only species in the United States; and probably, as *Pursh* suggested, not specifically distinct from the European V. *spiralis*.

In relation to this particular plant we are induced to add a remark in confirmation of the singular character here given of it. At various points on the Kentucky River we have seen large sheets of water covered over with the *Staminate flowers* of this plant, detached from their parents and floating on the surface of the water, but after the most diligent search at different times and places, we have never met with single *pistillate plant*.

The length to which we have carried our extracts from, and remarks on this work, now compel us to end them: and we do so with the more regret because we are conscious of having bestowed upon it but a small part of the commendation it deserves. The botanist who enters upon the study of the plants themselves, with this book as his *vade mecum*, will alone be able to appreciate its many excellencies—nor will its utility be by any means restricted to an examination of the plants of Chester county. On the contrary it must be decidedly the best manual extant for the Botanist of the Middle Eastern States; and it will answer a valuable purpose in determining many of the plants of the Northern, Southern and Western States. Would that every county and district in our widespread land could boast of a history as faithful of their vegetable productions, as that given by Dr. Darlington in his FLORA CESTRICA.

S.

ON THE CULTIVATION
OF CERTAIN MEDICINAL PLANTS

Art. V. *On the Cultivation of certain Medicinal Plants.* By Charles W. Short, M. D. &c.

The deterioration of many vegetable medicines, by long keeping, exposure to light and air, the depredations of insects and the injury of moisture; together with their adulteration by admixture with inert or injurious articles, are notorious to all who are conversant with them, and a frequent cause of regret and disappointment, in their practical applications to the cure of disease. As respects many of these medicines, for our supplies of which we are compelled to rely on foreign importation, the difficulties alluded to are only to be remedied by a careful selection of them, from druggists of approved standing and knowledge in their business; and afterwards by a diligent preservation and seclusion of them from the access of all injurious agents. These methods of protection are in some degree peculiar to each article, and need not here be pointed out. In every instance, however, the physician who has a proper respect for his own character, or regard for the safety of his patients, will promptly reject from his stock any substance whose excellence may even be suspected, and supply its place with the best of the kind which he can possibly obtain. For surely the most inexcusable of all kinds of parsimony is that, which would influence a practitioner to prefer an inferior article to one of decided excellence, merely on account of a few dollars difference in the price. In every well regulated drug-store or private shop the supplies of all drugs of a perishable nature should be frequently renewed, although no positive evidence of their deterioration may exist; for it is certainly erroneous to suppose, that any dead vegetable substance can improve, either in flavour or effect, by long keeping. As soon as articles of this kind are, by exsiccation sufficiently deprived of their sap and other vegetable juices to prevent decomposition, they have attained all the perfection of which, in that state, they are susceptible; and perhaps every day afterwards detracts in some degree from their virtues. The truth of this principle is constantly recognized in the common concerns of life, by the selection of the newest hay for the stall, and the freshest tea for the table. Why should less attention be paid to those more important, but equally perishable agents, upon which we venture the lives of human beings?

Fortunately, however, as regards many important articles of the vegetable materia medica, it is in the power of most physicians, and particularly of those who reside in the interior of country situations, where opportunities of resorting to good drug-stores are rare, of commanding a supply of these medicines, upon which they may at all times rely with confident assurances of their freshness and purity—by their own cultivation of them.

With the view of drawing to this subject the attention of the profession, and especially those members of it whose time and opportunity enable them to undertake it, the present paper is written. The objects it proposes, are not matters of conjecture; they have been practically tested by the writer, and their feasibility satisfactorily established: he, therefore, confidently recommends them to his professional brethren. To such of them as are engaged in farming, or are fond of horticultural pursuits, an attention to the culture of the plants alluded to, independently of their intrinsic utilities, will be found a source of pleasurable relaxation, from severer duties.

Digitalis purpurea.   Purple Foxglove.

This powerful medicine has had its day of reputation, followed but too soon, we are convinced, by the night of neglect. That it is possessed of most active properties, and is capable of being made to produce signal impressions on the human system, none are prepared to deny; and although its virtues are still highly extolled by some, as exercising a most controlling agency over diseased action, its use is vehemently denounced by others, of high standing in the profession, as always uncertain, and frequently unsafe. Perhaps these discrepant testimonies, and conflicting opinions, in relation to its employment, are in some degree to be accounted for, from the circumstances already alluded to—its deterioration by age, and other noxious agents. As frequently met with in the shops of western practitioners, the Digitalis is found to be a mass of faded worm-eaten leaves, which have, perhaps, for years been exposed, in open jars or drawers, to the injurious influence of air, light, moisture, insects, &c. and from it, in such a state, very different and inferior effects are to be expected, to those of the recent leaf, when properly prepared. It is, however, in the power of every physician to use this medicine in its purity, since the plant is one of the easiest cultivation in all parts of the Union.

In the different countries of Europe, to which it is indigenous, the Foxglove prefers dry, chalky, loamy or gravelly soils; indeed, is it found in all except such as are too damp, or marshy. In cultivating it, in this country, the situation chosen should be dry and not too much shaded, nor exposed too directly to the power of the sun. The seed may be put into the ground towards the last of April; but being very minute they are apt to be sown too thick; attention is consequently necessary to thinning the plants, when they have attained any size; care being taken not to leave them nearer than two feet apart. The Foxglove being a biennial plant, does not arrive at perfection, or flower until the second summer; but in this latitude it requires no protection during the intervening winter, and even in the severest weather the leaves retain some degree of verdure. About June of the second year, it sends up from a dense tuft of large root-leaves, a long, graceful spike of beautiful, purple flowers, elegantly dotted in the interior with eye-like spots, which continue unfolding for a number of weeks, and are succeeded by small capsules filled with minute seed. The largest and first of these seed-vessels should be reserved for further culture, securing them as soon as they turn brown and begin to open.

The directions given by Dr. Withering, (who has paid more attention to the preparation and exhibition of this article than any other physician,) for the collection and preservation of the plant are, that, " the leaves be gathered when the flower-stems are shot up, but before the time of flowering; and the largest and deepest coloured leaves are to be preferred. These are to be carefully dried in a warm room through which a current of air is passing; and when perfectly crisp and dry, they are to be reduced to powder, and kept in bottles closely corked, and not exposed to the light. In this state the digitalis has a fragrant smell, not unlike new hay. The dried plant, well kept, will preserve its virtues for a considerable time, but as uniformity in strength is always desirable; and as all herbaceous plants gradually lose their medicinal properties, it will be right for the apothecary to prepare it afresh every year."*

A variety of this species is sometimes met with, having white flowers, which is less esteemed for medical use than the purple flowered. A dozen thrifty plants of the latter, raised on the borders of a garden, where they are highly ornamental, will afford leaves enough for the supply of any physician of the most extensive practice.

Cassia Senna. Senna.

The seeds of this most valuable cathartic plant were probably first introduced into the U. States by imported parcels of the leaves, in which ripe capsules are occasionally found: and the plant has consequently been cultivated for several years in different parts of the country.

In a number of the *Raleigh Star* printed in the Spring of 1813, and republished in the *Eclectic Repertory* for January, 1816, is a short paper on the cultivation of this article; by which it appears that, some years previously, the Medical Society of North Carolina had offered a premium for the production of the largest quantity of Senna, exceeding forty pounds, raised by one person in one year; and that in consequence thereof the writer cultivated one quarter of an acre in the plant, and obtained therefrom between fifty and sixty pounds of Senna, which physicians said was much superior to that imported from the coast of Barbary, and equal to the best from the Levant As this is the only article, of which I am apprized,

---

* Rees' Cyclopedia, article, Digitalis.

that has been published in this country, on the culture of this plant; and as the directions given by the writer, (whose name is not known to me,) have been succesfully followed by myself, in recent experiments, I will give the substance of them in his own words, adding some remarks on particulars in which my own observations do not agree with his.

"It is a delicate plant, sensible to cold, rains and drought: the seeds should be committed to the earth about the first of May; the ground should be mellowed and the seeds planted in rows, covered an inch deep and four inches asunder. The rows should be a foot or two apart, so as to admit of being worked, and the only tillage necessary is to keep it clear of weeds and to earth it moderately. If the season is dry or the soil thirsty, it would be benefitted by an occasional watering. The plant in good soils grows to two-thirds of the height of indigo, but spreads more. The leaves (the valuable part) grow on long stems issuing from the trunk and branches.

"Besides a drought, the Senna is exposed to another formidable enemy. When in bloom it is visited by a yellow butterfly which deposites its eggs upon the leaves in vast abundance. The eggs in a few days become worms, which destroy the leaves. I know no means of preventing the visitation of these troublesome flies, or any expeditious mode of staying the advances of these eggs to the animal state. Sprinkling ashes over the shrubs has been recommended by some, and has suggested itself to me, as a probable means of being useful in both cases, but I have never tried it. The only means which I have attempted was to brush off the eggs with a wing where I have detected them. This is a work of some labour. The eggs are small and white, and will not be observed without minute inspection. The later in the season the plant is in coming to maturity the more liable it is to the depredations of this butterfly progeny. Hence the propriety of bringing it forward as early as the season and its tender nature will permit.

"The Senna is to be gathered once or twice a week as the plant is going on to maturity. When the lower leaves have gained their full size, and begin to change their colour a little.

pluck off a few courses of the lower stems; wilt them two or three hours in the sun, then spread and dry them in the shade, pick out the stems, and put up the leaves in bags suspended in an airy dry situation.

"The seeds are contained in pods which grow at the extremity of the stalk and its branches. As the ripen they become black and fall off. Gathering the leaves does not at all injure the production of seed.

"A light rich soil is best. If sandy, it is liable to suffer from drought."

My own experience would so far differ from the above as to suggest the sowing of the seed at an earlier period, even in this latitude; for they are slow in vegetating, at whatever season they be sown, (sometimes, indeed, requiring four and six weeks for this process,) and unless the plants are urged forward as early in the Spring as possible, they do not yield an abundant harvest of leaves, before they are killed by the frost.

In the course of three or four years experience with it, I have never once seen the butterfly alluded to in the communication above, nor ever noticed the slightest injury to the plant from any insect whatever; a circumstance from which we may infer that this latitude is even more favourable to the growth of the Senna, than that of the neighbourhood of Raleigh.

I have observed it moreover, to flourish best in a rich soil, having a small admixture of sand, and that the product of leaves was the greatest in warm, dry summers.

If, as would appear from the observations of Mons. Hippolite Nectoux,* that even the best Alexandrian Senna, as exported from Egypt, consists not only of the leaves of different species of Cassia, viz. *Cassia Senna* and *C. Lanceolata*, but even of other plants of different genera, it is surely desirable, with a view of avoiding these adulterations and admixtures, that the true Senna be more extensively introduced and cultivated among us. Whatever may be the relative virtues of the different components, which go to make up our parcels of imported Senna,

---

* Barton's Vegetable Materia Medica of the United States, vol. i. p. 143.

there can be no question but that the plant, to which in this paper we particularly invite the attention of the profession, and which is the true *Cassia Senna* of Linnæus, is every way worthy of their attention, as a cathartic medicine; to our indigenous Senna, (*Cassia Marilandica,*) it is in every respect superior.

Ricinus communis. Castor-oil plant.

Although the oil obtained from the seeds of this plant, in consequence of its great cheapness, is but little subject to sophistication, and is almost always to be had in a state of great purity and freshness, yet as it is a medicine of very general use, and such deserved reputation, both in the hands of the physician, and in domestic practice; and as it is, moreover, becoming an article of considerable traffic in many parts of the country, a few words on the subject of its culture and manipulation, derived from experience in them, may not be amiss in this place.

This plant, commonly called *Palma Christi*, and so frequently raised in country gardens, under the idea of its protecting other vegetables from the ravages of the mole, is subject to considerable varieties. Three sorts are most generally met with;—one having a deep purple stock, and leaves tinged with the same colour, growing luxuriantly and bearing large purple seed, of which, however, in this latitude it does not mature a great many. A second variety has a faint blush of purple on the stalk, but the leaves are entirely green; it does not grow so luxuriantly high as the preceding, but matures a greater number of seeds, which are smaller and of a less deep colour. The third kind is of still humbler, more diffuse and branching growth; it is entirely of a bluish green, and bears a great profusion of seed; these however are smaller than either of the others, consequently more troublesome to gather, and less profitable in the outturn. From these circumstances the second mentioned variety has been uniformly prefered for cultivation; and an opinion has even been entertained that the first kind yields an oil much more acrid than either of the others, but with what truth I am unable to determine.

The cultivation of the Palma Christi is of the easiest nature, being very similar to that of corn. A piece of ground being selected (which should be light and loamy, but not of the richest quality,) it should be deeply ploughed in the fall, and subjected, undisturbed throughout the winter, to the influence of frost. As soon in the Spring as it is dry enough, and the earlier the better, it should be again ploughed, harrowed and laid off by furrows five or six feet apart, crossing each other at right angles. Three or four seeds are then dropped at each intersection of the furrows, and lightly covered. When they have come up, and the danger of injury from the frost is over, they must be thinned, leaving one plant only in each spot. Whilst small they may be cultivated with the horse and plough, but when attaining any considerable size, they branch out laterally to such a degree that the hoe alone can be used. Throughout the whole of the season, from the first planting until the last gathering, it is necessary to keep them clear of weeds and well cultivated. When the seeds begin to ripen, which is shown by the seed-vessels becoming dry, and discharging their contents elastically, the gathering of the crop should immediately commence. This is best done by passing along the rows with large baskets and cutting off, with a strong knife, those bunches of seed which are beginning to open; and this operation must be repeated daily, (in the morning or evening,) until the whole crop is collected; for successive flowers are formed, and seeds ripened from mid-summer, until farther vegetation is arrested by the frost.

The separation of the seed from the husk or vessels is the next step in the process, and this is attended with no little trouble; for the seeds, being exceedingly brittle, cannot be threshed, and if not properly guarded they are lost; being thrown to a great distance by the sudden bursting and contraction of the capsules. To prevent this they should be laid, as soon as they are gathered, upon a tight floor, surrounded by close walls, admitting, in dry weather, all the air and sun-shine possible. A preferable plan is to select a garret room, not lathed or plaistered, but having a close floor, and several windows. In this room a number of light scaffolds are to be erected, one above another, and covered with lathes at a few inches distance. Upon these frames the bunches are laid as they are gathered; the heat and air of the situation favour their drying, and when the seeds pop out they are secured. When this process is over, the seeds are separated from the husks by sieves of a proper size, and are then ready for the manufacturer.

Formerly, as is well known, these seeds were mashed in large mortars, and the pulp subjected to the action of boiling water, by which means the oil was separated and skimmed off. The oil thus obtained has a deep amber colour, is unpleasant to the taste, and disposed to rancidity. Of late, however, its extraction by pressure in a mill, in the same manner with the lintseed-oil, has become general in this country; and the oil thus obtained is known as the cold-drawn or cold-expressed Castor-oil. When first extracted it is turbid or muddy, but by processes, known only to the manufacturer, it is rendered perfectly transparent and colourless, with little or no taste or smell. It may, however, be a matter of question whether the modern improvements, in the purifying and clarification of this oil, be not really a disadvantage;—a sacrifice of practical utility to fastidious taste; for every practitioner who has made use of both, must have observed the difference in their action; that while the pale oil is sometimes scarcely laxative, the red is generally an active purgative. So entirely, however, has the former superceded the latter, that a bottle of the red oil is now scarcely ever to be met with.

An acre of ground, well cultivated, will ordinarily yield about 20 bushels of clean seed, each bushel of which will afford a gallon and a half of clear oil.

Papaver Somniferum. Poppy.

All this extensive tribe of plants, of which twelve or fifteen distinct species are enumerated by botanists, together with their innumerable varieties, yield, when their capsules or heads are wounded, a milky juice, which on concreting becomes first brown and then black, and forms pure opium without farther preparation. Nor does the article, as obtained from any of these species or varieties, differ essentially in sensible, chemical, or medical properties. Nevertheless one particular species has been always preferred for culture, with the view of making opium; and that species is the *P. Somniferum*, called generally white poppy, from the more usual colour of its flowers, or from the whiteness of its seeds. The preference given to this species, for this purpose, arises solely from its more luxuriant growth, and larger capsule or seed-vessel; which, in consequence of its greater comparative bulk, may be made to yield a larger amount of opium than any of the other kinds, the capsules of which vary in size from a hen's egg to a garden pea.

The white poppy is a native of the fields, and waste grounds in the South of Europe, and of the same parallels of latitude throughout Asia. It was early introduced into England and has even been said to be found there indigenous: certain it is that it bears the temperature of that country well, and has been there profitably cultivated. In the year 1796, the "Society for the encouragement of Arts" granted premiums of 50 guineas each, to two gentlemen for their success in raising British opium.* Experiments made in the United States fully warrant the conclusion that the Poppy plant may be advantageously cultivated even in the northern States;† and in the southern become a source of considerable revenue. Some trial has lately been made with it at the Shaker settlement in this neighbourhood; and although not extensively pursued, the result was altogether encouraging; the opium produced being of the purest and finest kind; yielding on chemical analysis a greater amount, in a given quantity, of the active constituents of the drug, than the common Turkey samples.

The Poppy will grow in almost any soil, but it flourishes best in rich, loamy ground, well manured with thoroughly rotted dung, and frequently ploughed or turned so as to render it mellow. Towards the 1st of March, or during the month of February, if the ground be sufficiently dry, the seeds should be sown. For the purpose of collecting the opium most conveniently, this is done in shallow drills, eighteen inches or two feet

---

* Annals of Medicine for 1796.   † Medical Repository, vol. i, and vol. iii.

apart, strewing the seed very thinly in them: the young plants are not easily injured by frost, but do not bear transplanting well. About the middle of April, or when the plants are two inches high, they should be thinned, so as to leave them ten or twelve inches apart in the drills; and then frequently weeded, and occasionally watered, if the season be dry. In this manner they grow luxuriantly: each plant producing from four to ten flowers, and each flower being succeeded by a large capsule, or *head* as it is called. When these heads are fully grown, but whilst they are still green, the opium is obtained from them, by making slight incisions into them. This is best done with a small instrument, somewhat like a scarificator, having three or four cutting points, which will make as many incisions through the exterior epidermis, without penetrating the cavity of the head. With this instrument a person passes along the rows, and scarifies each ripe poppy head *on one side*. As soon as the incisions are made a juice of milky whiteness exudes, sometimes so abundantly as to drop on the leaves below, but more commonly it merely trickles to the bottom of the cut, where adhering it soon becomes brown and viscid. This operation should be done in the morning; and in the evening of the same day the small adherent masses of opium are scraped from the sides of the heads with the blade of a knife, or more conveniently, with a piece of iron having a circular edge, by which the exudations from all the cuts may be removed at one application. On the ensuing morning the opposite sides of the heads are treated in the same way, and in the evening, the produce being gathered, it is put with the previous parcels into a porcelain, or earthen dish, and exposed to the action of the sun until it attains the requisite spissitude, being occasionally worked up with a wooden spatula.

This is the process which from all testimony is pursued in Turkey: it is that which has been most successfully followed in the experiments which have been made in England; and that by which, no doubt, the purest opium is obtained. It is but proper to remark, however, that a somewhat different plan has been adopted, and recommended, by a gentleman of New York, which is here given in his own words.

"I have tried the Asiatic method, with several others; but none have ever succeeded so well with me as, in a sunshining day, to cut off the stalks at about an inch distance from their flowers, or capsules, and, as soon as the juice appears, which it does, at first, equally well on that part of the stalk cut off with the capsule, or flower, as on the standing part, to collect it with a small scoop or penknife, the last of which I have found to answer the purpose very well. After the juice ceases to appear on the top of the standing stalk, it should be cut off about an inch lower, when it will be found to yield almost as freely as before, and repeated as long as any juice appears.

"Since which, as it had been suggested that the method I recommended was not equal to the Asiatic, I made a number of experiments, to determine the matter with greater certainty: but what is necessary to add, and which is sufficient for the present purpose, is, that in every experiment, made under equal circumstances, I obtained the largest quantity in the former way, that is, by cutting the stalk, though it may require rather more care and labour."*

The harvest of opium-making lasts but for a short time, as the plants all flower and mature their heads sufficiently in a few weeks; the labour of gathering it, however, is so light that children, capable of exercising the proper amount of carefulness, are able to perform it. How far the product of one season may be augmented, by having different parcels of the plants to come on successively, remains to be determined by experiment.

Particular care should be taken not to permit any other species of the Poppy to grow in the neighbourhood, whilst cultivating the P. *Somniferum*, since it becomes easily adulterated, and even with the best care is apt to degenerate. Hence a few of the largest and first heads should be reserved for seed, and not tapped at all, and every few years the stock should be renewed from fresh parcels of seed.

---

* Experiments on the cultivation of the Poppy-plant, and the method of procuring opium, &c. By Dr. Shadrach Ricketson, in the New York Medical Repository, vol. i, and vol. iii.

OBSERVATIONS ON THE BOTANY OF ILLINOIS, MORE ESPECIALLY IN REFERENCE TO THE AUTUMNAL FLORA OF THE PRAIRIES— IN A LETTER TO DANIEL DRAKE

THE
WESTERN JOURNAL

OF

MEDICINE AND SURGERY.

MARCH, 1845.

ART. I.—*Observations on the Botany of Illinois, more especially in reference to the Autumnal Flora of the Prairies.* In a letter to Daniel Drake, M.D., &c.

MY DEAR SIR:

The interest which you have long taken in every thing relating to the Natural History of the Western States, and the desire which you have so frequently expressed to connect the study of Botany with the pursuit of medicine, will, I trust, be a sufficient apology for my addressing these observations to you. Having, moreover, very recently yourself traveled over a part of the country to which they refer, you will be the better enabled to judge of their correctness.

In a tour which I took through the State of Illinois, a few years previous to your own, I had the pleasure of being accompanied by my brother, and one or two other individuals, who took a considerable interest in the objects which mainly prompted my journey; and traveling in a light covered wagon, well prepared for making extensive collections, and vigilantly on the look-out for every object of interest, I may safely say that few such escaped our observation. Our visit to this interesting region was made in the latter part of summer, and extended so late into the fall, that severe frosts had put an end to vegetation before our return; so that my remarks must be considered as referring to the *autumnal Flora* of the Prairies, and may not be applicable to that of the spring, or early summer. We entered the State of Illinois from Terre Haute on the Wabash river, near the line dividing that State from Indiana; thence we traveled in nearly a north-western direction to Peoria, on the Illinois river; through Paris, Urbanna, Bloomington, and Mackinaw: and returning we took a more southern route through Tremont, Springfield, Hillsborough, Maysville, and Lawrenceville to Vincennes; where we recrossed the Wabash, which here forms the boundary between the States of Indiana and Illinois. This trace extending over a distance of nearly 400 miles, led us through the central portion of the State in two different lines, at a considerable distance apart, and gave us an opportunity of seeing and examining the face of the country and its productions under a great variety of aspects.

In a Geographical point of view, the surface of Illinois may be very appropriately, as it is naturally, divided into three districts. First—The heavily timbered tracts which for the most part occupy the southern portion of the State, bordering on the Ohio river, and which, extending into the middle and northern portions, are found in detached bodies surrounded by prairies, and in these situations are called 'Groves.' These groves are, for the most part, contiguous to, and often bounded by water-courses, which have preserved them from the action of fire. Secondly—The open prairies, of from one to twenty miles in diameter, entirely destitute of

trees, and indeed of all other woodly plants, except along
the margin of water courses which occasionally pervade them.
Thirdly—'The Barrens,' or tracts somewhat intermediate
between the two former, being sparsely covered with oak
trees of several different kinds, and of considerable size, with
a dense undergrowth of various shrubs and annual plants.
This third region bears a close relationship, both in appearance and productions, to those districts in Kentucky, which
are called 'Barrens'—tracts of country which seem to be in
a state of transition from more open prairies to densely timbered forests.

The vegetation of these three districts is, of course, essentially different; but apart from the presence or absence of
trees, which constitute the grand feature of distinction, the
annual and suffruticose plants are widely different, and indeed
in many respects entirely dissimilar. It is, however, to the
productions of the open prairies that I shall chiefly confine
myself in this communication: and even they vary greatly as
the surface of the prairie may be high, rolling, rich and dry,
or low, flat, wet and clayey.

The first sight of a prairie with which we were greeted
was in the neighborhood of Terre Haute, on the eastern
side of the Wabash, and consequently in the State of Indiana. In approaching this new and apparently thriving town,
from the east, over the national road, the eye is filled with
the prospect of an extensive plain entirely destitute of all
timber-trees, and stretching to a great distance both above
and below the town. Such a view, agreeable at all times,
was peculiarly so as it opened suddenly upon us just after
emerging from the heavily wooded forest through which we
had traveled all day. The Terre Haute prairie, however,
has been all reclaimed, or rather, botanically speaking, dese-
crated by the hand of man, and no portion of it now remains
in a state of nature. Corn, grass, small grain, and other
cultivated crops now occupy the hundreds of acres, which
lately bloomed and blossomed with indigenous productions;
and almost the only relics of these to be seen, were occasion-

ally on the road-side, or in fence-corners, a few plants of *Verbena stricta* and *Vernonia corymbosa*.

Twenty miles west of the Wabash at this point, we met with the first prairie in a state of nature; and from this, extending northward to the Lakes, and westward to the Mississippi, they continue, increasing in magnitude, and interrupted only by occasional groves of timber, so as to occupy by far the largest portion of the central, eastern, western, and northern portions of the State of Illinois.

On fairly entering the prairie region, and reaching the centre of one of these immense natural meadows, the view presented to the eye of a novice in such scenery, is one of the most pleasing sort. But beautiful, imposing, and even grand as is this spectacle, I must own, that in a botanical point of view, I was disappointed! The Flora of the prairies—the theme of so much admiration to those who view them with an ordinary eye,—does not, when closely examined by the Botanist, present that deep interest and attraction which he has been led to expect. Its leading feature is rather the unbounded profusion with which a few species occur in certain localities, than the mixed variety of many different species occurring any where. Thus from some elevated position in a large prairie the eye takes in at one glance thousands of acres, literally empurpled with the flowering spikes of several species of *Liatris*, among which the most predominant are *L. spicata*, *L. squarrosa*, *L. scariosa*, *L. cylindracea*, and *L. pycnostachya*. In other situations, where a depressed or flattened surface and clayey soil favor the continuance of moisture, a few species of yellow-flowered *Coreopsis* occur in such profuse abundance as to tinge the entire surface with a golden burnish. The species of this genus more commonly met with in such situations, were *Coreopsis trichosperma*, *C. senifolia*, *C. tripteris*, *C. palmata*, &c., &c. This peculiarity of an aggregation of individuals of one or more species, to something like an exclusive monopoly of certain localities, obtains even in regard to those plants which are the rarest and least frequently met with; for whenever one specimen was found there generally occurred many more in the same immediate neighborhood. The *Dalea alopecuroides*, (Willd.), which I met with but once, was found in that locality in the greatest abundance. The *Satureja hortensis*, which I believe is not regarded as indigenous to North America, was seen once by us in the greatest profusion, and that, too, in a situation the least favorable to the idea of its having been introduced—the centre of a large prairie, where no settlement could have been made. At some places between Peoria and Springfield the road-sides and even the beaten path, were so completely covered over with the little *Boebera chrysanthemoides*, that, trodden under our horses' feet, it exhaled a strong and nauseating odor. In many such localities this noisome weed seems to take the place of the *Anthemis cotula* and *A. arvensis* (Mayweed and Dog-fennel,) in the more settled portions of the Western States. In the neighborhood of Springfield, again, and especially in the out-lots of that town, we found the ground covered, to the exclusion of almost every other vegetation, with a small species of *Ambrosia* (*A. bidentata*) which, at the season in which we saw it, being out of flower, and ripening its dark-colored seed, gave to the common an aspect as dreary as "the bleak and blasted heath where Macbeth met the witches." In illustration of this peculiarity of the Botany of the prairies, I will only further remark that we did not observe the little *Erigeron divaricatum* until we reached Bloomington, in the commons of which town it is extremely abundant; and that it ceases to occur, or is but rarely seen, a few miles south of that.

There are, indeed, comparatively speaking, but few plants, except the grasses, (which are gregarious every where, and are intermixed in greater or less degree and variety among all the other plants of the prairies,) which may be considered as indigenes of the prairie region generally.— Among these we may mention, as occurring most constantly, and under greater diversity of soil and situation than any others, the *Silphium gummiferum*, *Parthenium integrifolium*, *Kuhnia critonia*, *Ceanothus intermedius*, (which here takes the place of *C. Americanus* in the Barrens of Kentucky.) *Prenanthes Illinoensis*, *Eryngium aquaticum*, *Petalostemum violaceum*, *Dracocephalum Virginianum*, *Baptisia leucantha*, several species of *Liatris*, *Coreopsis*, *Aster*,* *Solidago*,† *Rudbeckia*,‡ *Helianthus*,§ *Pycnanthemum*, *Gerardia*, *Pedicularis*, *Gentiana*, &c., &c. Those two beautiful plants, for our knowledge of both of which, I believe, we are indebted to Mr. Nuttall, the *Aster sericeus*, and *Amorpha canescens*, are very generally diffused, but not in the same abundance with many others. Indeed, they constitute an exception to the habit of congregation which obtains among so many of their associates.

As is the case, I believe, with the American Flora throughout the United States, and, indeed, the whole Continent, the autumnal botany of the prairies exhibits a large preponderance of the *Compositæ*. Besides those already mentioned, we may here enumerate, as of frequent occurrence, *Chrysopsis mariana*, *Helenium autumnale*, *Boltonia glastifolia* and *B. asteroides*, *Bidens frondosa* and *B. chrysanthemoides*, *Eupatorium serotinum*, *E. aromaticum*, *E. ageratoides*, *E. purpureum*. *E. perfoliatum*, &c., *Cnicus glutinosus*, *C. Virginianus*, *C. muticus*, *C. altissimus*, &c., *Silphium laciniatum*, *S. integrifolium*, *S. terebinthinaceum*, &c., *Prenanthes aspera*, *P. virgata*. *P. racemosa*, *P. serpentaria*, &c., *Vernonia fasciculata*, *V. corymbosa*, and one or two other species.

In a farmer's, or rather a grazier's estimation, the grasses would be regarded as the most valuable of the natural productions of the prairies; and we will next mention some of

---

* *Aster lævis*, *A. Novæ Angliæ*, *A. rigidus*, *A. gracilis*, *A. phlogifolius*, *A. concolor*, *A. azureus*, *A. undulatus*, *A. multiflorus*, *A. oblongifolius*, *A. turbinellus*, *A. carneus*, &c.

† *Solidago rigida*, *S. nemoralis*, *S. graminifolia*, *S. Ridellii*, *S. serotina*, *S. speciosa*, *S. Ohioensis*, *S. neglecta*, &c.

‡ *Rudbeckia purpurea*. *R. laciniata*, *R. hirta*, *R. subtomentosa*, *R. pinnata*, &c.

§ *Helianthus angustifolius*, *H. rigidus*, *H. occidentalis*, *H. grosse-serratus*, *H. tomentosus*, *H. mollis*, *H. pubescens*, *H. microcephalus*, *H. tomentosus*, *H. lætiflorus*, &c.

those which are of most frequent occurrence, omitting all reference to the allied tribe of *Cyperaceæ*, but few of which were observed, in consequence, perhaps, of the late season at which our visit was made. Among the most predominant of the *Gramineæ*, on the rich, dry, and rolling prairies are several species of *Andropogon*, as *A. furcatum*, *A. ciliatum*, *A. mutans*, *A. scoparium*, &c., *Aristida tuberculosa*, *A. stricta*, *A. gracilis*, &c., *Elymus Canadensis*, (var. *glaucifolius*.) *E. Virginicus*, *E. mollis*, &c., *Trichodium laxiflorum*, and *Vilfa heterolepsis*. In flat and marshy situations these give place to various species of *Panicum*, as *P. geniculatum*, *P. agrostoides*, *P. dichotomum*, *P. virgatum*, *P. latifolium*, and the universally diffused *P. crus-galli*, *Leersia Virginica*, and *L. oryzoides*, *Spartina polystachya* and *S. cynosuroides*. All these grasses in their young and tender states are eagerly devoured by cattle: as they become harder and less succulent by age, the coarser are rejected and the more tender are sought for. Among these, I believe, the *Vilfa*, before mentioned, is a general favorite, both for grazing and for hay. All of them, however, are cut promiscuously for this purpose, and when they occur, as frequently they do, in large natural meadows, occupying the ground to the almost entire exclusion of other vegetables, they yield a productive return to the labor of the mower; and when well cured make excellent hay. Our horses, which had never before been accustomed to any other than the cultivated grasses, ate this natural hay with great avidity. The quality of these grasses, both for pasturage and mowing, is much improved by the burning of the prairies during the winter, which, destroying the dead and dry stems, affords a better and earlier bite in the spring, as well as a cleaner swath for the scythe: and by protecting certain portions of the prairie from the action of fire until the spring or early summer, vegetation is then so much retarded by a 'late burn,' as the settlers call it, as to afford good pasturage throughout the latter part of the season.

To this action of the fires, which probably for ages have annually passed over these plains, consuming in their progress all relics of vegetable matter, both woody and herbaceous, is perhaps to be mainly ascribed the color of the soil, which for the most part is literally as black as coal, and in some situations of two or three feet in depth. And to this excess of carbonaceous matter, imparted to the soil of these prairies, is it perhaps to be ascribed that their productions, both in cultivated crops and natural growths, are by no means so rank or luxuriant as one might be led to expect. The Indian corn, though well-eared, was not so tall as I have frequently seen it in Kentucky and Ohio, on lands apparently much inferior in fertility; the different kinds of small grain, though heavily-headed, had a much shorter straw; and many of the natural productions, common to the Illinois prairies and the barrens of Kentucky, were less luxuriant in growth than I have observed them to be in the latter district, though the soil of the barrens has not the same appearance of fertility. This subject deserves particular investigation, and an accurate analysis of the prairie soil might lead to very useful practical deductions. One of our fellow-travelers, a farmer by profession, ascribed the appearance, above mentioned, to a 'sourness' in the soil. But the amount of carbonaceous and alkaline matters resulting from such frequent burnings would rather lead to an opposite conclusion.

Among the œconomical and medicinal plants of the prairies may be mentioned *Gentiana ochroleuca*, the roots of which have somewhat the bitterness of the officinal species, (*G. lutea*, of Europe,) *Prenanthes serpentaria*, several species of *Liatris*, the tuberous roots of which are possessed of acrid pungent qualities, and *Eryngium aquaticum;* all these plants have a considerable reputation, which perhaps is but little deserved, against the bites of poisonous serpents, and hence they are known indifferently by the names of 'snake-root,' 'button snake-root,' rattle-snake's masterpiece,' &c. *Frasera verticillata* is not so frequently seen in the more open prairies as in the thinly-wooded barrens. *Polygala Senega* and *Asclepias tuberosa* are abundant in both these localities. The different species of *Silphium* mentioned, exude from their stems a pearly resinous matter, very similar in appearance and sensible properties to turpentine, and used for the same purposes. The roots of the beautiful *Petalostemum violaceum* have a warm pungent quality, which suggested its employment, among the thousand other articles, in the treatment of cholera, and the plant is now known on the prairies as the 'cholera-weed.' Our two most valuable indigenous bitters *Eupatorium perfoliatum* and *Sabbatia angularis* are abundant, and *Aristolochia serpentaria* is seen occasionally in the groves, where various species of dogwood (*Cornus*) are also of frequent occurrence. Mr. J. A. Lapham, of Wisconsin, informs me that in that territory, the *Amorpha canescens* is called 'lead-plant,' from the circumstance of its growth being considered indicative of the presence of that mineral. If the same sign should hold good in Illinois, the whole of the prairies may one day become a mining region.

Ferns are remarkably rare on the prairies; indeed I do not recollect having met with a single specimen of any species of that extensive tribe in the more open prairies. This may, perhaps, be owing to the absence of that shade and constant moisture in which most of these plants delight. On the skirts of the timbered tracts, several kinds occur, which are usually found in the barrens, as *Pteris aquilina*, *Polypodium dryopteris*, and *P. hexagonopterum;* and in the 'groves' I observed many other species common in the Western States. The same remarks will apply, in a good degree, to the tribe of mosses.

I deem it improper to close these desultory remarks, without giving a catalogue, at least, of other common plants, which presented themselves at different places on our route through the prairies. Some of them may have been already incidentally mentioned, but the most of them occurred under circumstances not calling for particular note or comment. They are given as I find them in my note-book, without any kind of order or arrangement.—

Verbena stricta,
V. hastata,
Gerardia purpurea,
G. flava,
G. erecta,
G. auriculata,
G. quercifolia,
Petalostemum candidum,
Desmodium, }
Lespedeza,   } of various species.
Euphorbia corollata,
Gaura angustifolia,
Typha latifolia,
Cassia chamæcrista,
C. marilandica,
Monarda fistulosa,
Leptandra Virginica,
Lythrum hyssopifolium,
Pedicularis pallida,
Gillenia stipulacea,

Parnassia palustris,
Gentiana rubricaulis,
G. quinqueflora,
Sium latifolium,
Archemora rigida,
Artemisia caudata,
Polygala verticillata,
P. ambigua,
P. incarnata,
Linum rigidum,
Potentilla fruticosa,
Psoralea floribunda,
Boottia sylvestris,
Plantago cordata,
P. aristata,
Cissus Canadensis,
Chelone glabra,
Angelica triquinata,
Epilobium lineare,
Lysimachia revoluta, &c.

Doubtless many other species came under our observation, but being so common in other parts of the Western country, I omitted to note them.

In relation to the botany of the prairies, I have only to add a few remarks on the shrubs which are found among them; for although in the more open districts of this kind no ligneous or perennial stems are permitted to escape the ravages of the annual fires which sweep over them, yet on the margins of 'sloughs,' and along the courses of the small streams which occasionally meander through them, clumps of bushes and clusters of shrubbery are always to be found. These 'roughs,' as they are called, furnish welcome retreats to grazing cattle, and sometimes to the traveler's horse, from that annoying pest of these regions—the prairie fly.* In these thickets the more common productions are the hazle, (*Corylus Americana,*) three species of sumach, (*Rhus glabrum, R. copalinum,* and *R. aromaticum,*) several dwarf kinds of plumb, (*Prunus,*) of which the species were not ascertained, two or three varieties of dogwood, (*Cornus sericea, C. asperifolia, C. alba, &c.*) several species of undetermined willows, (*Salix.*) Besides these, may be mentioned the *Amorpha fruticosa, Zanthoxylum fraxineum,* (prickly ash,) *Prinos verticillata, Ilex prinoides, Aronia melanocarpa, Spiræa tomentosa* and *S. salicifolia, Symphorea racemosa, Cephalanthus occidentalis, Rubus*

---

* I regret that I am not Entomologist enough to give the scientific name of this fly. It is, however, but too well known, both by name and its effects, to all those who have had the misfortune to pass through their haunts during the season of their prevalence, which begins in June, and only ends with the recurrence of hard frosts in the fall. I cannot do better, in this place, than to extract from the note-book of one of my fellow-travelers, his account of this tormenting insect:—

"At length fairly on the prairie, its ocean-like expanse—its multifloral hues, and the strange aspect of everything around us, especially of the far-off head-lands of timber, melting into the horizon with 'the mist of blue' which distance gave them, caused us all for some moments to be mute with rapture and admiration; from which delightful trance we were soon aroused by observing the woeful condition of our panting and stamping horses. In fact every part of them not protected by cloths, was covered by blood-thirsty—blood-sucking flies. These insects, unlike all others of their kind I have ever seen, fall upon their prey without buzzing, circumvolation, or prelude of any sort: they dart with the rapidity of shot from the fowler's gun, and as soon as they have touched the animal on which they alight, seem already bedded in his skin, from which they are not to be dislodged but by main force and violence. So greedy were they, and so intent upon one sole object, that they suffered themselves to be pinched off the horses; and so perfect seemed their blood-sucking apparatus, that hardly had they alighted an instant, when on being brushed off, they appeared already gorged with their sanguine food. Vengeance on our part, and commiseration for our horses, induced us frequently to stop, for the purpose of slaughter; and in a few moments our blood-stained hands, and the heaps of slain in the road, gave evidence that we spared not, and were as merciless as the foe whom we encountered.

villosus, (blackberry,) *Ribes rotundifolium,* called Illinois gooseberry, of which the fruit, though spinous, makes a delicious tart; together with various species of wild roses, grape-vines, &c.

Though not properly falling within the compass of this communication, the object of which has been to give some account of the autumnal botany of the prairies, yet before I close it, I will venture to add a few remarks on the forest trees of Illinois. These, in the main, do not differ from the productions of similar districts in the timbered lands of Indiana, Ohio, Kentucky, and Tennessee. In Illinois, the richest groves, interspersed through the prairies, are constituted mainly of the same kind of trees which indicate the best soils generally in the Western States, as black walnut, hickories, hackberry, (*Celtis crassifolia,*) sugar-maple, pawpaw, (*Porcelia triloba,*) &c. The thinner lands are clothed chiefly with oaks of various species, hickories and gums, (*Liquidambar*

We thought, too, at first, that we were relieving our horses, *pro hac vice* at least, of their torturing assailants; but a very little observation soon made it manifest that where we killed one, a dozen more keen and insatiable would arrive. So there was no way of stopping with a view to relief—the gauntlet had to be run, and the sooner it was over the better. Indeed, an old prairie traveler afterwards told us, in answer to our wonder, expressed at the naked condition of his horses, that the worse the flies were the more rapidly he drove. Such a course, however, appeared to us inhuman; and our horses, good and true though they were 'as ever looked through a halter,' gave evidences that they were not used to such leeching; and we were truly glad when, nine or ten miles on our road, a resting-place presented itself on the skirts of a forest. It is a most fortunate circumstance that these flies do not infect the woodlands, though immediately adjoining their haunts in the tall, thick herbage of the prairies; and we were told that so disgusted are they with the odor of a stable, they will not pursue an animal that takes shelter in one, however rudely and openly constructed of common round logs, without any *chinking* of its various apertures. From my recollection of Western stables generally, I think this fly evinces a great deal of good sense in avoiding them. It is, indeed, a clean, bright, and beautiful insect, of variegated green-and-golden burnish, about the size of, and not unlike the Spanish blistering fly."—*MSS. Notes on a Tour through Illinois, by* J. CLEVES SHORT.

styraciflua and *Nyssa* of two or three species,) whilst the poorest soils, those especially of the 'bushy barrens' and 'oak openings,' are occupied mostly with the different kinds of oak, among which the post-oak, (*Quercus obtusiloba*,) and blackjack, (*Q. ferruginea*,) are most prominent. I am able, indeed, to indicate but two trees which are in any way peculiar to the forests of Illinois; and these are the paccan and catalpa. Of these the paccan (*Carya olivæformis*,) is found abundantly on the southern borders of the State, where about Shawneetown and other points on the Ohio river, it constituted a large portion of the original forest; and from these districts great quantities of the nuts have been exported. They are not considered, however, to be equal, either in size or flavor, to the paccan-nuts of Texas. The other tree—the catalpa, (*Catalpa cordifolia*,) I have the authority of General Harrison for saying, is found occasionally, and of large size, in the alluvions of the Wabash river, where he considered it to be certainly a native; in opposition to the opinion of the Abbé Correa, who thought it more probable that the seeds may have been derived from trees planted by the early French settlers of Vincennes and other posts. I have seen this tree in similar alluvions among the dense forests of Henderson county, Kentucky.

Whilst walking over the prairies adjoining the town of Bloomington, in company with our friend Dr. John F. Henry, who resides there, he pointed out to us an extraordinary phenomenon in connexion with vegetation, and one only visible, I suppose, in a prairie country. It was a semicircular, or rather horse-shoe-shaped line of herbage, distinguishable very plainly from the surrounding and included growths, by its darker or deeper green hue. He said that these circles or segments of circles, usually of fifteen or twenty feet diameter, were frequently to be seen in summer, and that it was generally believed they were occasioned by lightning. He described the thunder-storms of this region as sublimely majestic and terrific. We had no opportunity of witnessing this display of Heaven's artillery, during our journey; but in two or three instances afterwards, I think, we observed this singular appearance of the grass on the prairies, indicating what might, perhaps, without impiety, be called 'the foot-prints of the Deity!'

Very respectfully and truly, I am,

My dear Sir, yours,

C. W. SHORT.

Professor DRAKE,
Medical Institute of Louisville,
February, 1845.

INSTRUCTIONS FOR
THE GATHERING AND PRESERVATION
OF PLANTS FOR HERBARIA;
IN A LETTER TO A YOUNG BOTANIST

Art. III.—*Instructions for the Gathering and Preservation of Plants for Herbaria; in a letter to a young Botanist.* By Charles W. Short, M. D.

My dear friend:

You ask me for instructions as to the best mode of preserving and arranging plants in your collection. This, although purely a mechanical part of the study of botany, is a very important one, since it is manifest that no one individual, at any season of the year, however favourably situated, can immediately refer to a large number of living plants at once; much less can he have them growing before him, at all seasons of the year. This difficulty is then most conveniently remedied by forming a collection of dried specimens, which, if well selected and preserved, and conveniently arranged, offers to our study and examination, at any moment, all the plants of a whole district, or even of the world. To this may be added, as the testimony of a very competent witness, and indeed, as the result of universal experience, that "no one can be a botanist without collecting plants, and making up an herbarium with his own hands." The utility of such a collection, however, in a great degree depends upon the care and labour bestowed in forming it: and as I know of no full and specific directions to this object to which I can refer you, in any of the common systems of botany, I am the more willing to communicate to you the result of my own very considerable experience in this business. I know from my own case, and that of many others, that beginners in this study are apt to lose the fruits of several first years' labour, from a want of that kind of definite and precise instruction so necessary on the subject. You will therefore be fortunate, and I shall be well rewarded, if your first essays in this line should be so well executed as to be worthy of future preservation.

The manual labour of a botanist in forming his collections, may be arranged under three heads, as there are three several stages in the process: these are,

I. The collection of plants in their living state.
II. The drying of them for preservation.
III. The arrangement of the dried specimens in some suitable manner for convenient reference.

I. The first of these labours constitutes, perhaps one of the most delightful pursuits which can be engaged in, as no pleasure can exceed that of an enthusiastic botanist, when thrown into the midst of the wilds of nature; and whilst his senses revel on the beauties of 'herb and fruit and flower,' his bodily powers participate in the invigorating enjoyment; for by this healthful exercise

"O'er hills, through vallies and by mountain tops,
" Is life both sweetened and prolonged."

But to return to the business on hand. Before commencing your herborizing excursions, you must provide yourself with a tin-case, technically called a *vasculum;* a small trowel, or a strong knife. The vasculum is very similar to a common tin candle-box; it should not be less than eighteen inches long and six inches in diameter, having a narrow lid opening on the top nearly its whole length, and secured by a hasp or catch. If this box is somewhat flattened on two sides, so as to assume rather an oval than a perfectly circular form, it will be more conveniently carried under the arm; and for this purpose it should be provided with two loops for a strap, by which it is suspended from the shoulder. The peculiar excellence of this apparatus is that plants shut up in it are effectually protected from evaporation, or injury of any kind; for collections made in the morning are taken out at night in a state of perfect freshness; and they will even continue so for several days. The protecting influence of this case is still the greater if it be not painted or japanned; as the sun, being more effectually reflected from the bright surface of the tin, will be less injurious to the plants contained within it. Some prefer taking with them on these excursions an oiled bag of silk; and some a large book of bibulous paper; but the tin vasculum is decidedly preferable to either. The use of the trowel, or the knife, is that of taking up small plants by the roots, or cutting larger ones into convenient lengths.

Thus equipped you start upon an herborization: and here the young botanist is apt to commit his first error; for, supposing that the common and unsightly productions of his neighborhood—those which he has been accustomed to consider as mere *weeds*, are of no interest whatever, he passes over all such, in search of those which are more rare, more imposing in appearance, or more beautiful in flower. This is a radical error which you must avoid, and it should be your aim to collect every thing growing in your reach, and especially all such as are natives of the country; for when you come to exchanging specimens with distant botanists you will find, that they take more interest in your common weeds, than in some others which you deemed more worthy of preservation. Collect then every thing which you meet with.

Another difficulty to the beginner arises from the great diversity in the sizes, and habits of plants, from the diminutive moss to the giant oak. As a general rule in this matter, the smaller are to be collected whole; the larger ones must, of necessity, be divided. As the length of your box has been directed in reference to the size of the paper in which your specimens are to be preserved and arranged, all plants which you can get into it without doubling or bending, should be gathered entire, even with their roots; those too large for this may be cut into two, or even three pieces of the proper length; which in general is preferable to bending or doubling them. Of those which are still larger it will usually be sufficient to gather a specimen from the summit, or part bearing the flower, together with a few leaves growing on different parts of the stem, and those of the root; for often the leaves on different parts of the same plant, are different in shape, or modes of attachment to the stem, from each other, and these differences should always be shown in the specimens preserved. Of trees and the most of shrubs you must, of necessity, content yourself by gathering the smaller twigs alone, selecting such, however, as bear the most perfect leaves and flowers.

As a general rule all plants should be gathered when their flowers are most perfectly developed; and it is always desirable when the flowers appear before the leaves are unfolded, as in the most of our forest trees, that specimens be gathered, both when in flower and in full-grown leaf: and moreover, when the fruit is of a kind which can be preserved in the manner presently described, that specimens of the fruit should accompany those of the flower and leaf. Some flowers are so exceedingly fugacious as to shed their petals within a few hours after unfolding, as the common *Sanguinaria*, *Jeffersonia*, and *Hydrastis;* these and some others, although they be put into your vasculum with full blown blossoms, will probably be found on taking them out, to have dropped them. This is best remedied by gathering specimens of such individuals as are not quite fully expanded, and if they should not have opened by the time you are prepared to preserve them, a few hours standing in a vase of water will bring them to the proper point.

Some very extensive tribes of vegetables are so very similar in their flowers, and other parts upon which distinctions are usually founded, that it is only by referring to their fruit, or ripe seeds, that they can be satisfactorily determined. Such are the large family of *Umbelliferous* plants, and the extensive grass-like genus *Carex*, not to mention some other tribes with which you will hereafter become better acquainted. These, therefore, should be gathered when their seeds are fully grown, but before they become so ripe as to shatter off too easily. Yet even of these I would advise that specimens be gathered also in flower, for then their leaves are generally most perfect. In selecting specimens of all plants for preservation, you should take such as are fair samples of the most common height, habit and appearance of the species; rejecting stinted dwarfs on the one hand, or luxuriant monsters on the other: at the same time if any peculiar circumstance is found to characterise particular individuals of the species, constituting what are called *varieties*, specimens indicating these variations should be collected.

Having in this manner, with well selected specimens filled your vasculum, which may be packed with gentle pressure, so as to hold a large number, not only without injury but rather with advantage to their keeping, you return home and are prepared for the second step in the process.

II. The drying of them for preservation. This is done by subjecting them to pressure between folds of dry paper. For this purpose you must be provided with two or three reams of unsized printing paper, and some sort of machinery for making considerable pressure. This object is well effected by a press, in miniature, made after the fashion of the common tobacco or cotton press, and may consist either of a stout lever eight or ten feet long, playing in a fixed mortice and bearing upon a firm stand; or a wooden screw of two or three inches diameter, and as many feet in length, fixed in an appropriate frame-work. Some content themselves merely with the pressure exerted by large stones, or other heavy weights, placed upon their plants; but the lever press is altogether the most convenient, and by it a much greater amount of force may be exerted than by either of the other plans. It is well to be provided, moreover, with several loose boards of different thicknesses, but of uniform size with the paper employed: and the best size for the paper is that called by printers *medium*, which should be of a good, thick and substantial body. Divide one of your reams into parcels of four or five sheets, and prevent these sheets from becoming detached by passing a few stiches through them. These parcels, thus being eight or ten double, are called *dryers;* and they may be more economically made, and answer the purpose equally well if made of old news-papers, or other kind of waste paper, provided it be smooth and bibulous. If such are used they should be trimmed to the medium size, and stiched together by means of a thread running around the entire margin. The number of these dryers required will of course be in proportion to the number of plants which you undertake to preserve. In the extensive collections which I have made during the past season, I have not found less than one hundred sufficient; but when once prepared they will answer for several seasons' constant use. Unsized paper is prefered, because it absorbs moisture from the plants, much more readily than that which has been sized.

With these fixtures you are prepared for the task before you, which consists in placing your plants in single sheets of paper, putting these sheets between alternate dryers, and subjecting the whole to pressure. This is the nicest part of the entire process, and as upon the mode in which it is done, the value and usefulness of your collection will depend, particular instructions will be given on this head. Take then any one plant from the vasculum and lay it between the leaves of a single sheet of your paper, taking care to spread it out so as to have its parts as little confused as possible. In doing this, however, you must give to its parts no unnatural direction; for instance, do not give to a flower which naturally droops an erect position: flower stalks which are attached to but one side, must not be turned to both: a crooked or a tortuous stem must be left so, and a straight one must not be bent: in short avoid all unnatural stiffness, formality, or artificial arrangement of its several parts, and preserve as nearly as possible the natural habit of the plant while growing—for as it is now dried it must forever afterwards remain. This sheet, with the plant or plants so arranged in it, is then placed on one of the dryers, and another dryer laid on it. Of the smaller plants a number may be placed in one sheet; of the larger, several sheets may be required by the different parts of the same plant; but care must be particularly taken in arranging them, that the different plants thus placed in the same sheet do not over-lap or over-lay each other, lest under pressure they should adhere together and otherwise interfere with the drying. Of such plants as have their stems very thickly set with leaves, some of these may be removed, so as to preserve and exhibit the remainder more perfectly. Where a number of stems arise from one point, and thus interfere with the equable pressure of the specimen, some from the under and upper side may be removed. Where the stems are thick, crooked and unyielding, the knife should be employed in removing projecting points and in thinning them; and in very large and succulent stems, as those of the *Frasera* or *Sonchus*, it is sometimes necessary to split them in two, and to press the halves with their attached leaves, flowers, &c. separately. Some flowers are so crowded on their branches as to require that some be stript off for the better exhibition of the rest, as in *Vernonia*, and some of the *Eupatoriums*; and some flowers are so bulky, hard, and unyielding, as to render it necessary to divide and press them separately, as in some species of *Helianthus, Rudbeckia, Cnicus, Silphum, &c*.—a part of one of these large compound flowers, well pressed shows its character better than the whole badly preserved. It is a matter, moreover, of much consequence that the specimens be so flattened by pressure, as that they will occupy as little room as possible, and lie smoothly together in your Herbarium. Any obstacles, therefore, to this equable pressure of all its parts must be removed, when it can be done without interfering with the characteristic habit of the plant.

In this manner you proceed arranging your plants in single sheets and placing these between your dryers, until you have exhuasted your vasculum, and formed a considerable pile. They are now ready for the press. Place the pile under your lever, screw, or weights; lay a thick board over it, of the proper size, and begin the pressure, making it at first moderate, so that the plants may gradually yield to its influence, without suffering violence or injury to their texture. In two or three hours the pressure may be increased, but not yet to the full amount of your power. After remaining in this situation for three or four hours longer, you will find on examining them, that all the papers, both single sheets and thick dryers, have become quite wet with the moisture absorbed from the plants; and they should now be changed. This is done simply by shifting the single sheets, without opening them or disturbing the plants, into fresh dryers, and immediately placing them under the press again, which should now be made to bear somewhat more heavily on them. Your moist dryers are then to be spread out in the open air, and in a hot sun-shine, (upon boards, or on a flat-roof preferably,) until they are thoroughly dried. In this way you continue transferring your sheets with their contents from moist to fresh dryers, at first twice and afterwards once a day, increasing the pressure at each renewal, until all moisture is extracted from them, and they are rendered, flat, thin and perfectly dry.

The time required for this process will vary according to the nature and peculiarities of the plants acted on. As a general rule, and for the most of plants, three days will be sufficient; yet some, as most of the grasses, are sufficiently dried in two days; others, more succulent, and tenacious of life, as the *Sedums* and *Talinum*, require as many weeks. These latter and some analogous plants even make efforts to grow for some days after being subjected to the influence of a powerful press; others in drying cast off their leaves, as the fir tribe, the *Diospyros, &c.* and some shed their flowers, as the *Agave Virginica*. To destroy this vegetating principle, and to dry such plants more speedily, and without a loss of their parts, it is advised to dip them in boiling water, and wipe them, before they are placed in the sheet. Some botanists prefer with such plants the yet more expeditious process of pressing them between folds of paper, under a hot smoothing iron, or a flat stone heated—the more expeditiously, indeed, all plants are dried the better do they retain their original colours; yet it is improper to subject them whilst drying to the influence of a hot sun, since they become thereby crisped and brittle. Notwithstanding, however, the utmost care, some plants cannot be made to retain their natural colours, but become black in drying; this is especially the case with the *Drosera, Buchnera, Gerardia, Podalyria, &c.* and many others assume this hue, if allowed to remain too long in damp papers.

In pressing at the same time a great variety of plants it is always well to examine them once a day, and to remove from the parcel such as are sufficiently dried; continuing to act upon the remainder until all are finished. It is, however, by no means necessary that one parcel should be entirely disposed of before another is commenced with. On the contrary, you may have under press at the same time, plants in every stage of the drying process, only taking care that thin boards are interposed between the different parcels to prevent the moisture of a fresh collection from affecting those which are dryer.

We come now to the last stage of our operations, which consists in

III. The arrangement of the dried specimens in some suitable manner for convenient reference. A collection of plants so arranged is called an *Herbarium* or *Hortus Siccus*, and various plans have been devised for their formation, and very different directions are given by different authorities on this head. Some direct us to fasten the specimens to sheets of white paper by means of weak glue; others to attach them by means of a needle and thread, or strips of paper pasted across the specimens, or by loops cut into the sheet itself. One party—(for there are parties in Botany as well as in every thing else,) direct the species to be arranged according to the natural order of Jussieu, and another prefers the artificial system of Linnæus. In this matter, as in others, I can only be here expected to give my own preference, without taking time to discuss the relative merits of the different plans.

My instructions to you, then, are these. Still using the same thick medium printing paper, of good quality, you trim the edges of it, so as to have every sheet of the same size, that they may lie more neatly together, and be more conveniently handled, than with the rough edges, as they come from the mill. Into these new sheets, you next transfer your specimens, from those in which they have been dried; and in my opinion it is decidedly better to leave them loose, than to have them attached in any manner to the sheet because you can examine them much more conveniently; you may at any time substitute a better specimen for a more indifferent one; you can more effectually protect them from the injury of insects; and save the time and trouble required for fixing them. It is only necessary, for your own Herbarium, that one good characteristic specimen of each species be put up in this manner; unless, in the cases before specified, where varieties obtain in the species; where they produce flowers and leaves at different times; or where it is necessary to preserve specimens in fruit; in these cases, of course, specimens must be preserved, showing the species in these different stages. Any duplicates which you may have pressed over and above these, may be left in their original sheets for purposes presently to be mentioned.

This is perhaps the most convenient time for a very important, and indeed an indispensably necessary step in the business—the *labelling* of your plants. For this purpose, as you proceed in shifting your specimens, take slips of writing paper of convenient size, and write upon them, first the systematic name of the individual species—then its synonyms, and next its common English name or names, if it have any. Where any doubt exists as to the genus or species of your plant this must be expressed by the mark of interrogation (?) following after the name. To these it is always proper to add, especially if the plant be rare or peculiar to your district, various other items in relation to its history—the situation in which it is found—the character of the soil it prefers—whether marshy or dry, sandy or argillaceous, mountainous or plain, &c.; together with the usual height it attains—whether annual, bienniel, or perennial—time of flowering, and maturing its fruit or seeds. This label should be laid in the sheet with the species to which it belongs; and a similar one should be left with any duplicates of the same which you may have on hand. If these particulars are not noted at the time, whilst they are fresh in your memory, you may forget them, and afterwards have occasion to regret the want of such knowledge.

Your plants thus dried, placed in sheets and labelled, are now to be systematically arranged into different parcels of convenient size for handling and examination; for if they all remain promiscuously mixed together, the *rudis indigestaque moles* would be comparatively of no value; as more time and trouble would be required, in looking through such a chaos for any one individual, than the object, perhaps, would be worth when arrived at. Some systematic arrangement of them then is required, and here I decidedly prefer, for the young botanist, the system of Linnæus. After having become more deeply initiated into the general principles and philosophy of the science, by enlarging your knowledge of plants, you will be the better enabled to appreciate the advantages, if it really has any, of the natural method, as it is called; and may then, if you prefer it, very easily modify your collection according to its rules.

Following then the Linnæan system in the arrangement of your collection, you first put together all the species belonging to one genus, and enclose all the sheets belonging to this genus in one common sheet, of still stouter and sized paper, on one corner of which is written the name of the contained genus; and having reduced your plants to genera, you arrange the genera according to the classes to which they belong; and thus, however small your collection may be at first, or however extensive it may ultimately prove, you will have it comprised within twenty-one groups or classes,* which may afterwards be sub-divided into orders when your collection becomes very large.

Some plan must now be devised for keeping these classes separate, preventing the plants and labels from falling from the sheets, and preserving the whole in neat order for convenient reference. This is also effected in various ways, but perhaps as convenient a method as any other is to have a number of *port-folios* made of thick binder's boards, with leather backs and corners. The leaves or boards of these folios should be a little larger than your trimmed medium paper, that they may the more effectually protect their contents from injury. Each board is furnished with three ties of tape or braid, by which, when filled with sheets, they are so firmly bound together, that plants and labels are prevented from falling out.

In these port-folios you arrange your plants, allotting one book to each class, which at first you will find sufficient, but as your collection increases, several such will be required for the larger classes, as *Pentandria, Syngenesia, &c.* whilst one will probably continue to serve for the smaller classes, as *Heptandria* and *Enneandria.* If the leather backs of these folios are gilt and lettered, in the manner of a book, they will have, when arranged on the shelves of a cabinet or case, the appearance of large folio volumes; and the class or order which each contains being marked upon it, any genus may be in a moment referred to, and any given species in that genus speedily produced.

It must now be your care to protect this collection from two very noxious and destructive agents, *damp* and *insects.* For this purpose the case in which you keep them must be perfectly tight; and pieces of camphor, or bits of sponge moistened with some of the pungent aromatic oils, should be placed on each shelf among the volumes, and occasionally renew-

---

* We here allude to the classification of Linnæus as modified in *Eaton's Manual,* which seems to meet every requisition, and by rejecting three classes is rendered more simple.

ed. The more certainly still to prevent the depredations of insects, which will be found the more troublesome as you proceed southward, the collection should be looked over frequently in dry weather; and where their presence is detected they should be brushed away, and the affected specimen gently passed over with a camel-hair pencil dipped in a solution of corrosive sublimate in spirit. This not only protects it from farther injury in this way, but even brightens its colour.

One word on the subject of exchanges, and we are done with this long epistle. It should be the constant aim of every botanist not only to increase his own knowledge, by every possible opportunity, but to add something to the general stock; and this is most readily and effectually done by a free and liberal interchange of specimens with other botanists. Whilst, therefore, you are collecting and preparing one specimen for your own use, collect and prepare a half dozen for your correspondents. This is the more particularly incumbent on you with regard to those plants which are in any way peculiar to your district, and which of course will be highly interesting to those at a distance; and in return for such you may receive specimens of many which you might never meet with in a living state. Thus will your collection be constantly enriched by new acquisitions, and in proportion to the number of species in each genus which you get together, will you find it more and more easy to identify with positive certainty any plant you meet with, by comparing it with those you have. Of such as you are unable to ascertain the name by reference to the proper books, it will be only necessary to affix corresponding numbers to the specimens which you reserve, and those you send to your correspondent, who, if a competent botanist, will thus be enabled to furnish you the names. All specimens intended for the purposes of exchange, should be well secured in a light and tight box, of the exact size with the paper in which the plants are included, the top of which should make considerable pressure on them, when fastened down, so as to prevent all displacement of specimens or labels, by transportation. Such packages addressed to Mr. Thomas Nuttall, Boston—Dr. John Torrey, New York—Dr. Charles Pickering, or Dr. William P. C. Barton, Philadelphia—Dr. William Darlington, West-Chester, Pennsylvania—Dr. Thomas R. Ingalls, Jackson, Louisiana*; will meet, I am sure, with a hearty welcome from these gentlemen, who will not only furnish you with the names of such plants as you do not know, but will cheerfully exchange with you those of their neighbourhoods for yours; and thus in time you may form a collection of the vegetable productions of all the United States. In this way you will contribute essentially towards the formation of that great desideratum in our Botany—AN ACCURATE AND COMPLETE FLORA OF THE AMERICAN UNION.

In conclusion, my dear Sir, of this dry detail of particulars, which I have thought it necessary to give, and which you will find it important to observe, permit me to urge upon you an attention to the study of nature in this delightful department. You must necessarily have more or less leisure from labours and duties more imperiously incumbent on you, and credit me when I assure you, as the experience of one who has in some degree tasted of its pleasures, that you will never have occasion to regret the time devoted to this enchanting pursuit. Listen, moreover, to the testimony of another, far more competent than myself to bear witness to its charms. "The study of natural history," says the lamented Elliott, "has been for many years, the occupation of my leisure moments; it is a merited tribute to say, that it has lightened for me many a heavy, and smoothed many a rugged hour; that beguiled by its charms, I have found no road rough or difficult, no journey tedious, no country desolate or barren. In solitude never solitary, in a desert never without employment, I have found it a relief from the langour of idleness, the pressure of business, or from the unavoidable calamities of life."

* Mr. Robert Peter, Henry I. Griswold, or myself, Lexington, Kentucky.

PART II

BOTANICAL NOMENCLATURE, HISTORY AND BIBLIOGRAPHY

REMARKS ON THE NOMENCLATURE OF BOTANY

Art. V.—*Remarks on the Nomenclature of Botany.* By C. W. Short, M. D. &c. Read before the Lexington Medical Society on the evening of the 2d of January, 1835, and published at their request.

Nomenclature is a term employed to denote the language peculiar to any particular science or art.

It is to the modern nomenclature of chemistry, so admirable for its ingenuity and comprehensiveness, that the rapid progress which has been made in this department of science, during the last forty years, is in a great measure to be ascribed. Nor need we be surprised at this, for " as ideas are preserved and communicated by means of words, it necessarily follows that we cannot improve the language of any science, without at the same time improving the science itself: neither can we, on the other hand, improve a science, without improving the language, or nomenclature which belongs to it. However certain the facts of any science may be, and however just the ideas we may have formed of these facts, we can only communicate false or imperfect impressions of these ideas to others, while we want words by which they may be properly expressed."* Such is the remark of the celebrated Lavoisier, and in all the circumstances attendant on the reform in the science and language of chemistry his reasoning is most fully verified.

Nor is it by any means to chemistry alone, that these remarks and these reasonings are applicable. In the pursuit of all the other sciences, though less exact in their details than this, is a fixed and settled nomenclature indispensable to proficiency and success. This is even true of the mechanic arts, as well as all the humbler avocations of life; and the engineer and architect—the brick mason and house-joiner—the farmer and the gardener have each their own nomenclature—their peculiar technicalities, which for the most part is an unknown tongue to all except the initiated.

* Ree's Cyclopœdia, article Nomenclature.

I propose, therefore, in the remarks which are to follow to enter into some defence of that technical nomenclature which is used in one of the branches of natural history, to which I am especially devoted; and in this defence I trust that I shall be able to show that the language of this science is not so harsh, unmeaning or arbitrary, as some have imagined; and by doing away this unfounded objection to its study, I hope I shall be in some measure instrumental in opening the door for some of those who hear me, to an entrance upon the most captivating, delightful and innocent of all pursuits—the study of nature.

It is objected by many to the study of BOTANY that its oracles are delivered in antiquated tongues—that its nomenclature is couched in hard Latinity, or yet harder derivatives from Greek; and a complaint which frequently meets me from students of medicine is, that they could get along very well in *Materia medica*, were it not for the long botanical names, which so frequently cross their paths, like the ghosts of a grave yard, frightening away all recollections of doses, modes of exhibition, uses and effects. But the same objection might certainly be made, and with equal propriety, against the study of anatomy, where we find the same barbarous tongues prevailing; since in all the treatises and lectures on this branch of medicine, the names of all the component parts of the human body, are either given in Latin, or are of Latin or Greek derivation; and yet no student, on this account, objects to the study of anatomy. This objection to the nomenclature of Botany must be in a great measure removed, when it is recollected that an imperative necessity existed that one uniform medium of communication should be established, whereby its votaries in all portions of the world might correspond; and by which, as on a neutral ground, they might meet for interchange of thought and opinion. How much greater, for instance, would be the difficulty in acquiring a knowledge of the vegetable productions of the world at large, if their names were alone given in the dialects of the countries where they are found; or even in the most extensively prevailing of the *modern* languages—the English—the French—the German—the Spanish—or the Italian; nor would this difficulty have been much lessened if any *one* of these modern languages had been selected as the uniform language of Botany; since it is clear that no one of the modern languages is so well understood by the world at large as is the Latin. Added to this consideration the Latin language possesses a terseness of expression, and brevity of definition, of which most of the living, and our own language in particular, is lamentably deficient. To illustrate this by a reference again to anatomy, what three words of any language could possibly have been selected so appropriate as *Sterno-cleido-mastoideus,* for the name of that muscle? A name which at once and of itself, without further description, conveys to us as perfect a knowledge of the origin, insertion, and offices of that muscle, as could have been given in half a page of English description.

In farther illustration of the necessity which existed that some uniform language should be adopted for the nomenclature of Botany, and of the especial adaptation of the Latin for this language, permit me to adduce a supposititious case— a case by no means without the pale of probability. We will suppose then that I, or any other American physician, having tested the efficacy of some western plant, say the Puccoon for instance, in certain diseased affections, wish to give to the world the result of my experience with it. I publish a treatise on the subject, and call the plant by that name which it universally bears in this portion of the country—so universally indeed that that every negro child in any farmer's quarter can tell us what the Puccoon is. So far, then, my name answers well enough, since it serves to designate with precision the plant I mean. My treatise travels to the north, where it is read by a New-Englander, who is somewhat at a loss to identify my remedy, because the plant I allude to is there more frequently called "Red-root" and "Blood-root" than Puccoon. Still following the fate of this publication we will suppose that it, or a notice of it, crosses the Atlantic, and is read in Great Britain. There the reader is utterly at a loss to know what remedy I am recommending, for there they have not the plant, and know not this American name for it; —and referring to his dispensatory—his dictionary, or manual of Botany, he finds no such name, and therefore possesses no clue by which he can ascertain what I allude to. The treatise finds its way into Europe, but the farther it goes the greater confusion it carries with it, from the increased impossibility of ascertaining what is the precise remedy I wish to recommend. Now, if I had only said in my treatise that the Puccoon was the *Sanguinaria Canadensis*, not the least doubt or difficulty could have been entertained in any portion of this country, or elsewhere about it; for all the world knows, or may easily ascertain, what precise plant I mean; since there is but the one plant in all the world known by that name, and under that is described in all the general works on Botany. And thus we see that even in the same country, the same plant is know by a variety of common names, and by none of these is it recognised in foreign countries.

The Latin has, therefore, been properly adopted by the naturalists of all countries, as the nomenclatural and descriptive language of all the natural sciences; and Linnæus, the illustrious Swede, who is justly considered as not only the reformer but the founder of these sciences, willingly relinquished the language of his native country, to impress upon the myriads of objects which were offered to him, from every department of nature, and from every quarter of the world, those classic Latin names which they were destined to transmit to the latest posterity.

'The Swedish sage admires in yonder bowers,
His winged insects, and his rosy flowers;
Calls from their woodland haunts the savage train
With sounding horn, and counts them on the plain—
So once at Heaven's command the wanderers came,
To Eden's shade, and heard their various name.'

Having thus, as I trust, shown that the cause of science demanded that some one language should be adopted as the language of science, in the nomenclature of its objects, and that none other could have been so appropriately selected as the Latin; we go on in the next place to show, that the names which are selected from this language, to designate the objects of Botanical pursuit, are not so harsh, arbitrary or unmeaning as those who are uninformed on the subject might at first sight suppose. But here we must content ourselves for the present with a defence of the *Botanical names* of *plants* alone. An exposition and explanation of the *general* language of Botany, in its elementary, anatomical and physiological departments, would far transcend the narrow bounds prescribed for this paper. And here the first step in the task before us is that we all distinctly understand what is meant by two terms which will frequently occur in the course of our remarks. I allude to the terms *genus* and *species*, for it is to a defence of the generic and specific names alone of Botany that we now restrict ourselves.

It must then strike the most casual and inattentive observer that there are certain resemblances in some vegetable productions, which enable him to say that they must be nearly related. Thus the merest tyro in Botany, nay even the most unlettered woodsman, or uncivilized savage, will place together in three different parcels, from their general resemblances, all the oaks, ashes, hickories, &c., because there are certain marks of similitude among these, and other plants, which enable all "who have eyes to see" to group them together as accurately, merely from their general habit and appearance, as the most profound botanist could do, by reference to their fruit and flowers, which are the parts upon which he relies for his nicer discriminations. Now all those plants which from their general resemblances, and yet more certainly from resemblances in their fructification (i. e. their flower and fruit,) show their close relationship, are placed together in one group, and this group is called a *genus*. Thus all the oaks belong to one genus, all the ash-trees to another, all the hickories to a third, and so on; nor would a savage any sooner than a sage consort together an ash-tree with an oak, or an oak with a hickory.

Whilst however these general and minute resemblances obtain among all the oaks, and other genera, yet the same casual glance is sufficient to show that there are shades of differences among the individuals thus consorted together which forbids the idea that they are identically the same.— Thus the forester perceives that one oak has a white smoothish bark, with a leaf nearly entire and a large fruit or acorn; another oak has a black, rough bark, with leaves much divided and a smaller acorn; whilst a third kind never attains the stature of a tree, but is a low shrub, much disposed to multiply itself by its horizontal roots. The first of these kinds he will call, for the purposes of distinction, the white oak, the second the black oak, and the third the running oak. These three kinds of oak are, then, three different species of the oak genus; for they differ specifically in their leaves, the relative size and situation of their fruit, and in their mode of growth. Thus also the blue-ash differs from the black-ash, the scaly-bark hickory from the pignut hickory; and these are, therefore, different species of the ash and hickory genera: and so on throughout the whole vegetable world. Now give to these genera and species appropriate and distinctive Latin names, and you have the whole secret of Botanical nomenclature.

When Linnæus undertook a reformation in the language of Botany, he found that many genera as well as species had already received their names from his predecessors. Some of these names were appropriate and characteristic; others were objectionable on the score of abstruse derivation, indelicate allusion, or want of euphony, and a third set were barbarous, unmeaning, or arbitrary. The first of these, with becoming courtesy to their framers, he adopted—the second he modified and amended—the third he expunged altogether, substituting better in their places. This part of the science of Botany seems, indeed, to have been much at heart with this great expounder of nature; and to its elucidation he has devoted a considerable part of his two works the *Philosophia* and *Fundamenta Botanica*. His great object was, in the first place, to promote uniformity and simplicity in the nomenclature already established; and in the next, to provide judicious regulations, for the contrivance and application of new names for future discoveries. And the rules laid down by Linnæus on these heads have been, in part, or in whole, adopted by all succeeding botanists.

Let us now see how these labors have eventuated, and these regulations have been adopted, in the formation of the Latin names of Genera first, and then of Species. It is an established axiom of the Linnæan school that any peculiar characteristic in a genus, as regards its properties—uses—form—appearance—resemblance—locality—mode of growth &c. &c. constitute appropriate grounds on which to form the generic name; and accordingly we find many genera named from all these, and many other analogous circumstances. In illustration of this we will adduce a few examples of each kind, deriving them as far as possible, from medical plants, and, in the most of instances, from American Genera.

I. Genera named from supposed properties, or qualities, or uses.

Sanicula, (from Sano, to cure) from its supposed vulnerary qualities.

Tussilago, (*tussis*, a cough) from its supposed efficacy in coughs and catarrhs.

Lavendula, (*lavo*, to wash) from its being used in baths and washes on account of its fragrance.

Herniaria, (*hernia*, a rupture) from its once esteemed efficacy in ruptures.

Matricaria, (*matrix*, the womb) from its surposed virtues in diseases of that organ.

Pulmonaria, (*Pulmones*, the lungs) from its reputed properties in diseases of the chest.

Saponaria, (*sapo*, soap,) from the cleansing qualities of its leaves which are substituted for soap.

Scrophularia, from its supposed utility in scrophulous affections.

Sanguisorba, (*Sanguis*, blood, and *sorbeo*, to drink up or absorb,) from its reputed virtues in hæmorrhagies.

II. Form—appearance—resemblance &c.

Companula, (*Campana*, a bell) from its bell-shaped flower.
Pyrola, (*pyrus*, a pear) from its pear-shaped leaves.
Clavaria, (*clavus*, a club,) from its habit and appearance.
Detaria, (*dens*, a tooth) from its roots bearing some fancied resemblance to teeth.
Globularia, (*globus*, a globe or sphere) from the figure of the flower.
Lunaria, (*luna*, the moon) from the figure of its fruit or seed-vessels.
Sagittaria, (*sagitta*, an arrow) from its arrow-headed leaves.
Sanguinaria, (*sanguis*, blood) from its juice which is of a blood-red colour.
Stellaria, (*stella*, a star) from the figure of its flower.
Hepatica, (*hepar*, the liver) from the figure of its leaves.
Digitalis, (*digitus*, a finger) from its flowers resembling the finger of a glove.
Uvularia, from the fancied resemblance of its fruit to the uvula of the throat.
Lactuca, (*lac*, milk,) from its abounding in a white milky juice.
Urtica, (*uro*, to burn,) from its stinging qualities.

III. Locality—mode of growth, &c.

Limosella, (*limus*, mud) from this genus delighting in muddy situations.
Sedum, (*sedeo*, to sit) from its station on walls and rocks.
Ranunculus, (*rana*, a frog) from its growing in marshy places which are frequented by frogs.
Arenaria, (*arena* sand) from its native soil.
Convallaria, (*convallis*, a valley) from its favourite place of growth.
Parietaria, (*paries*, a wall,) from its growing on old walls.
Saxifraga, (*saxum* a rock, and *frango* to break) from its growing out of the clefts of rocks.
Calendula, (*calenda*, the first of every month) from its flowering during every month of the year.
Primula, (*primus* first) from its early flowering in the spring.

Convolvulus, (*convolvo*, to twist together) from the spiral twisting of its stems.
Salix, (*salis* to leap) from its quick growth.
Sempervivum, (*semper* always, and *vivo*, to live) from its continued verdure.
Fontinalis, (*fons*, a fountain) from its place of growth.

IV. Some genera are named from particular countries where they may have been first discovered, or to which they are exclusively restricted, as

Samolus, from the island Samos.
Parnassia, from the celebrated monut Parnassus.
Iberis, from the kingdom of Iberia or Spain.
Smyrnium, from the city of Smyrna.
Arabis, from Arabia.
Arethusa, from the celebrated fountain of that name near Syracuse.
Punica, from the Carthagenian city.
Colchicum, from Colchis a country of Asia.
Marrhubium, from a town in Italy.

Particular countries, however, more commonly give specific than generic names to plants, as we shall presently see.

V. Some generic names are borrowed from the fables of the classic poets of antiquity, and among those of poetical origin are the following:

Ambrosia, Protea, Actœa, Achillea, Narcissus, Hyacinthus, Amaryllis, Adonis, Circœa, Medeola, Andromeda, Daphne, &c. &c.

VI. A very prolific source, from which many generic names are drawn, is found in the long list of eminent men who, in every age of the world, have devoted their time and their talents to the study of this department of nature: and surely no names can be more appropriate than those which are intended to hand down to posterity, by engraving their names on the temple of nature, a memorial of those who have themselves contributed to elevate and adorn it. This has been called the APOTHEOSIS of Botanists; and no honor which it is in the power of the brother-hood to bestow, is greater than that of dedicating a newly discovered genus to a deserving botanist. Accordingly botanists in all ages have eagerly coveted this honor, and have narrowly watched its desecration, by withholding it from all who have not richly deserved it. During the Augustan age of Napoleon, the French Botanists were anxious to honor their imperial patron in this manner, and therefore named after him a splendid genus of plants brought from Egypt. To this name, however, their brethren in other portions of the world objected, because the Emperor of France, however eminent as a Legislator, or celebrated as a General, was no Botanist; the name was consequently annulled, and another given to the genus. Thus may the humblest votary of nature arrive at an honor which was denied to the Conqueror of nations!

Names of Genera derived from the source now under consideration, are rendered more euphonous by terminating the name of the individual in *a* or *ia;*—and although to the unpractised ear some of these may sound unharmoniously, yet by use we soon become accustomed to them—a few of these we will mention.

Hippocratea, from Hippocrates, the father of Physic.

Dioscorea, from Dioscorides, the celebrated Greek physician, and Botanist.

Monarda, from Monardes, a Spanish physician much devoted to the study of plants.

Lobelia, from de L'Obel, a French author of a history of plants.

Gerardia, from Gerard, a celebrated apothecary and herbalist of England.

Robinia, from Robin, a Frenchman, among the first who visited America, and introduced our black-locust into Europe.

Tillandsia, from Tillands, a swedish Botanist, the friend and cotemporary of the great Linnæus.

Linnæa, from that father of Botany—and, as if destined to perpetuate his name throughout the world, even when the remembrance of his labors shall have passed away, this plant has been found in every quarter of the globe.

Magnolia, from Magnol, professor of Botany at Montpelier, in France.

Rudbeckia, from Rudbeck, another eminent Swede.

Boerhaavia, from the distinguished professor of Botany and Medicine at Leyden.

Halleria, from the learned Albert Von Haller whose treatise on Physiology is well known to all of us.

Spigelia, from Spigel, an Italian Botanist of some distinction.

Kalmia, from Kalm professor of Botany at Abo in Finland, and author of travels in North America.

Solandra, from the late Dr. Solander who accompanied Capt. Cook around the world as naturalist to the expedition.

Claytonia, from Dr. Clayton of Virginia who discovered this genus.

Bartramia, from John Bartram an amiable man and excellent Botanist, the founder of a Botanic garden near Philadelphia, and author of travels in Florida.

Jeffersonia, in honor of our late venerable Chief Magistrate, who to the wisdom of the Statesman, added much of the learning of the man of Science.

Kuhnia, from the late Dr. Kuhn, of Philadelphia, the only American pupil of the great Linnæus, to whom he sent many of the plants of America.

Bartonia, in honor of the late professor of Medicine and Botany in the University of Pennsylvania, Dr. Benjamin Smith Barton.

Hossackia, from Dr. Hossack of New-York.

Michauxia, from Michaux father and son, authors of able works on the Botany of our country.

Nuttallia, from that indefatigable naturalist and able author, Thomas Nuttall, now engaged in exploring the Rocky Mountains.

Darlingtonia, from Dr. Darlington of West Chester, Pennsylvania, author of a Flora of that region.

VII. When a Botanist has made any particular tribe of vegetables the object of especial study, there seems to be a peculiar propriety in dedicating a genus of that tribe to him. Thus we have.

Buxbaumia, from Buxbaum, a German professor at Amsterdam, who was especially fond of the study of the *mosses*.

Hutchinsia, from Miss Hutchins, of Great Britain, distinguished above all her male associates, themselves pre-eminent, in the study of the *sea-weeds*

Muhlenbergia, from the late Dr. Muhlenberg of Pennsylvania, celebrated for the accuracy of his knowledge of American *grasses*.

Hookeria, from Dr. Hooker, Regius Professor of Botany in the University of Glasgow—a gentleman whom I am proud to call my friend and correspondent—a botanist pre-eminently distinguished for his acquirements in all the departments of the science, but perhaps especially so for his *Muscological* researches.

VIII. Generic names of *Greek* origin, expressive of the character, habit, place of growth, and virtues or sensible qualities of the genus, are, in the opinion of Linnæus, preferable to all others. In these, however, the terminations and the spelling are so altered as to suit the idiom of the Latin language. The following genera are of Greek derivation.

Glycirrhiza, (from *glukus** sweet, and *riza*, a root) from the sweetness of the roots of Liquorice.

Hydrophyllum, (*udor*, water, and *phyllon*, a leaf) from the leaves being spotted, as though waved with water.

Helianthus, (*elios* the sun, and *anthos* a flower,) from the disposition which the flowers of this genus have to follow the motions of the sun.

Liriodendron, (*leirion*, a lilly, and *dendron*, a tree) from the large lilly-like flowers borne by this splendid tree.

Rhododendron (*rhodon*, a rose, and *dendron* a tree,) from the resemblance of its flowers to those of a rose.

Cynoglossum, (*kunon* a dog, and *glossa*, a tongue) from the leaves resembling in shape the tongue of a dog.

Podophyllum, (*pous*, *podos*, a foot, and *phyllon* a leaf) from the leaves resembling the webbed feet of some water animals.

* For want of Greek types the Latin characters and spelling are substituted.

Galanthus, (*gala*, milk, and *anthos*, a flower,) from the milky whiteness of its flowers.

Polygala, (*polus*, much, and *gala*, milk) from the milky juice with which some of the genus abounds.

Lithospermum, (*lithos*, a stone, and *sperma*, a seed,) from the stony hardness of its seeds.

Aster, (*astær*, a star) from the figure of its flowers.

Oxalis, (*oxus*, sour) from the acidity of its leaves.

Geranium, (*geranos*, a crane,) from the fancied resemblance of its permanent style to a crane's bill.

Dracocephalum, (*drakoon*, a dragon, and *kephale*, the head,) from the figure of the flower.

Panax, (*pan*, every, and *akoos*, a medicine) from its boasted powers to cure all diseases.

Rheum, (*reo*, to flow) from its purgative qualities, &c. &c.

So much, Gentlemen, for our generic names; and perhaps some apology may be due you, for having dwelt so long on a subject so barren and uninteresting as that of *mere names;* but as the chief object of the present paper is to defend these very names from the charge of being arbitrary and unmeaning, I trust you will excuse the time devoted to their explanation—especially since the chief labor has been on my part in pronouncing them.

Next of *specific* names, by which we mean those names by which the different species of the same genus are distinguished from each other. Some genera have but a single species, and other genera may contain an hundred species; it is therefore clear that each one of these hundred, must have some distinctive name by which it may be recognized from all the other ninety-nine. If I say *Sanguinaria*, every body who knows any thing of American botany, knows what I mean, because there is but one species of that genus known; but if I say *Quercus*, it can only be known that I mean some kind of oak, of which genus at least forty different species are found in North America; but what kind or what particular species I refer to, can only be learnt by giving that specific name by which the particular kind or species alluded to is distinguished from all the rest: and when I say Quercus *alba* every botanist knows the precise tree I mean—that kind of oak which is with us called white oak.

The *generic* name is in every instance applied and prefixed to the *specific* name, that the genus as well as the species may be at once designated. Indeed, without the name of the genus, the specific name is of no significancy. Thus, if I say *alba*, alone, I convey no definite idea of any thing; but if I prefix a generic name and say Quercus *alba*, all ambiguity at once vanishes.

Now these specific names are, for the most part, *Latin adjectives*, signifying some property, quality, peculiarity, form, habit, mode of growth, &c. The specific name ought, indeed, to be expressive of characters inscribed as it were by the hand of nature upon the species named; and the more fully the name expresses the character the better. Thus we have Quercus *alba*, the specific name referring to a characteristic whiteness in the bark of that tree—Quercus *nigra*, from the blackness of its bark—Quercus *palustris*, from the species so named being found most commonly in wet land—Quercus *pumila*, from the low and shrubby growth of that particular species. Thus we find monarda *mollis*, and monarda *fistulosa;* the former species of monarda having a *soft, velvety leaf*, the other a *hollow stem*.

Magnolia *glauca*, and magnolia *grandiflora*; one species of this tree having that kind of leaf which botanists call *glaucous*, another a very *large flower*.

Arethusa *bulbosa*, and arethusa *pendula*, one species of this genus having a *bulbous root*—another a *pendent flower*.

Amaryllis *formosissima*, and amaryllis *vitata*, one species of this genus having a *superlatively beautiful*—the other a *striped flower*.

Andromeda *arborea*, and andromeda *nitida*—one species attaining the *stature of a tree*, another having a *shining polished leaf*—&c. &c.

Medical virtues, supposed or real, not only stamp generic, as we have seen when speaking of generic names, but these are frequently alluded to in the specific names also. Thus we have Cephaelis *emetica*—Juglans *cathartica*—Spigelia *anthelmia*—Bromus *purgans*—Cynoglossum *officinale* &c. &c.

Species are sometimes named from the time of the year at which they flower—thus Primula *veris*—Adonis *æstivalis*—Adonis *autumnalis*—Colchicum *autumnale*—Solidago *serotina*—Cymbidium *hyemale* &c.

Peculiarities of situation, soil climate, exposure &c. in which particular species delight, are often brought into their specific names. Thus Quercus *palustris*—Quercus *montana*—Linnæa *borealis*—Ranunculus *aquatilis*—Galanthus *nivalis*—Scilla *maritima*—Convolvolus *aquaticus*—Draba *muralis*—Convolvolus *arvensis*—Stellaria *arctica*—Tussilago *frigida*—Arbutus *alpina*—Eupatoreum *rupestre*—adjectives whose meaning is familiar to the most of you, and intelligible to all by a moment's reference to a Latin dictionary.

The *form* of leaves, which frequently differ in different species, affords also very appropriate marks by which one species may be distinguished from another. These forms are most generally expressed by a Latin adjective in connexion with the word *folium*, a leaf: thus three species of Cinchona used in medicine are distinguished by the specific names Cinchona *lancifolia*—Cinchona *cordifolia*—Cinchona *oblongifolia*. Two species of Laurel are thus distinguished, Kalmia *angustifolia*—Kalmia, *latifolia*; thus too we frequently find a Latin abjective of form, alone, as Eupatoreum *ovatum*—Eupatoreum *lanceolatum*—Asclepias, *obtusa*—Pyrola *eliptica*, referring to the oval, lance-shaped, obtuse and eliptic forms of the leaves of these species.

Sometimes the *manner in which leaves are attached* to the stems afford very proper marks of distinction, and is therefore frequently taken into consideration in the specific name. Thus we have Eupatoreum *sessilifolium*—Eupatoreum *perfoliatum*—Eapatoreum *verticillatum*—Hypericum *petcolatum*—Ludvidgia *alternifolia*.

The *number of leaves* upon particular species, when they are few, or the *number which grow together* when there are many, also afford good grounds of distinction, and of specific names. These names are compounded of Latin numerals with the word *folium,* as Convallaria *bifolia*—Gillenia *trifoliata*—Asclepias *quadrifolia*—Panax *quinqefolia, &c. &c.*

The relative *size of the flowers,* together with the *number* growing upon one plant, or grouped together, is often refered to in specific distinctions: thus we have a Magnolia *grandiflora*—Stellaria *parviflora*—Pyrola *uniflora*—Convallaria *biflora*—Galium *triflorum*—Lysimachia *quadriflora*—Rosa *multiflora*—Valeriana *pauciflora, &c. &c.*

Species are frequently named from the countries where they were first found, or where they occur most abundantly. Thus we find Lycopus *Europæus,*—Rosa *Gallica*—Primula *Scotica*—Genista *Anglica*—Gnaphalium *Germanicum,*—Saxifraga *Laponica*—Lichen *Icelandicus*—Hydrophyllum *Canadense*—Prunus *Virginiana*—Spigelia *Marylandica* &c.

Species as well as genera are frequently dedicated to distinguished botanists who may have discovered the species, or are deemed deserving of the honor. In this case the name of the individual is most generally given in the genitive or dative case, so far as it is convertible into declinable Latin; or sometimes the proper name is made an adjective; of the latter we have examples in Monarda *Bradburiana,* and Carex *Torreyana.* These two species of Monarda and Carex being named in honor of *Mr. Bradbury,* an English gentleman who travelled up the Missouri some years since, on a botanizing voyage, and *Dr. Torrey,* the distinguished botanist of New York. Instances of the former termination in the genitive or dative case are more numerous, and they occur indeed, in almost every page of botanical works. We will notice but a very few of them.

Hieracium *Gronovii*—a species of Hieracium named in honor of Gronovius, a physician and botanist of Holland, and author of the *Flora Virginica,* which he compiled chiefly from specimens sent him by by Dr. Clayton of that State.

Jeffersonia *Bartonis*—a name which at once unites the

memory of the distinguished patriot and statesman, with the learned physician and naturalist.

Viola *Nuttallii*, so named from Mr. Thos. *Nuttall*, before mentioned.

Arenaria *Richardsoni*, an arctic species of arenaria named, and most justly, in honor of Dr. Richardson, of G. Britain, who accompanied, as naturalist and Surgeon, the late perilous expeditions of Sir John Franklin in the arctic regions of North America.

Pinus *Douglasii*, a gigantic species of pine, discovered on the river Columbia, by Mr. David Douglass, sent to that country by the Horticultural Society of London.

Dryas *Drummondi*, in commemoration of Mr. Thomas Drummond, an indefatigable Scotch naturalist, now engaged in exploring Texas, &c. &c.

Thus, gentlemen, have we attempted to show that an absolute necessity existed for the selection of one single language, as the language of science in its technical nomenclature; that no one language would have answered this purpose so well as the Latin; that the Latin names which have been adopted in the science of Botany for the discrimination of genera and species of plants, are by no means so senseless, arbitrary, and unmeaning as many have supposed; but that on the contrary, the most of these names have been classically formed from Greek or Latin, with appropriate references to their properties, qualities or uses, discoverers, localities, &c.

If, by this attempt, I have succeeded in removing from the mind of a single individual who has heard me, an objection to the study of this science, growing out of these names, I am amply rewarded, and I trust that you will not have occasion to regret the time which you have spent in listening to me.

A SKETCH OF THE PROGRESS
OF BOTANY IN WESTERN AMERICA

ARTICLE XII.

A Sketch of the Progress of Botany in Western America.—
By C. W. SHORT, M. D., &c.

In the rapid increase of knowledge which has distinguished the close of the eighteenth and the commencement of the nineteenth century, every department of science has felt the animating influence of improvement. In every branch of knowledge, and particularly in those which depend on facts and observations for their support, the increase and improvement has been great and rapid; and in every branch of Natural History these results are particularly striking. Zoology is no longer the study of one individual; quadrupeds and birds, and fish and insects are become distinct pursuits; even the different orders of insects have attracted and fully occupied different observers, and their forms and habits and splendid drapery have been noted and delineated, until the imagination is almost become wearied with contemplating the boundless variety of organized beings, and the variety scarcely less boundless of habits, instincts and qualities. Mineralogy and Geology, though each treating of the same inorganic portions of the globe, have become divided into distinct studies, each fully occupying all the powers of the most gifted minds.

It is scarcely a century since Botany began to claim any of

the distinctions of a science; at a much later period it was considered as so small a branch of the department of Natural History, that it was generally included in it as a subordinate, although always a favorite study. Even now it may be correctly viewed under the same aspect; but so wonderfully have the branches of this great stock expanded, that Botany may now be said to comprehend many ramifications dependent on itself, each of which may occupy and amuse the leisure hours of a long life. Vegetable physiology, the distribution of plants into definite groups, comprehending the principles of classification, descriptive botany, or an examination and description of all the species of which the vegetable kingdom is composed, and even the history of the science, are each of them inquiries of great extent. In descriptive Botany, instead of the limit which was once supposed to circumscribe its objects, instead of ten thousand species which Linnæus, with all his knowledge, and in the height of his enthusiasm, believed would comprehend all the existing forms of vegetable life, we will not say in the language of Poetry, that ten thousand times ten thousand are rising up before us, but it is well known that the ascertained species are rapidly approaching to one hundred thousand, and new species, we may safely say, new genera, if not new families, are annually added to the long catalogue of recorded names.

Nor should the perpetual expansion of this circumference deter the lover of natural history from engaging in its pursuit. It should rather be a gratification and an incentive to him, that his occupation will be interminable, that curiosity in itself insatiable, shall be supplied by fountains in themselves exhaustless; and whilst the conquerer of the world wept that he had no more to do, the student of Nature need never apprehend, that with the most industrious devotion, of the longest life, he will ever exhaust the sources of his enjoyment. In no pursuit, perhaps in which man engages, does he enter with so pure and disinterested an enthusiasm, with such devoted and exclusive ardour. There is none in which successful results appear to give more unmingled pleasure. *Labor ipse voluptas,* is the motto which is always inscribed on his banner.*

Amidst this ample range which Botany now opens to our view we must on the present occasion necessarily restrict our researches within very narrow bounds, and we, therefore, propose devoting this paper to a sketch of the progress of Botany in Western America. In doing this we will advert to the labours of those only who have been instrumental in forwarding the march of this science, and promoting its discoveries in the more recently explored and newly settled portions of our continent: and for the sake of greater convenience will mention them in the order of chronological occurrence.

The first scientific Botanist who visited this portion of the Union was Andre Michaux, the elder, who having studied the science under the great Jussieu, and other eminent teachers, having visited various portions of France on botanical excursions, and accompanied the Persian consul to the East, where he spent two years in the exploration of its vegetable treasures may be supposed to have been well qualified for the task to which he was selected by his royal master, Louis the Sixteenth—that of exploring the continent of North America. In 1785 he sailed from France, on this mission, and for ten years was industriously engaged in examining various portions of the continent, from Hudson's Bay, to the Bahama Islands; and from the Atlantic seaboard to the banks of the Mississippi. For the purpose of assisting him in transporting his collections of living plants and roots to Europe, he formed establishments at New York, and Charleston, in South Carolina, for their cultivation; and spent a considerable portion of his time in the latter city, when not engaged on his excursions. These establishments were soon brought into a flourishing condition, and besides effecting the objects for which they were especially instituted, did much towards advancing the science of Arboriculture in the United States.

*Elliot in the Southern Review, No. viii.

In the year '93, Michaux crossed the Alleghany mountains, and visited many portions of the Western country; he traversed Kentucky, and spent some time in this place. In the following year '94, he again descended the Ohio river, and pushed his investigations into the interior of Illinois, even to the borders of the Mississippi. The difficuities, privations and dangers to which this enthusiastic naturalist was exposed, at that early day, in these unsettled wilds, may be easily imagined; but we can as readily conceive that these all were more than balanced in his mind, by the delights which he experienced in traversing an heretofore untrodden region, through which, in reference to the lights of Science and the labours of civilization, it may truly be said,

"He bent his way where twilight reigns sublime
O'er forests silent since the birth of time."

In 1796, this father of American Botany returned to Europe, richly laden with the materials for a comprehensive work on the Flora of North America. But finding his country in a distracted state, growing out of the Revolution, he was induced to postpone the publication of his works, and to join an expedition then about to sail for New Holland; on which, after having visited Teneriffe, and the Isle of France, he died at Madagascar, in November, 1802.

Previously to this, however, his son Francis Andre Michaux, commonly styled Michaux the younger, who had been with his father in America, returned hither in the year 1801, under the auspices of M. Chaptal, Minister of France for the interior, and spent nearly two years more, in further investigations of the natural productions, especially of the Carolinas, Kentucky and Tennessee. These were made during a journey from the city of New York as far west as Nashville, and thence to Charleston. On this travel, he diligently examined that portion of our State bordering on the Ohio river above Maysville; and thence through the interior by the way of Lexington, to the Barrens. A narrative of this journey was published by him on his return to Paris, in which he speaks, in terms of respect and gratitude, of the civilities and assistance which he received, during his stay in Lexington, from Dr. Samuel Brown, late Professor of the Theory and Practice of Medicine in Transylvania University.

Soon after the return of Michaux the younger to Europe, he published in Paris two works of which his father had left the MSS. These were the *Flora Boreali-Americana*, in two volumes, 8vo. and one volume on the Oaks of North America, in folio. The former of these was the first publication ever given to the world on the general Botany of North America; for although partial Floras of particular districts had been previously given by Cornutus, Catesby, Walter, Clayton, Gronovius, Marshall and others, yet these were all necessarily imperfect and limited. The work of Michaux comprised descriptions of 1700 plants, and about 40 new Genera. Of these acquisitions made by Michaux to the Botany of America, our own State and her sister Tennessee has the honor of having furnished a due proportion; and among them some curious in their economy, and others imposing in appearance. We have only time at present to allude to the *Pachysandra procumbens*, flowering among the snows of February —the aquatic *Hydropeltis purpurea*, defended from the action of the water by a thick glutinous covering—the humble but useful *Podostemum ceratophyllum*, confined to the shoals of the most rapid rivers, where it serves to protect the channel from the fury of the current, by binding together gravel, shells and stones on one impenetrable mass—the little *Poa reptans* performing the same office by matting together the dry sands of the river bank—the graceful *Virgilia lutea* decorating our calcarious cliffs with its long pendent racemes of snow-white flowers, &c.

His characteristic descriptions given in pure and classic Latin are exceedingly faithful; and subsequent investigations have but served to confirm the fidelity of these descriptions and the accuracy of his localities. Of this we will adduce but a few proofs out of the many which might be cited. In speaking of the *sedum pusillum*, Michaux mentions it as being found in North Carolina, at a place called "The Flat-Rock." Pursh, the author of another and later work on American Botany which we shall presently mention, in describing the same plant after Michaux, but without his precise accuracy, says, that it is met with "on flat rocks in North Carolina" and elsewhere. Now, although this little latitude in the most of instances might safely be indulged in, as similar plants are for the most part found in similar localities in the same countries, yet in the present instance it has proved unfavorable to Pursh; for Mr. Nuttall, of whom we shall hereafter speak more particularly, writing to us some years ago, on the subject of this particular plant, and its peculiar and restricted locality, thus expresses himself. "On this singular rock of Granite of nearly five acres area, I had for the first time, during my numerous perigrinations in the United States, the satisfaction of meeting with this extremely rare plant, and upon the same rock where so long before the unfortunate André Michaux had found it; from that time to the present no one except Michaux and myself had ever collected or met with it—it has never yet been any where found, but on the 'Flat-Rock' near Camden, in North Carolina." The *Bellis integrifolia* or American daisy, first described by Michaux in the work now noticed, the existence of which was even questioned by some American Botanists, has since been found abundantly in Kentucky and Arkansas. And it has been our good fortune to detect the original *Cunila glabella* of this author, in the neighborhood of Lexington, though long confounded with a totally distinct species growing around the falls of Niagara.

Besides the *Flora Boreali-Americana* and the volume on American Oaks by the elder Michaux, we are indebted to the younger for a splendid work on the forest trees of our country, the *Sylva Americana*, forming with the Oaks, three large volumes, with beautiful and highly accurate coloured engravings. Of this work, which should be in the library of every intelligent farmer and physician, two or three editions have been published in Europe, and one in America.

The estimable and venerable author of this work is now living in the neighborhood of Paris, in France; and to him we had the pleasure, a short time since, of sending by Dr. Campbell of Tennessee, a small parcel of plants, being chiefly such as have been discovered in this country, since the travels of his father and himself.

Soon after the purchase of Louisiana, the Government of the United States wisely determined upon taking measures to explore their newly acquired territory, and the immense wilderness included within its limits, in order to learn its geographical boundaries—its soil and natural productions. As intimately connected with the investigation before us, and as next in the order of their occurrence, we must mention the labours of those intrepid explorers Lewis and Clark, who at the instance of President Jefferson were sent in 1803 to the Western portions of our Northern continent, up the Missouri, over the Rocky mountains, and down the Columbia to the shores of the Pacific. Of the fitness of Capt. Lewis for the command of such an expedition, the President thus expresses himself in his recommendation to Congress. "Of courage undaunted; possessing a firmness and perseverance of purpose which nothing but impossibilities could divert from its direction; careful as a father of those committed to his care, yet steady in the maintenance of order and discipline; intimate with the Indian character, customs and principles; habituated to the hunting life; guarded by exact observation of the vegetables and animals of his own country, against losing time in the description of objects already possessed; honest, disinterested, liberal, of sound understanding, and a fidelity to truth so scrupulous, that whatever he should report would be as certain as if seen by ourselves: with all these qualifications, as if selected and implanted by nature in one body for this express purpose, I could have no hesitation in confiding the enterprise to him. Under this leader was this daring enterprise accomplished in three years, to the entire satisfaction of the government.

It is much to be regretted, however, for the cause of Natural Science, that the wisdom of President Jefferson had not perceived the necessity of attaching to this expedition some thoroughly competent naturalist; for whatever may have been the tact and discernment in observation, possessed by Capt. Lewis, he was not prepared by previous education for making those accurate and minute observations, collections and reports on the Botany, Mineralogy and Zoology of those unknown regions, which would have proved most interesting and useful to his own country, and to the world at large. For making these, facilities and opportunities were enjoyed by this expedition which have not been possessed by any subsequent party. Nor were they entirely unimproved by our travellers; for a large collection of plants was made during their slow and tedious ascent of the Missouri, which, however, was most unfortunately lost by being deposited among other things at the foot of the Rocky mountains. A much smaller, but still highly interesting collection, made during the rapid return of the expedition, was placed in the hands of Pursh, a distinguished botanist, of whom we shall presently speak, for the purpose of figuring and describing such as might be new. Of this parcel, Pursh, thus speaks:—"The loss of the first collection is the more to be regretted when I consider that the small collection communicated to me, consisting of about one hundred and fifty specimens, contained not above a dozen plants well known to be natives of North America; the rest being either entirely new or but little known, and among them at least six distinct and new genera. This may give an idea of the discerning eye of their collector, who had but little practical knowledge of the Flora of North America, as also of the richness those of extensive regions in new and interesting plants, and other natural productions." What then might not have been the acquisitions made to the Flora of Western America," had this expedition been provided with competent naturalist!

At the same time that Capts. Lewis and Clark were performing their arduous and important services, in exploring the unknown sources of the Missouri, Capt. Zebulon Pike, another highly meritorious officer, was despatched on a similar expedition, for the purpose of tracing the Mississippi to its head; and although but illy provided with the proper outfit, and labouring, consequently, under many disadvantages, he nevertheless effected the main object of his mission in nine months, to the satisfaction of Government; and immediately on his return was selected by Gen. Wilkinson for a second expedition to the interior of Louisiana, which he prosecuted even into the Spanish Territory. A narrative of these two expeditions was published in 1810, which although rich in geographical and other valuable information, is comparatively barren in its notices of the Botany and natural history of the unknown regions through which he passed; no one conversant with these subjects having been associated with him. This we have the greater reason to regret, because we know that one gentleman at least, of pre-eminent attainments, applied to the executive for permission to accompany these expeditions, but applied in vain!

A few years after the return of the party under Lewis and Clark, the same country which they explored was visited as far up as the Mandan Villages on the Missouri, by Mr John Bradbury, an English gentleman of very respectable attainments as a naturalist, who had been sent to America, by an association in England, as a collector of objects in natural history, and of seeds and roots, for introduction to the gardens of that country. Descending the Ohio from the East, he examined the productions of its borders; and at St. Louis, where he remained during the entire season of 1810, he diligently explored the region roundabout, and despatched in the fall a rich collection of plants to Europe. Early in the Spring of 1811, he joined a fur-trading company and ascended with them the Missouri to the point we have mentioned. On this voyage still larger collections, and some new discoveries were made, which being sent to England fell into the hands of Pursh, and were published in his Flora, as it appears, without the consent of Mr. Bradbury. In 1817, this traveller published in London a journal of his travels in America during the years 1809–10–11, in which is contained a great deal of interesting information, on the Botany of the Missouri country.

It is now time that we notice more particularly a work, whose publication forms a considerable epoch in the annals of American Botany, and whose author on several occasions we have already mentioned.

Frederick Pursh, a German by birth, and educated at Dresden, left that country in 1799, with the determination, as he states, not to return, until he had explored North America to the utmost of his means and abilities. From the time of his arrival until the year 1811, when he returned to Europe, he seems to have been variously engaged, and at different points of the Eastern and Southern States, in prosecuting his design; but his most extensive explorations were made during the years 1805 and '06, in one of which he visited and examined the Northern States, and in the other, the Southern from New Hampshire to Georgia.

"Both of these tours," as he says in the preface to his work, "I made principally on foot, the most appropriate way for attentive observation, particularly in mountainous countries; travelling over an extent of more than three thousand miles each season, with no other companions than my dog and gun, frequently taking up my lodgings in the midst of wild mountains and impenetrable forests, far remote from the habitations of men." It does not appear, however, that Pursh ever crossed the Alleghanies or descended into the Western Valley; consequently in the present enquiry we would not be so much interested in tracing his foot-steps, or noticing his labours, except that they resulted in the publication of a work, by far the most comprehensive which had ever yet appeared on the subject of American Botany.

In 1811, after an absence of twelve years, Pursh returned to Europe with an ample stock of materials towards a Flora of North America, which, in 1814, he published in London under the title *Flora Americæ Septentrionalis*. In the compilation of this work he seems to have availed himself industriously of the aids furnished him in that great emporium of all Science, the British capital, and particularly in referring to the extensive Herbaria there collected of American plants.

In this work of Pursh, frequent references are made to Western plants, and Western localities; but for all such he must have been indebted to the Michauxs, Nuttall, Bradbury, Menzies, Lyon, Lewis and other explorers of Western America; of the labours of all of whom he appears to have freely availed himself in enriching his work, and too often, as I am constrained to believe, without making the proper acknowledgments. Nevertheless, whatever may be the minor inaccuracies of this work, or the reprehensible mode in which some of its materials may have been collected, it must be confessed that it was, and indeed still continues to be, the most complete and extensive Flora ever yet published of our country.

About the year 1815, this country was visited by the abbe Correa de Serra, a man of distinguished attainments in natural science, as well as general literature, whom Jeffery, the former well known editor of the Edinburgh Review, calls "the learned Portugese." On his return to Philadelphia, where he then resided, Mr. Correa, spoke to us in rapturous terms of the Botany of our native State, Kentucky; and especially of his astonishment at finding in our mountains, an arborescent *Andromeda*, having never before seen any other than shrubby species. We are not aware, however, that this gentleman ever published anything on the natural history of this region, except a paper in the Transactions of the American Philosophical Society, more particularly on the Geology of the West.

We come in the next place to notice the labours of an individual, much more immediately identified with the interests and advancement of Western Botany than any of those who had preceded him. I allude of course to Mr. Thomas Nuttall, whom we have already mentioned more than once. An

Englishman by birth, he was at an early age, thrown on our shores, where he soon became enraptured with its natural productions, and has since devoted his life exclusively to their investigation. In 1811, he accompanied Bradbury on his then perilous voyage up the Missouri; soon afterwards he travelled extensively in the Arkansas Territory—then an unknown region. In 1816, we had the pleasure of meeting with this gentleman in this country, and enjoyed the happiness of making with him several herborizations, in the neighborhood of this place and Cincinnati. At that time, in addition to his zeal for botanical acquisitions, he was much interested in the examination of the aboriginal relics of this region, and we assisted him in taking plans and measurements of an extensive fortification at the confluence of the great Miami and Ohio rivers, and of another in this vicinity.

In 1818, this Botanist published his *Genera of North American Plants*, the result of personal collections and observations made during nine years active research, throughout most of the States and Territories of the Union; during which time he more than once visited the Western section of it. Though differing essentially in character and scope from the works of Michaux and Pursh, since it professes only to give generic characters, together with a mere catalogue of species, and detailed descriptions of such only as are new, yet the Genera of Nuttall is not a less useful or excellent production than either of the former; whilst in point of accuracy and minuteness, it is even more so. The testimony of the public to this assertion is manifested in the fact, that a second edition of it has been long demanded.

By this work the American Flora has been enriched with many acquisitions of interest, utility and beauty, made by its author in every portion of the Union. Time would fail me were I to attempt an enumeration of them, but I cannot pass them by without a notice of a few of those—the more exclusive natives of our Western woods. Among these are the early flowering *Erigenia bulbosa*, the first harbinger of our spring—the beautiful parti-colored *Collinsia verna*, dedicated to his friend and fellow botanist, Zaccheus Collins of Philadelphia—the *Phalanguim esculentum*, as ornamental as the cultivated Hyacinth, and having a large edible and nutritious bulb—the gay and graceful *Hesperis pinnatifida*—the Osage apple or orange of Arkansas, most appropriately named in honor of William Maclure, the American patron of the Natural Sciences, &c. Of late Mr. Nuttall's predilections seem to run chiefly in the line of ornithology, on which he has published in Boston two volumes, illustrated with very neat woodcuts of many of the birds of America. Recently, however, he has given to the public two lengthy papers on the subject of American Botany, one in the Transactions of the American Philosophical Society, entitled "Contributions towards a Flora of Arkansas," containing descriptions of the plants, which he had detected in his travels through that Territory; the other, "Notices of new and rare species from various parts of the American Union."

The lovers of Natural Science will be gratified to learn that Mr. Nuttall is now engaged in making further explorations of the Rocky mountains, the river Oregon, and the contiguous islands of the Pacific Ocean; from which, in addition to his already well-earned reputation, he will doubtless acquire a distinguished character, as an enterprising naturalist.

The order of our enquiry next leads us to notice the labours of another expedition of discovery sent by the general Government to the Rocky mountains, by way of the Platte branch of the Missouri, and thence homeward by the Arkansas river. This expedition, under the command of Major Long, had attached to it several gentlemen eminently qualified to observe, collect and report on the natural productions of the interesting and unknown regions through which they passed. These were Drs. Baldwin and James, Messrs. Say, Peale and Jessup, the botanical investigations being particularly entrusted to the two former. This party left Pittsburgh in May, 1819, and in October of the following year, assembled at Cape Gerardean, on the Mississippi, where it was dispersed.

At Franklin, on their outward journey, this party was deprived of the professional and scientific services of Dr. Baldwin, by the lamented death of that gentleman, whose ardor in the pursuit of botanical knowledge, led him to undertake an expedition to which his declining health was totally inadequate; and on the banks of the Missouri, far from the bosom of his family, and the circle of his friends, he found an untimely grave.* "His Diary, in which the latest date is only a few days previous to his death, shows with what earnestness, even in the last stage of weakness and disease, his mind was devoted to the pursuit, in which he had so nobly spent the most important part of his life. He has left behind him a name which will long be honored; his early death will be regretted, not only by those who knew his value as a friend; but by all the lovers of that fascinating science, to which his life was dedicated, and which his labours have so much contributed to advance and embellish."† His Herbarium and communications, it is well known, have contributed to enrich the works of Pursh and Nuttall. He was the friend and correspondent of Muhlenberg and Elliott, and contributed materials for the copious catalogue of the former, and the excellent "Sketch" of the latter. In South America, where he had travelled extensively, he met with Bonpland, the celebrated companion of Humboldt, and a friendly correspondence was there established between them which continued until his death. His notes and collections made during frequent journeys through Georgia, Florida and other parts of North America, are extensive and valuable. During the short period of his connexion with Long's expedition, the infirmities resulting from a long established and incurable pulmonary disease, then rapidly approaching its fatal termination, could not overcome the activity of his mind, nor divert his attention from his favourite pursuit. Though unable to walk on shore, he caused plants to be be collected

*Dedication of the *Florula Cestrica*, by William Darlington, M. D.
†Account of the expedition by Dr. James, Phila. 1823.

and brought on board the boat; and not disheartened by the many vexations attending this method of examination, he persevered throughout the course of the voyage from Pittsburgh to Franklin, detected and described many new plants, and added many valuable observations relating to such as were before known.*

After the death of Dr. Baldwin, the botanical duties of the expedition devolved upon his successor Dr. James, who discharged them in a highly satisfactory manner, as will appear from a reference to an account of the expedition, drawn up by himself and published in two volumes, 8vo. in 1823. In this work will be found a vast amount of general information in regard to the countries explored, and especially on the subject of its vegetable productions. Previously to the appearance of this work, however, the botanical results of the expedition were given by Dr. James in the 2d volume, (N. S.) of the Amer. Philos. Trans.; and more recently a fuller account of the plants found exclusively on the Western side of the Mississippi, has been published by Professor Torrey in the annals of the Lycæum of Natural History, of New York.

Within a short time past, Death has robbed the Republic of Science of another member of this expedition—another naturalist of pre-eminent attainments—Mr. Thomas Say. This gentleman, whose acquirements in some of the most difficult departments of natural history were perhaps superior to those of any other individual on the Continent, published some years since three volumes on American Entomology, which in point of elegance of execution, and accuracy of matter, will challenge a comparison with any similar production. For the last few years Mr. Say had resided at New Harmony, Indiana, whither he had been invited by his friend, the proprietor, Mr. William Maclure. Here he undertook the publication periodically of a work on the shells of North America, illustrated with coloured engravings from the pencil of his accomplished lady. This work, which is highly spoken of by those best conversant with the subject of which it treats, is the

*Account of the Expedition, &c.

first work on any department of natural history which has yet been published in the Mississippi Valley, and constitutes, therefore, a memorable epoch in the annals of Western Science. We proceed, however, with the investigation now immediately before us—the progress of botanical discovery.

The British government having failed to effect the long cherished scheme of discovering a North Western passage by sea to the Pacific ocean, although successive naval expeditions, liberally outfitted and ably conducted by Captains Ross, Parry, Lyon and Beechy had each made most energetic and daring efforts to accomplish it, determined upon other plans of exploration, by which this long-sought and anxiously desired channel might still be found.

Among these none seemed so feasible, or so full of promise, as that of sending an expedition *over-land* from Hudson's bay to the Arctic ocean, and the exploration of its coast quite across the Continent. With this view two several expeditions under the command of Capt. Sir John Franklin, of the Royal navy, were successively despatched on this new and venturous project. And although they also failed to effect the main object of Government, yet as they contributed greatly towards a knowledge of the natural history, and especially the Botany and Zoology of the arctic and North Western portions of our continent, a brief notice of each will not be deemed irrelevant to the enquiry before us.

The first of these *over-land expeditions*, under the command of Capt. Franklin, accompanied by Dr. John Richardson as surgeon and naturalist, disembarked at York Factory on Hudson's bay in August, 1819; and notwithstanding the long detention, occasioned by an intervening winter of nine month's duration, by the end of the second season they had penetrated northward to the Polar sea. Here winter, clothed with all the horrors of an arctic climate, overtook the party early in September. They suffered dreadfully from cold and famine; to a degree indeed unparalleled in the annals of human misery; most of the party perished, and the survivors were on the verge of the grave; when the Indians brought them supplies of provisions, and conducted them to the nearest post of the Hudson's bay company.

By this disaster all the extensive collections made on their outward journey were lost—the enterprise was abandoned, and in the summer of 1822, the small remnant of the party returned to Europe.

On the return of Capt. Franklin and Dr. Richardson from an expedition where they had purchased so dearly the glories of discovery, it was not asked, or even expected by their Government that they should again brave the perils of those distant and terrible shores. Yet so high was the ardor with which they were inspired, that scarcely had they breathed from their voyage, before they presented a new scheme for completing the outline which they had only begun to sketch. The British government cordially embraced the proposal, and furnished most liberally every means of prosecuting the undertaking with success, and escaping the evils which had before pressed on them so heavily. Three large boats were constructed of mahogany, so light that they could be carried on men's shoulders across the portages, yet so firmly knit together that they were able to face the waves of the Northern ocean. Provision was laid in (consisting chiefly of pemmican, a light, portable and highly nutritious article) calculated for two years subsistence; and the boats being sent forward by the way of Hudson's bay, the officers took the more agreeable route of New York.

In the Spring of 1825, Franklin and Richardson, accompanied by Mr. Thomas Drummond, as assistant naturalist, proceeded from New York along the chain of inland seas from Ontario to Lake Winnepeg, where meeting with their boats and the rest of the detachment, they proceeded northward until they fell on the Mackenzie river, and embarking on its waters, reached in due time the Polar sea; the shores of which through more than 40 degrees, and under the 70th of latitude, were diligently explored during the brief interval of one arctic summer.

In the progress of this expedition Mr. Drummond visited the Rocky mountains, by the route of the Saskatchawan river, and reached them at that interesting and important point which must be considered as the most elevated of that lofty chain, for here the *four mightiest rivers of the continent, interlocking their primary rills, descend in the four cardinal directions, seeking their different and far distant ocean-homes*— the Saskatchawan runs eastward to Hudson's bay—the Mackenzie northward to the Polar sea—the Columbia westward to the Pacific ocean, and the Missouri southward to the Gulf of Mexico; whilst in the same quarter, though comparatively in a much lower region, arise the St. Lawrence and the Mississippi proper.

From the most elevated portion of the Rocky mountain chain, at this interesting point rise, in towering majesty, two rival peaks to the height of 15 and 16000 feet, between which a passage of comparatively easy ascent is offered across the mountains. These guardian giants of the pass-way are named in honor of two illustrious botanists of Great Britain—Drs. Brown and Hooker; and thus are the Pelion and the Ossa of the Rocky mountains—the Chimborazos of the Northern Andes, dedicated to the cause of Botany; and whilst they rear their towering summits to the skies, clad in eternal snows, they proclaim the pure and elevated delights of our science, and stand themselves everlasting monuments of the zeal and daring of its votaries!

Whilst this portion of British America was thus diligently explored by this party, that section of it lying west of the Rocky mountains, on the Pacific coast, and contiguous to the Columbia river, was undergoing a similar investigation by Mr. David Douglas, a very competent Botanist who was sent out by the London Horticultural Society.* Thus a zone of at least two degrees of latitude in width, and reaching en-

*The fate of the indefatigable and lamented Douglas was melancholy in the extreme. From the American coast he passed over to the Sandwich islands; and whilst exploring one of these, he fell into a pit, prepared by the natives for entrapping the wild-bull, and by one of these animals was gored to death!

tirely across the Continent, from the mouth of the Columbia to Hudson's bay, has been explored by three of the ablest and most zealous collectors that England has ever sent forth; while a zone of similar width extending at right angles with the other, from Canada to the Polar sea, has been more cursorily examined by these expeditions.

The botanical results of these explorations are now publishing in London, under the title of *Flora Boreali-Americana*, by that able and distinguished naturalist, Sir William Hooker. The British Government, actuated by a most laudable desire of encouraging our science, has lent a liberal aid to the undertaking, and has granted one thousand pounds to be applied towards defraying the expense of the engravings alone. About one half of this splendid work has reached us, and when completed it will be an invaluable acquisition to the American Botanist. It will, indeed, identify the names of Douglas and Drummond, of Richardson and Hooker with the cause and progress of Western American Botany.

The order of our enquiry next leads us to notice the further labours of one of the naturalists of this expedition, in a different quarter of the Continent. Having published in England, a work exclusively on the subject of the American Mosses, chiefly the result of his late explorations, in 1825-6-7, Mr. Drummond again sailed for America, at the instance, and through the liberal pecuniary aid chiefly of Drs. Hooker and Graham, for the purpose of exploring the less known parts of the Southern and Western United States. Commencing his tour again at New York, in the Spring of 1831, he passed through Philadelphia and Washington, where every facility was afforded him by naturalists and official agents, for a successful prosecution of his undertaking. He crossed the Alleghanies on foot, descended the Ohio from Wheeling to its mouth, and thence up the Mississippi to St. Louis. Here and in the neighborhood, he remained until the winter, and although his labours were greatly interrupted by an attack of fever and succeeding bad health, he made very extensive collections of plants, shells and Zoological specimens.

During the succeeding spring and summer Mr Drummond explored the neighborhood of New Orleans with his accustomed zeal, and thrice examined the opposite shore of Lake Ponchatrain. From this he extended his explorations into the neighbouring Southern States, where amidst many dangers, and notwithstanding the severest attacks of fever and cholera, he amassed a collection of upwards of one thousand species of plants.

Mr. Drummond next visited Texas, from the floral riches of which *El dorado* of the botanist, he promised himself a rich reward: nor was he disappointed. For although his visit to that country was ill timed, in consequence of the unprecedented wetness of the season, (1833-4,) its consequent unhealthiness, and the unsettled position of its political affairs; still he made very extensive collections, among which were many new and beautiful plants. Of these a number have been introduced to the gardens of Great Britain, and several have been figured and described in *The Botanical Magazine;* whilst in the *Companion* to that work a general account has been given of the labours of Mr. Drummond in the Southern and Western States, by his friend and patron Sir William Hooker.

It appears from some of his last letters to his friends in Scotland, that Mr. Drummond had determined upon a permanent settlement in Texas; and to this end had made arrangements for returning home to remove his family. Desirous, however, of still further extending his explorations, and increasing his collections, he touched at Havanna on his way homeward: he was there soon seized with fever, of which he died in the fall of 1834. Deeply has science to deplore the martyrdom of this intrepid traveller and indefatigable collector: had he lived, much would, doubtless, have been effected by him, in making known the vegetable treasures of his adopted country; and few have done more for **the Botany of Western America than Thomas Drummond.**

About this time our Western borders were visited by another foreign naturalist, Prince Maximillian de Nenweid, who having spent some time in the Eastern States and in Pittsburgh, determined to explore the upper Missouri, and to extend his tour to the Rocky mountains. The hostility of the Indian tribes prevented him from realizing his original plan to the full extent; nevertheless he ascended some distance beyond the confines of civilization, and made a very fine collection of plants and animals; and what is also a matter of much interest considering how fast the native sons of our forests are being exterminated, he made a series of drawings of some of the most distinguished chiefs and warriors belonging to about twenty different tribes, who are as yet but imperfectly known to the whites.

Next in chronological order, we come to make mention of of Mr. Charles Beyrich, a Prussian gentleman of science, who, under the auspices of that government, came to America about four years since, and spent the greater portion of that time in the diligent exploration of its botanical treasures. He passed the summer of 1833 chiefly in the Carolinas and Georgia, where, and in some of the adjoining States, he amassed a collection of thirteen hundred species in one season. Visiting the City of Washington during the succeeding winter, and learning that a military expedition would be sent, the ensuing spring, into the Indian territory west of the Mississippi, he applied for, and readily obtained permission from Secretary Cass to accompany it. He joined the detachment at St. Louis in the Spring, proceeded with it to the different frontier posts; and was with the U. S. Dragoons in their engagements with the Pawnees and Cumanches. On the return from this expedition, richly ladened with the fruits of extensive and diligent observation and collection, in a new and unknown region, he was seized with Cholera and died at Fort Gibson, in September, 1834. Mr. Beyrich is represented by those who knew him to have been an amiable, liberal, communicative and unpretending man, and a profound botanist—Science will long and deeply deplore his untimely end!

Last in our notice of foreign labourers in the field of Western Botany, we must mention Dr. Joseph Frank of Germany; who after having made extensive explorations andcollections in his own country and Switzerland, came over to America with the same object in view. He spent a year or two in Cincinnati and other parts of Ohio; when he was commissioned by the Grand Duke of Baden to travel in the Southern and Western States. On this service he ventured to New Orleans early in the fall of 1835, where he speedily fell a victim to yellow fever. What was the extent of his collections in this country, or what disposition has been made of them we are uninformed.

Whilst these things were doing towards the elucidation of the Botany of the West, by travellers from abroad, and explorers from other portions of the Union, a few of our own citizens were not entirely inattentive to, or unobservant of it. Among these Dr. Daniel Drake was foremost. In "A natural and statistical view or picture of Cincinnati and the Miami country," which he published in 1815, quite a copious catalogue is given of the forest trees found in that quarter; and another of such herbaceous plants as are useful in Medicine or the Arts; to these are appended a Floral Calendar, or Journal of the progress of vegetation in and about Cincinnati. During his subsequent engagements as Professor of materia medica in Transylvania University, he devoted a due share of attention to medical Botany, and both in his teachings and writings he has ever strenuously advocated the cause of Botany, as an important collateral branch of the science of Medicine.

In 1819 a work of somewhat a similar character to that just mentioned, was published by Dr. McMurtrie of Louisville, in which among a variety of other matter is given a catalogue of the plants growing in the neighborhood of that city. We cannot, however, vouch for the accuracy of that catalogue; though the locality is confessedly a rich one, a number of the species mentioned by Dr. M. have never been found there by succeeding botanists.

From about this time to 1826, Lexington was the residence of Mr. C. S. Rafinesque, who held for some portion of that time, if we mistake not, the professorship of modern languages in its University. This gentleman, in the general scope of his survey of all the natural sciences, paid much attention to Botany; and during his frequent and prolonged excursions, through various portions of Kentucky, and the adjoining States, he formed large collections of animals, shells, plants, minerals and organic remains. It is to be regretted, however, that his discoveries, of which he professes to have made many —very many—in each of these departments, have been published, either in foreign journals or ephemeral magazines, so as to be lost, or rendered inaccessible to the majority of readers; and consequently are of little or no use to the students of our country.

From this hasty and very imperfect sketch of the labours of our predecessors and cotemporaries, we come next to mention the humble efforts of ourselves and a few friends in this immediate field. For the last twenty years we have paid some attention to the Botany of Kentucky; and whilst actively engaged in the practice of medicine, in that portion of the State most inaptly called "The Barrens," opportunities were constantly presented for noting and admiring the varied vegetable productions of that interesting region. In many a long and solitary ride through these natural flower-gardens, have our fatigues been lightened, and our spirits cheered by their floral beauties. Here at one point, the ground was carpeted with the flame-colored flowers of the dazzling *Euchroma;* and there enamelled with the parti-coloured blossoms of *Violets, Gentians,* and *Trilliums.* In this spot, from amidst a tuft of humbler beauties, the majestic *Frazera* was seen shooting up its pyramidal head, crowned with wreaths of its very peculiar flowers; and in that, various *Sumachs* overhung the path.

emitting from their clumps of berries a shower of acid on the traveller. Now, would burst upon the view a placid sheet of water, skirted with the blue and purple hues of the *Pontederia* and *Decodon*, intermixed with the scarlet berries of the *Prinos*, whilst its surface was covered over with the large and floating leaves and splendid flowers of the *Cyamus;* and then, in endless vista, was stretched before the eye, a waving sea of gigantic grasses. In such a field as this, none but a recreant to nature, and undeserving of its pleasures, could remain indifferent to the charms, spread in such lavish profusion around; and, although we were not idle, inattentive or unobservant of them, yet do we now find cause for bitter regrets, that we did not then more industriously avail ourselves of the opportunities there enjoyed, for studying, examining and collecting the productions of that rich and interesting region.

In our subsequent efforts in the cause of Western Botany, it has been our good fortune to be associated, at different times, with a few fellow-labourers, whose devotion and industry have contributed greatly to our perseverance. Of these, the late Mr. Eaton must first be mentioned; whose amiability of character, and zeal in the pursuit of natural science, greatly endeared him to us, and gave an additional incentive to our own. That zeal in him, alas, but too soon lighted the fire which consumed him! for of our departed friend it may with much truth be said, that

"Science 'self destroyed her favourite son."

Having in another place* attempted an eulogy of this excellent young man, we will only here pause a moment to pay the passing tribute of a sigh to one so rarely endowed—so deservedly esteemed.

About the time of the death of Mr. Eaton, his loss to the cause of Science in the West, was fortunately supplied by two individuals, one of whom had been his fellow-student in the Rensselaer institution, and in the other he had been instru-

*A Biographical Memoir of H. Hulbert Eaton, A. M., late Assistant Professor of Chemistry in the Medical Department of Transylvania University—Transylvania Journal; vol. 5.

mental in exciting a relish for the charms of Botany—these were Dr. Robert Peter, and Mr. Henry A. Griswold. In connexion with one or both these gentlemen, we have been diligently engaged, for the last five years, as leisure and opportunity permitted, in exploring various portions of Kentucky. Of those localities, which have been for the most part very thoroughly examined, and which have yielded us the richest harvests, may be mentioned the precipitous lime-stone cliffs of the Kentucky river at various points—the sand-stone hills and swampy bottoms bordering the Licking river—the mountainous region roundabout the Olympian Springs, and the Blue Licks—the elevated point in Madison county called the "Big Hill"—the Knobs around the Crab Orchard, being the first spurs of the Cumberland mountains—the country bordering the Ohio river at Maysville, Cincinnati, North Bend, and especially the marshy tract around Louisville—the Barrens of Kentucky, &c., &c. The results of these explorations have been published in the form of Catalogues of the Plants of Kentucky, in several preceding numbers of the Transylvania Journal of Medicine, from which it appears that about one thousand species have been detected by us, as natives of the State, which number will probably be extended by future examination to fifteen hundred. The fruits of these collections in the shape of well prepared specimens have been liberally distributed among our brother botanists; and within the time just specified not less than twenty five thousand specimens of Western plants, have been forwarded by us to various correspondents in different portions of Europe and America. Nor have these offerings been unrequited. On the contrary we have great pleasure in acknowledging valuable and acceptable returns in exchange, from Sir William Hooker, of Glasgow; Dr. Greville, of Edinburgh; Mr Bentham, of London; Mr. Parker, of Liverpool; M. Mirbel, of Paris; and Dr. Fischer, of St. Petersburgh. Whilst our countrymen, Professor Torrey and Dr. Gray of New York; Mr. Oakes of Massachusetts, Dr. Griffith and

Mr. Durand of Philadelphia; Dr. Darlington of Pennsylvania; Dr. Aikin of Baltimore; Rev. Mr. Curtis and Dr. Loomis of North Carolina; Rev. Dr. Bachman of Charleston; Dr. Chapman and Mr. Croom of Florida, have been prompt and liberal in exchanging specimens from their several districts with us.

By the addition of these contributions to our own collections, we have been enabled to form a very extensive Herbarium which is daily increasing; and thus are we becoming gradually possessed of materials and information, out of which we trust may be ultimately compiled a full and faithful Flora of Kentucky.

Nor is Kentucky, by any means, the only Western State in which resident Botanists are actively engaged. In Ohio, on the contrary, the number of labourers is greater than with us. Of these Dr. Riddell has published quite a comprehensive Catalogue of Western Plants.* In Cincinnati he is assisted by the co-operation of Drs. Eberle, Locke, and Colby, and Messrs. Buchanan, Lea and Clark; in Dayton, by Mr. Vancleve; and in Worthington, by Mr. Paddock. In Western Virginia we hear of Mr. Townsend, at Wheeling; in Michagan, of Dr. Houghton, at Detroit; and on the borders of Lake Michigan, in the new Territory of Wisconsin, of Mr. Lapham, at Milwauke, all engaged in bringing to the light of day, the hidden treasures of their several districts. Of our South Western States we regret not to be able to give a more favorable account; but we have not the pleasure of knowing personally, or by report, a single botanist, or collector of plants, resident in Tennessee, Alabama, Mississippi, Arkansas or Missouri. What a wide, interesting and almost exhaustless field for future exploration! In Louisiana Dr. Clarendon Peck has made some investigation into the plants of Sicily Island; and Drs. Hale and Ingalls are respectively engaged in the exploration of the country adjacent to Alexandria and New Orleans. Whilst the extreme limits of our frontier borders have

*A Synopsis of the Flora of the Western States; by John L. Riddell, M. D. &c. Cincinnati, 1835, pp. 116.

been occasionally more or less attentively examined and explored by Drs. Leavenworth and Pitcher, Surgeons in the U. S. Army, as they have happened to be stationed at the different outposts. This list of labourers in the wide-spread field of Western Botany we trust is far from being complete—at all events we hope it may be rapidly augmented, by the addition of zealous devotees in all quarters, until the vegetable riches of this vast territory are fully ascertained!

In connexion with these desultory remarks on the progress of Botany in Western America, it may not be irrelevant to observe that, some two or three years ago, at the instance of the Lexington Medical Society, we read before it a paper on the subject of collecting and preserving plants for Herbaria, which, having been printed and extensively circulated, has received the commendation of those best qualified to judge of the matter; and we trust the directions therein given, will be found useful in diffusing a general knowledge of that important point in practical Botany—the formation of perfect specimens.

In conclusion, we regret not to have been able to give, in the proper place, some account of the discoveries of Dr. Scouler and M. Chamisso, on the Western coast of the Continent. The former of these gentlemen accompanied one of the British expeditions of discovery; and the latter was naturalist to a Russian voyage of exploration under Kotzebue.— Both have contributed valuable materials towards a Flora of the Pacific coast; but we are not sufficiently acquainted with the particulars of them to enter into any detail. The same may be said of two other botanists of our own country, Dr. L. C. Beck, of New York, and Mr. Schweinitz, of Pennsylvania; both of whom have performed tours through Ohio, Illinois and a part of Missouri, of which some notice has been published, by the former, in Silliman's Journal.

Lexington, Kentucky, August, 1836.

BIBLIOGRAPHIA BOTANICA
A NOTICE OF SOME OF THE MORE RECENT WORKS ON AMERICAN BOTANY

ART. VIII.—*Bibliographia Botanica. A Notice of some of the more recent works on American Botany.*

1. *A Flora of the Northern and Middle Sections of the United States; or, a Systematic Arrangement and Description of all the Plants hitherto discovered in the United States, north of Virginia.* By JOHN TORREY, M. D. &c. &c. Vol. I. New-York, 1824. 8vo. pp. 519.

2. *A Compendium of the Flora of the Northern and Middle States; containing generic and specific descriptions of all the Plants, exclusive of the Cryptogamia, hitherto found in the United States, north of the Potomac.* By JOHN TORREY, M. D. &c. &c. New-York, 1826—1 Vol. 12mo. pp. 403.

3. *Musci Americani; or Specimens of the Mosses collected in British North America, and chiefly among the Rocky Mountains, during the Second Land Arctic Expedition under the command of Captain Franklin, R. N.* By THOMAS DRUMMOND, Assistant Naturalist to the Expedition.—Vols. 2. 4to. Glasgow, 1828.

4. *Flora Boreali-Americana; or, the Botany of the Northern Parts of British America; compiled chiefly from the Plants collected by Dr. Richardson and Mr. Drummond on the late Northern Expeditions, under the command of Captain Sir John Franklin, R. N. To which are added (by permission of the Horticultural Society of London) those of Mr. Douglas from North West America; and other Naturalists.* By WILLIAM JACKSON HOOKER, LL. D. Regius Professor of Botany in the University of Glasgow, &c. &c. &c. Published under the authority of the Right Honorable the Secretary of State for Colonial Affairs. Vol. I. 4to. London, 1833.

5. *Botany of the Northern and Middle States; or a Description of the Plants found in the United States, north of Virginia, arranged according to the Natural System. With a synopsis of the Genera according to the Linnean System—a Sketch*

of the Rudiments of Botany, and a Glossary of terms. By
LEWIS C. BECK, M. D. &c. 12mo. Albany, 1833.

6. *North American Gramineæ and Cyperaceæ.* By ASA GRAY,
M. D. Parts I and II. Folio—New York, 1834, 1835.

It must be in the highest degree gratifying to the naturalist, to witness the ardour with which the Botany of North America has been recently investigated, and the rapidity with which books of standard excellence, are multiplying on this branch of science. When we first entered on this pursuit, some twenty years ago, it was with extreme difficulty that a single copy of Michaux's Flora* could be obtained in Philadelphia, and the possession of that one we owe to the liberality of Mr. John Vaughan, the venerable and active librarian of the American Philosophical Society. At that time this work was the only one which had been published on the general Botany of North America, with the exception of Muhlenberg's Catalogue,† which was a bare enumeration of the plants then known as natives or naturalized. Some time before this, however, in 1785, the Arbustrum Americanum‡ of Marshall had been issued, in which was given a very good account of the forest trees and shrubs, then known as natives of North America; and this little work is now entitled to antiquarian veneration as being the very first book ever issued from the American press on American Botany.

We do not mean to say that the work of Marshall was the earliest work devoted to an elucidation of American Botany.

---

* *Flora Boreali—Americana,* sistens caracteres plantarum quas in America Septentrionali collegit et detexit Andreas Michaux. Tabulis Æneis 51 ornata. 2 vols. 8vo. Paris.

† A catalogue of the hitherto known native and naturalized plants of North America, arranged according to the sexual system of Linnæus. By Henry Muhlenberg, D. D. Minister at Lancaster, in Pennsylvania—1813.

‡ *Arbustrum Americanum:* The American grove, or an alphabetical catalogue of forest trees and shrubs, native of the American United States, &c. &c. By Humphrey Marshall, Philadelphia, 1785. 1 vol 8vo. pp. 174.

The Flora Virginica* of Gronovius preceded it nearly twenty years; Catesby's History of Carolina† more than ten; and the Flora Americæ Septentrionalis‡ of Foster, about the same length of time, viz. in 1771. The Flora Caroliniana of Walter§ was of still later date.

Some years after the publication of the Flora of the elder Michaux just alluded to, his son gave to the world his elegant work, the Sylva Americana;‖ in which many additional trees and shrubs are added to the list of Marshall, with full descriptions and beautiful figures of all; it is a work which should be in the hands of every educated farmer and physician of the country.

Next to these appeared two large and laboured works on the general botany of America—the excellent Flora of Pursh,¶ (for notwithstanding its many glaring defects, it is an excellent work), and the still more excellent Genera of Nuttall;**

* Flora Virginica exhibens plantas quas nobilissimus vir D. D. Johannes Claytonus, Med. Doct. &c. &c. in Virginia crescentes observavit, collegit et obtulit D. Joh. Fred. Gronovio, &c. &c.—Lugduni Batavorum. 1762—4to. pp. 180.

† The natural History of Carolina, Florida and the Bahama Islands; containing the figures of birds, beasts, fishes, serpents, insects and plants. By Mark Catesby, F. R. S. London: 1771. 2 vols. folio.

‡ Under this imposing name was published by John Reinhold Foster, F. A. S. a meagre catalogue of the then known plants of North America. London: 1771.

§ Flora Caroliniana, secundum systema vegetabilium perillustris Linnæi digesta, &c. &c. Autore Thomas Walter, Agricola. Londini: 1788.

‖ The North American Sylva; or a description of the forest trees of the United States, Canada and Nova Scotia, &c. &c. Illustrated by 156 colored engravings. By T. Andrew Michaux, Paris: 1819. 3 vols. large 8vo. (The English translation; the French copy was published some years before.)

¶ Flora Americæ Septentrionalis; or a systematic arrangement and description of the plants of North America. Containing, besides what have been described by preceding authors, many new and rare species, collected during twelve years travels and residence in that country. By Frederick Pursh. 2 vols. 8vo. with 24 engravings. London: 1814.

** The Genera of North American Plants, and a catalogue of the spe-

and subsequently down to this time the Manual of Professor Eaton* has passed through six successive editions, thereby giving the surest warrant of its usefulness. It has perhaps, indeed, contributed more to a general knowledge of the plants of North America than any other one book. In the meanwhile we have been favoured with the publication of several very valuable local Floras, or descriptions of the plants of peculiar districts; as the Florula Bostoniensis† of Dr. Bigelow—the Compendium Floræ Philadelphicæ‡ of Dr. Barton—the Florula Cestrica§ of Dr. Darlington, and the admirable sketch of the Botany of South Carolina and Georgia by Mr. Elliott. Whilst numerous detached papers, in the shape of monographs of particular genera and families; catalogues of the plants of peculiar districts; descriptions of genera and species newly discovered, &c. &c. have been given in separate publications, attached to other works, or through the pages of various period-

cies, to the year 1817. By Thomas Nuttall, F. L. S. 2 vols. 12mo. pp. 312 and 260. Philadelphia: 1818.

* *Manual of Botany* for NorthA merica; containing generic and specific descriptions of the indigenous plants and common cultivated exotics, growing north of the Gulf of Mexico. By Professor Amos Eaton. Albany: 1833. (sixth edition) pp. 644.

† *Florula Bostoniensis*. A collection of the plants of Boston and its vicinity, with their generic and specific characters, principal synonyms, descriptions, places of growth, and time of flowering. By Jacob Bigelow, M. D. Boston, 1824. (second edition) pp. 424.

‡ *Compendium Floræ Philadelphicæ;* containing a description of the indigenous and naturalized plants found within a circuit of ten miles around Philadelphia. By William P. C. Barton, M. D. &c. 2 vols. 12mo. Philadelphia: 1818.

§ *Florula Cestrica;* an essay towards a catalogue of the phænogamous plants, native and naturalized, growing in the vicinity of the borough of West Chester, Pennsylvania. By William Darlington, M. D. West Chester, 1826. 8vo. pp. 152. (An enlarged and improved edition of this valuable Flora is now in progress by the author.)

‖ A Sketch of the Botany of South Carolina and Georgia. By Stephen Elliott, L. L. D. 2 vols. 8vo.—pp. 606 and 744. Charleston, 1821–1824.

icals.* Among the contributors of this miscellaneous matter
to the general stock of our botanical science, may be found the
names of the Bartons, Bartram, Baldwyn, Cooper, Croom, Curtis,
Darlington, Dewey, the Eatons, Gray, Greene, Griswold, Gibbes,
Houghton, Hossack, James, Leconte, Leavenworth, Loomis, Muhlenberg, Mitchell, Nuttall, Oakes, Pickering, Peter, Rafinesque, Riddell, Schweinitz, Torrey, Short, &c. the most of
whom are well known to the world by their labours; and the
others, if they have not occupied the same distinguished station, have yet not laboured in vain.

Besides these efforts of American naturalists to diffuse a
knowledge of our vegetable productions, through the medium
of the press, their silent and unostentatious labours have been
both arduous and useful. Associations have been formed, and
are still forming, in various portions of the Union, for the
mutual instruction of their members and the public, in the
several departments of natural science, among which Botany
is deservedly a favourite in all. Individuals in different and distant situations are industriously engaged in the study and collection of the plants of their districts. A few of the surgeons
of our army, availing themselves of their stations on our frontier borders, are making known to us the rare and interesting
productions of these unknown regions; a decided improvement
is taking place in the manner of preserving specimens; a liberal interchange is going on among botanists in all parts of the
country: and from the particular quarter in which we write—
from Lexington alone—not less than fifteen thousand specimens

* A few of these papers have appeared in foreign journals. The pe-
riodicals of our own country in which botanical communications have
been chiefly published, are the Transactions of the American Philosophical Society—The American Journal of Science and Arts—The
New York Medical Repository—The Journal of the Academy of Natural Sciences of Philadelphia—The Annals of the New-York Lyceum—
The Journal of the Boston Society of Natural History—The Atlantic
Journal—The Western Review, (Lexington, Ky.)—The Western Journal of Medical and Physical Sciences, (Cincinnati, O.)—The Transylvania Journal of Medicine, &c. &c.

of western plants have been sent, in the course of the past year, (1835) to correspondents in various parts of Europe and America.

With these preliminary remarks on the progress of American Botany, we come now to the matter more immediately before us—a brief notice of some of the later publications on this branch of science; and this we give, not in the spirit of a critical reviewer, but mainly for the purpose of pointing out to the student of American Botany his best guides and helps: to give a detailed analysis of any one of the works, which head this article, would more than exceed the limits allotted to it.

The two works which head this paper are from the pen of one who is justly placed by his compeers at the head of American Botanists. They are devoted essentially to the same object—an elucidation of the Botany of the northern and eastern states: they are therefore *local Floras*, "the advantage of which," in the words of the author, "are now generally acknowledged; as their authors, it is presumed, must be better acquainted with the plants of which they treat, than with those of a more extensive district; they are the means of recording many facts and observations, and minute descriptions, which could not be introduced into general works." The works before us are based upon the Linnæan classification, and are intended to include all the phænogamous plants, as well as the ferns, of the district specified. Of the larger of these works, or the Flora, intended to occupy two volumes, the first has only yet been published, and it extends to the 11th Linnæan class, *Icosandria;* giving very full and satisfactory descriptions of all the known plants belonging to the eleven first classes, which are natives of, or naturalized within the prescribed limits. As this work from its necessary size may be inconvenient for reference in the field, the Compendium, comprising the essential generic and specific characters of all the plants described in the larger Flora, has been prepared: and whilst the Flora remains unfinished, the Compendium is complete within itself, embracing all the plants of all the classes down to the first order of Cryptogamia inclusive. As these works, though doubtless perfectly familiar to all our eastern brethren of the science, are yet comparatively unknown to western tyros, (for whose benefit chiefly we are induced to make this retrospective notice), we will give a specimen of description from each, to show their different scope and character. We take for example that common denizen of all the American continent, the

CLAYTONIA. *Gronovius.*

Calyx 2-leaved. *Petals* 5, emarginate. *Stigma* 3-cleft, *capsule* 1-celled, 3-valved, 3-5-seeded. *Seeds* reniform. *Gen. pl.* 402. *Nutt. Gen.* 1. p. 152. *Juss.* p. 314. *Lam. Ill.* t. CLIV. *Roem. & Schult. Gen.* 992. Nat. Ord. PORTULACEÆ *Juss.*

C. Virginica L. leaves linear-lanceolate; petals obovate retuse; leaves of the calyx somewhat acute; root tuberous. *Ait-Kew.* I. p. 284. *Willd. Spec.* 1. p. 1185. *Bot. Mag.* t. 941. *Mich. Fl.* I. p. 160. *Pursh Fl.* I. p. 175. *Elliott Sk.* I. p. 306. *Bart. Fl. Am. Sept.* t. 51. *Gron. Virg.* 25. *Roem. & Schult.* V. p. 433.

Root large, tuberous, fleshy. *Stem* erect or procumbent, very smooth, and a little succulent. Leaves on the stem about 2, opposite, thick, at first almost linear, but becoming broader with age, about 4 inches long. *Flowers* (6—12) in a loose simple raceme; peduncles gradually diminishing in length upwards; the lowest ones more than an inch long. Leaves of the *calyx* oblong, persistent. *Petals* twice as long as the calyx, pale rose-colour, with darker veins. *Stamens* shorter than the petals, and inserted at their claws; filaments dilated at the base; *anthers* oblong, 2-celled. *Style* longer than the stamens; *stigmas* linear, spreading. *Capsule* ovate-globose. *Seeds* compressed, black, shining.

HAB. In moist shady woods; common. April—May."

Flora, Vol. I. p. 259.

"CLAYTONIA. *Cal.* 2-leaved. *Pet.* 5, emarginate. *Stig.* 3-cleft. *Caps.* 1-celled, 3-valved, 3-5 seeded. *Seeds* reniform. PORTULACEÆ.

"*C. Virginica.* leaves linear-lanceolate; petals obovate, retuse; leaves of the calyx somewhat acute; root tuberous.

"HAB. moist woods. April—May. Perennial. Smooth, erect or procumb. leav. few, oppos.; fl. racem., rose-col."

Compendium, p. 94–119.

From these extracts it will be at once perceived, that whilst the first and larger work contains full and minute descriptions, with copious reference to authorities, and all the synonyms, where they obtain; those of the other are contracted and abbreviated within the narrowest compass compatible with accuracy. It is thus rendered a convenient and portable *vademecum*; for the pocket and the field; while the former is admirably adapted for the more minute investigations of the closet and the study.

We regard them both, then, as admirable works in their different lines, and have only to add our regrets to those of all Botanists of the country—we would not fear to add, to all Botanists of the world—that the Flora has remained so long unfinished. Twelve years have now elapsed since the publication of the first volume, and yet the second is not forthcoming; nor have we any assurances that it soon will be! This delay does not arise, we are sure, from any lessened interest, or abated ardour, on the part of its author, in the matters of which it treats: on the contrary, we have every reason to believe—to know indeed—that both his ardour and interest in the Botany of his country are still growing and increasing, with his growing years and increasing knowledge. Why, then, does he not complete an undertaking, which has already redounded so much to his reputation, and which is so well calculated to spread abroad an interest in this delightful science? Not only do the interests of the science call loudly for the second volume of the Flora, but also for a second edition of the Compendium; we believe that the first is entirely out of print.

It is said that our author is industriously engaged in an extensive work on the general Botany of North America; and it is hinted, moreover, that he has become so exclusively devoted to the *Natural system,* as to have lost all toleration for that of

Linnæus. But, surely, neither of these considerations should
be allowed to interfere with the completion of a work begun
upon the Linnæan—we do not like to say, the *Artificial system*—and half finished in so satisfactory a manner. A local
Flora of the character of that before us, is the best *avant
courier* of a general one; and there is no one to whose hands
we whould so soon confide a great work on the Botany of North
America as DOCTOR TORREY.

The Musci Americani of Drummond, though a very valuable and highly useful work on its peculiar branch of American
Botany, is, of course, a work altogether different in character,
from those just noticed. It consists of specimens of American
Mosses, collected chiefly in the British possessions, and mostly
among the Rocky Mountains, during a late tour of discovery
under the command of Captain Franklin of the Royal Navy;
to which expedition the author was assistant naturalist, his associate being Dr. John Richardson, Surgeon. These specimens, like all others, by the same hand, are well preserved; and
being neatly fastened to the leaves of two 8vo. volumes, are
very conveniently examined. They are accompanied with
printed labels giving the numbers, names, authorities, synonyms, habitats, &c. &c. as in the following:

230. Climacium dendroides. *Schwaegr. Richardson in Franklin's
Jour. ed.* 2, *app. p.* 41.
Hypnum dendroides. *Hooker et Taylor. Musc. Brit. ed.* 2. *p.*
168, *t.* 25. *Drummond, Musc. Scot. v. I: No.* 85.
HAB.—About Beaver Lake—the Columbia River, &c.

In the volumes before us we have specimens of two hundred
and eighty six mosses, whereof seventy-four are species and
varieties of the genus *Hypnum;* thirty-four of *Dicranum;*
thirty of *Bryum;* fourteen of *Splanchnum;* fourteen of *Ortho-
trichium;* twelve of *Polytrichium;* eleven of *Tortula;* &c. &c.
It is, therefore, easy to perceive how great the assistance which
the well authenticated specimens of this work are capable of
affording to the student, in this difficult, minute and interesting department of Botany.

The author was, perhaps, the most laborious, indefatigable

and pains-taking collector of this or any other age; and besides the work before us, the Flora Boreali-Americana of Professor Hooker, and the Fauna* of Dr. Richardson, as well as the valuable natural history details in the appendix to Franklin's Journal, are, in great part, the fruits of his collections in the various departments of natural science. The Herbarium, indeed, which was taken to Great Britain, on the return of this expedition, was so large as of itself to justify the publication of a Flora of the vast regions through which it passed. In the prosecution of the general objects of this enterprize, hardships, dangers and privations, of the most appalling nature, were suffered; and among these an incident, which occurred in the collection of materials for the present work, will serve to show the enthusiastic ardor of its author, and may not be uninteresting to the reader.

"Having crossed the Assinaboyne River, the party halted to breakfast, and I went on before them for a few miles, to procure specimens of a *Jungermannia*, which I had previously observed in a small rivulet on our track. On this occasion I had a narrow escape from the jaws of a grisly bear; for, while passing through a small open glade, intent upon discovering the moss of which I was in search, I was surprised by hearing a sudden rush and then a harsh growl, just behind me; and on looking round, I beheld a large bear approaching towards me, and two young ones making off in a contrary direction as fast as possible. My astonishment was great; for I had not calculated upon seeing these animals so early in the season, and this was the first I had met with. She halted within two or three yards of me, growling and rearing herself on her hind feet, then suddenly wheeled about, and went off in the direction the young ones had taken, probably to ascertain whether they were safe. During this momentary absence, I drew from my gun the small shot with which I had been firing at ducks during the morning, and which, I was well aware, would avail me nothing against so large and powerful a creature, and replaced it with ball. The bear, meanwhile, had advanced and retreated two or three times, apparently more furious than ever; halting at each interval within a shorter and shorter distance of me, always raising herself on her hind legs, and growling a

---

*Fauna Boreali—Americana; Or the Zoology of the Northern parts of British America; containing descriptions of the objects of natural history collected on the late northern land expedition; by John Richardson, M.D. &c. Surgeon and Naturalist to the expedition. 1 vol. 8vo. Part 1. containing the Quadrupeds, London, 1829-

horrible defiance, and at length approaching to within the length of my gun from me. Now was my time to fire; but judge of my alarm and mortification, when I found that my gun would not go off! The morning had been wet, and the damp had communicated to the powder. My only resource was to plant myself firm and stationary, in the hope of disabling the bear by a blow on her head with the butt end of my gun, when she should throw herself on me to seize me. She had gone and returned ten or a dozen times, her rage apparently increasing with her additional confidence, and I momentarily expected to find myself in her gripe, when the dogs belonging to the brigade made their appearance, but on beholding the bear they fled with all possible speed. The horsemen were just behind, but such was the surprise and alarm of the whole party, that though there were several hunters and at least half-a-dozen guns among them, the bear made her escape unhurt, passing one of the horsemen, (whose gun, like mine, missed fire,) and apparently intimidated by the number of the party. For the future, I took care to keep my gun in better order, but I found, by future experience, that the best mode of getting rid of the bears when attacked by them, was to rattle my vasculum, or specimen box, when they immediately decamp. This is the animal described by Lewis and Clark in their Travels on the Missouri, and so much dreaded by the Indians. My adventure with the bear did not, however, prevent my accomplishing the collecting of the *Jungermannia*. It is No. 17 of the "American Mosses."*

We come in the next place to notice the most splendid offering ever yet made at the shrine of American Botany; and those of our readers whose eyes have been blessed with the vision, can have no difficulty in understanding our allusion to be to the *Flora Boreali-Americana*, of Professor Hooker. In the compilation of this great work, ample materials were at the author's hands, and the manner in which they have been used is such as to redound, in the most signal manner, to his credit, as an accurate, industrious and philosophic Botanist. It is, indeed, a matter of no small astonishment, that so complete a Flora of so vast a region could have been given by one, who himself never visited any portion of it; and it must be supposed that the materials furnished by others for this work, were of the best possible kind, or such a structure, under such circumstances, could never have been built of them.

* Sketch of a Journey to the Rocky Mountains and to the Columbia River, by Thomas Drummond, &c. *Hooker's Botanical Miscellany*, vol. 1, p. 197.

Of these the most valuable were the extensive Herbaria carried to England by the return of the second exploring party under the command of Franklin, and which reached its destination "in the finest possible preservation." It included extensive collections made in three different portions of the country.

"1. That of Captain Franklin and his officers, upon the coasts of the Arctic Seas, from the mouth of the MacKenzie river, westward towards Behring's Straits. 2. That of Dr. Richardson, principally obtained from the shores of the same sea, to the eastward of the MacKenzie river, and between it and the Copper-mine river; and comprising among many other rarities, probably the whole of the species which were unfortunately lost in the former expedition. And 3dly, The portion collected by Mr. Drummond, the Assistant Naturalist; by far the most extensive as may be supposed, of the three, since his whole time was devoted to forming collections, and in the most fertile part of the country;—that is to say, from the whole extent of the inland route of the expedition, through Canada and the Hudson Bay Company's territories; and from that very interesting district, too, which Mr. Drummond alone was charged to visit; namely, the most elevated chain of the Rocky Mountains, a part of that vast ridge, extending in an almost uninterrupted line to the Andes of South America, and which no Botanist had previously explored. This combined herbarium is so extensive that it, alone, would justify the preparation of a Flora of that vast region. But with these he has the opportunity of incorporating all the previous discoveries of the same travellers on the former overland expedition; of Captain Parry, and other Arctic voyagers; together with the plants of Newfoundland and Labrador, gathered by Dr. Morrison, who afterwards fell a victim to his courage and love of science in exploring Central Africa; the botanical productions of Canada, which have been received from the Lady Dalhousie, Mrs. Percival, Mr. Sheppard and Mr. Todd, &c. those of Northwest America, gathered by Mr. Menzies and Dr. Scouler; together with herbaria which will be more particularly noticed in the work itself. All these, too, Dr Hooker is enabled to compare with a great number of the species of the United States, which he has received with their names from the authors of most of the Floras of that country, and will serve to clear up many points which must otherwise have remained doubtful."*

The publication of this work was commenced in 1829; and down to 1833 inclusive, six parts or numbers have been issued,

* Botanical Miscellany, vol. I. p. 93.—1829.

forming the volume before us—a heavy quarto of 350 pages of close letter-press, and 118 copperplate engravings by Mr. Swan, and consequently in the first line of the art, from drawings made by the author himself and his friend Dr. Greville, of Edinburgh; both of whom possess in an eminent degree the tact, so necessary to the Botanist, of admirable graphic delineation. These plates are chiefly devoted to the representation of new and interesting species, or such as have not previously been figured. We find among them many properly dedicated to individuals who have done and suffered much to advance the cause of American Botany; such as *Parrya macrocarpa, Picradenia Richardsoni, Viola Nutallii, Astragalus Drummondi, Silene Menziesii, Parnasia Kotzbuei, Clematis Douglasii, Rhamnus Purshianus, Saxifraga Jamesii, Bartonia lævicaulis*—a beautiful genus which we are gratified in seeing thus identified with one of the patriarchs of American Botany, in place of the humble *Centaurella*.

The matter of the work is arranged after the natural system; and this first volume reaches to the extensive order *Compositæ*, but part of which it includes. At what time the eager desires of the public are to be gratified with any part or the whole of the 2d volume, seems undetermined; but we fear that in consequence of the recent failure of the publishers, (Treuttel & Wurtz, London,) we shall have ample opportunity for the exercise of philosophic patience, and the enjoyment of the pleasures of hope deferred. When completed, however, it will be an invaluable addition to the library of the American Naturalist; and will identify the names of Hooker and Richardson, Douglas and Drummond with the cause of American Botany.

By the volume under notice, a great number of new species have been added to the American Flora; of these some which were published in the first part, have been introduced into the 6th edition of Eaton's Manual—the most recent work on the general Botany of this continent. The greater portion, however, have not yet appeared in any other work than that before us. Thus in the extensive tribe of *Leguminosæ*, which seems to abound in the high latitudes, we find 17 new species of *Lupinus*, 10 of *Phaca*, 8 of *Astragalus;* besides several belonging to the genera *Oxytropis, Hossackia, Psoralea, Trifolium*, &c. Among the *Rosaceæ* are 15 hitherto undescribed species of *Potentilla* and 13 of *Rubus;* of the *Saxifrageæ* 22 species of *Saxifraga*, and 5 of *Heuchera* are new; among the *Carophylleæ*, *Onograriæ* and *Grossulariæ*, we meet with 7 species of *Arenaria*, 6 of *Silene*, 6 of *Stellaria*, 12 of *Œnothera*, 7 of *Epilobium* and 10 of *Ribes*, not yet introduced into any other work on American Botany.

To give a specimen of the work we will extract the description of that common plant, the *Silene Virginica.*

"8. *S. Virginica;* viscoso pubescens, caule procumbente assurgente ramoso, foliis lanceolatis inferioribus longissime petiolatis basi longe ciliatis, floribus magnis paniculatis, calycibus amplo clavatis, petalis longe unguiculatis, latis bifidis coronatis. D. C.—*Linn. Sp. Pl. p.* 600! *Mich. Am. v. I. p.* 272. *Pursh. Fl. Am. v. I. p.* 316. *Elliott. Carol. v. I. p.* 516. *Torrey Fl. of U. S. v. I. p.* 450. *De Cand. Prodr. v. I. p.* 379.

"Hab. Lake Huron. Dr. *Todd*—There are several specimens of this plant in Dr. Todd's collection, but the corolla is so much withered and faded that I cannot satisfy myself whether it is the *S. Virginica* or *Pennsylvanica;* nor, indeed, do I understand the difference between the two species. The present individual has its petals deeply bifid, on which account I refer it to *S. Virginica;* but Elliott assures us that the petals vary in having the limb entire or divided. The colour of *S. Virginica* is said to be a bright crimson, that of *S. Pennsylvanica* a bright purple (*Elliott*), purplish white (*Bigelow*). Torrey unites the *S. Catesbæi*, of Walt. to this, which, judging from Dr. Schweinitz's specimens, is very different, and more allied to *S. regia*, Bot. Mag. t. 1724."

Flor. Bor. Am. Vol. I. p. 90.

We have designedly selected the above description and remarks because our author expresses doubts on a subject, about which no American Botanist has any; and to show the spirit with which he, in common with all great minds, acknowledges an error. Soon after the publication of the second part of the Flora, the writer of this article sent to Dr. Hooker a parcel of plants of Kentucky, containing specimens of both these *Silenes*, together with a drawing of *S. Virginica.* This drawing was promptly published in Curtis's Botanical Magazine, of which Dr. H. is editor, with the following remarks:

"In the Flora Boreali-Americana, v. I. p. 90, I expressed a doubt whether the *Silene Virginica*, of which I had then only very indifferent specimens at my command, were really different from the *S. Pennsylvanica*. But my valued friend———, of———, has cleared up all my difficulties on this point, and by a beautiful drawing of the former; (which though said in the Hortus Kewensis to be introduced to our collections by Mr. Loddiges in 1783, I have never seen in our gardens,) and by excellent specimens of both, with remarks upon them, has enabled me to give the accompanying representation and description."*

Every part, indeed, of the work before us bears honorable testimony to the courtesy and liberality of its author towards the Botanists of America; and scarcely a page occurs which does not make mention of Nuttall or Torrey, of Bigelow or Boott, Schweinitz or Elliott, in terms of commendation.

Lest, however, we should be accused of too great partiality for this *Magnus Apollo*, and of having given too unqualified eulogy to his *magnum opus*, we will in conclusion venture to find a fault or two with them. In the first place, then, we object to the *price* of the book. The single quarto volume before us, with uncoloured plates, cost us, even with University exemption from duty, forty dollars! This may suit well enough the princely purses of European Naturalists, but it ill comports with that *res angusta domi* which is unfortunately the fate of too many of those of America. Will not the publishers issue, in some shape, a cheaper edition, that its usefulness may be more generally diffused? In the second place we find fault with the *name* of the book; and we cannot but express a sincere regret that this work, in every respect so worthy of its author, should have been published under the same name with that of the elder Michaux. For although the title is more strictly applicable to the Flora now under consideration, yet having been so long ago adopted by the enterprising, accurate and unfortunate Frenchman, it should not, we think, at this day have been encroached on by the liberal, learned and magnanimous Briton. We much fear, morever, that confusion will grow out of future references to two such different works under the same name. Would not Dr. Hooker have found an equally

*Botanical Magazine, 3342. London, 1834.

appropriate title, and one free from all objections of this sort, in *Flora Britanico-Americana?*

The work of Dr. Beck next claims our attention; and its publication constitutes an era of some notoriety in the annals of American Botany; as it is the first work of the kind, in our country, based upon the *Natural orders*. In the year 1815 "the learned Portugese" M. Correa de Serra published a reduction of all the Genera of Plants contained in Muhlenberg's Catalogue, to the natural families of M. de Jussieu's system, for the use of a class in Elementary and Philosophical Botany in Philadelphia; and very recently Professor Torrey has appended to his edition of Lindley's Introduction to the natural system, a much more copious catalogue of North American Genera, arranged according to Lindley's modification of the natural orders; but Dr. Beck is the first American to found on this system a Treatise on the plants of a large district. He has consequently very properly given a few pages to "the Rudiments of Botany, and the characters of the natural orders, which are arranged according to the method of Jussieu as modified by De Candolle." "And, to accommodate those who wish to investigate plants according to the artificial system, a synopsis of the genera is also introduced, containing under each genus a reference to the natural order, and the page where the species are described." "In this part of the work it has been my object to give an accurate and sufficiently detailed description, together with the habitat and geographical range of each species, and such popular characters and illustrations as it was thought would be an additional guide to the beginner."* But here, as before, it will be best that we should allow the descriptions to speak for themselves; selecting, as usual, the most familiar illustrations.

"CLASS II. ENDOGENÆ OR MONOCOTYLEDONOUS PLANTS.

"*Trunk* usually cylindrical, with no perceptible distinction of bark, wood and pith, increasing in diameter by the addition of new matter to the centre. *Leaves* frequently sheathing at the base and not readily separating from the stem by an arti-

*Preface, pp. 6.7.

culation, mostly alternate, with parallel simple nerves and minute transverse veins. *Embryo* with but one cotyledon; if with two, then the additional one is imperfect and alternate with the other; radicle usually enclosed within the substance of the embryo, through which it bursts when germinating."

Subclass I. PETALOÍDEÆ. *Lind.*

"*Stamens* and *pistils* naked or covered by verticillate floral envelopes.

Order CXXIII. LILIACEÆ. *Juss. Lind.*

"*Perianth* coloured, regular, 6-divided. *Stamens* 6, perigynous, opposite the segments of the perianth. *Ovary* superior, 3-celled; *style* 1; *stigma* simple, or 3-lobed. *Capsule* 3-celled, 3-valved, with a loculicidal dehiscence. *Seeds* numerous, usually flat, packed one above the other in 1 or 2 rows, with a spongy dilated integument; *embryo* straight, in the axis of fleshy albumen; *radicle* next the hilum.

Plants with scaly *bulbs* or arborescent *stems*. *Leaves* with parallel veins."

ERYTHRONIUM. *Linn.*

"*Perianth* campanulate, 6-parted; segments reflexed; the 3 inner ones with a callous tooth on each side near the base, and a nectariferous pore. *Stamens* 6. *Capsule* substipitate. *Seeds* ovate.   *Hexandria. Monogynia.*

1. *E. americanum Smith:* leaves lanceolate, punctate; segments of the perianth oblong-lanceolate, obtuse at the point; inner ones bidentate near the base; style clavate; stigma entire.—*E. lanceolatum Pursh.—E. dens canis Mich.*

Hab. Wet meadows. Can. to Geor. April, May. Per.—Scape 6—8 inches high. *Leaves* 2, radical. *Flower* solitary, terminal, yellow.   *Dogtoothed Violet.*

2. *E. albidum Nutt.* leaves elliptical-lanceolate, not punctate; segments of the perianth linear-lanceolate, obtuse; inner ones without dentures, subunguiculate; style filiform; stigma 3-cleft; lobes reflexed.

Hab. Wet meadows. Can. and N. Y. W. to Miss. April, May. Per. *Scape* 6 inches high. *Flower* white, segments thick and somewhat obtuse.—Very abundant near Albany, N. Y. and also found in Canada by D. Thomas, Esq. I have observed a plant at New-Brunswick, N. J. which agrees with this in the absence of dentures and in the trifid stigma, but the perianth is yellow. It is probably the same which is alluded to by Mr. Nuttall, (Gen. Pl. i. 223,) and may prove distinct.   *White Erythronium.*

3. "*E. bracteatum* Big: leaves lanceolate, unequal; scape bracted. HAB. High mountains. Ver. June. Per.—*Leaves* very unequal, one being two or three times as large as the other *Scape* shorter than the leaves, with a narrow lanceolate bract 1—2 inches below the flower, which is yellow, half as large as in No. 1; the segments gibbous at base."—pp. 341. 361. 365.

Our author has adopted in this work all the most recent nomenclature, and, in some cases we fear, has given too ready currency to innovations perhaps too hastily proposed. We subscribe, with all readiness, to his opinion that "Botany is a progressive science, and it would be strange, indeed, if the labours of Botanists, since the time of Linnæus should not have resulted in a more correct knowledge of plants,"* as well in regard to their nomenclature as their affinities. But at the same time we venture to be old-fashioned enough to express an opinion that 'since the time of Linnæus' but few such masterspirits have appeared on the field of nature; and that many inferior ones, who have pretended to revolutionize and reform the science, have but rendered 'confusion worse confounded.'

We object not, of course, to many of the new or recent names which we find in the volume before us; the most of them are doubtless adopted on amply sufficient grounds; and we hail with pleasure, because it facilitates the enquiries of the student, the division of all extensive genera, when that can be done without a violation of nature, or a reference to hair-splitting distinctions. But when we see a genus of but limited extent, severed into as many distinct genera as there were species under it, and bare varieties converted into distinct species, we are compelled to enquire, *Cui bono, et quowarranto?* We candidly confess that it was not without some querulous misgivings of this sort, that we found in the volume before us our favourite, and as we fondly hoped, well-established genus *Prenanthes*, metamorphosed into *Harpalyce; Cleome* not sufficiently thinned by colonizing *Polanisia*, sending another to *Gynandropsis;* and the old unfortunate *Convallaria*, whose misfortunes appear to be increasing with its years, after being cut up

*Preface. p, 5.

into *Majanthemum, Smilacina, Polygonatum, Dracœna* and *Convallaria* proper, meets with still more merciless dissection, and is still farther dismembered into *Clintonia* and *Styrandra!* In justice to our author, however, it is proper that we should assign his reasons for the last named innovations. Under *Styrandra*, he says:

"After a most careful examination of the subject, I have determined to adopt the views of Mr. Rafinesque, in regard to the Linnæan genus *Convallaria*. The habit and flowers of these plants are so widely different, that it is almost impossible to present any collective characters. I am as much opposed as any one, to unnecessary division, but the very purpose of botanical arrangement is frustrated when a genus is allowed to have such an unnatural range.—See *Raf. Med. Bot.* ii. 84."

So much in regard to a few of the new names we find in the volume before us—a word or two more on a few old ones, and the plants bearing them, in reference to which we venture to differ from our author, and we are done. We are, then, yet to be convinced that *Dodecatheon Meadia* and *D. integrifolium* are really distinct species; and could we have the pleasure of our author's company in a single excursion, we doubt not we should be able to convince him that *Trifolium stoloniferum* differs as much from *T. reflexum*, as any other two clovers; nor would he hesitate to pronounce with us that our *Hottonia inflata* differs *toto cœlo* from the *H. palustris* of Europe, the testimony of Pursh to the contrary notwithstanding.

The volumes of Dr. Gray stand last in our caption. "The object of this work," as expressed in the introduction to the first volume," is "to place in the hands of our Botanists and others who take an interest in North American Plants, authentic specimens of the GRAMINEÆ and CYPERACEÆ of this country."

"The grasses and Cyperaceous plants appear to be less understood, both at home and abroad, than the other phænogamous plants of this country, except by a few who have made them a particular study; and the author has thought that a work like the present, would, in some degree, extend our knowledge of these plants, and be serviceable to those for for whom it was designed."

This work then is of the same character with that of Drummond already mentioned, though devoted to subjects of more universal interest; consisting of authentic specimens of the American Grasses and the allied Cyperaceous tribe, well selected and preserved, and fastened to the leaves of folio volumes. This plan is certainly well adapted to extend an accurate knowledge of these vegetable tribes which are obtainable in sufficient number for the purpose; and which, like the grasses and mosses, differ from each other in such minute particulars as almost to defy sufficiently accurate description. Such specimens are, indeed, in many respects better than coloured engravings—the cost of which, besides, is so great as almost to preclude their use in our country.

In the two volumes or parts before us, we have specimens of two hundred grasses and cyperoid plants, one hundred in each volume; generally two specimens of each species are given, and frequently more where they are small, and exhibit any marked variety. They are accompanied by printed labels, giving the established name of the species, according to the most recent and approved authorities in this line of Botany, together with full synonyms, habitat, &c. This will be best seen by exhibiting one of these labels.

"14 Muhlenbergia Mexicana. *Trin. Gram. Unif. p.* 189.
  Agrostis Mexicana. *L. Willd. Spec. vol. I. p.* 374. *Spreng. Syst. Veg. vol. I. p.* 263. *Roem. & Schult. v. II. p.* 373. *Muhl. Gram. p.* 67.

A. lateriflora. *Mich. Fl. v. I. p.* 53. *Spreng. Syst. Veg. v. I. p.* 258.
 Roem. & Schult. v. II. p. 353. *Torrey, Flora, v. I. p.* 86.
A. filiformis. *Muhl. Gram. p.* 66.
A. lateriflora, *var. filiformis. Torrey, Fl. v. I. p.* 86.
A. foliosa. *Roem. & Schult. v. II. p.* 373.
Muhlenbergia foliosa. *Trin. Gram. Unif. p.* 190.
M. clandestina. *Trin. Gram. Unif. p.* 190.
 Agrostis clandestina. *Spreng. Mant.* 1. *p.* 82. *Roem. & Schult. v. II. p.* 369. *non Muhl. Elliott & Torrey.*

HAB.—Western part of the State of New York."

We have selected one of the longest labels, for the purpose of showing their value in regard to the synonyms, but we beg our western neophytes not to suppose that all our grasses are loaded with the same multiplicity of names. It must be honestly confessed, however, to the beginner in the study of this difficult but important tribe, that no other families, have been so much confused by conflicting names. We trust, however, that all this confusion will now soon be done away, considering the very able hands which are now engaged in the work of reform; and although in this revolution we must expect to have much, (as we thought,) well settled nomenclature, up-rooted, still we submit cheerfully for the general good. Thus in the work before us we find our old acquaintance the *Cinna arundinacea*, ranked under the banner of *Muhlenbergia*, and several of the *Agrostes* turned over to *Vilfa*.

The two published volumes of this valuable work contain specimens of sixty-three species of *Carex*, fifteen of *Poa*, fourteen of *Panicum*, fourteen of *Scirpus*, eight of *Cyperus*, eight of *Muhlenbergia*, five of *Rhyncospora*, four of *Vilfa*, &c. &c. A few new species are given which are accompanied by descriptions, and a full index is appended to each volume. We are delighted to find that it is the intention of the author to prosecute the undertaking "if sufficiently encouraged," until a complete Herbarium of American Gramineæ and Cyperaceæ is given. Surely no more acceptable service could possibly be rendered to the Botanical public; and surely no Botanist will refuse the aid necessary to carry on and complete so laudable an undertaking. We are informed that arrangements have been made with Botanists in different sections of the United States, for the collection of the grasses that are peculiar to their several districts: and it has afforded the writer of this notice much pleasure to contribute, for the ensuing volume, many of those of Kentucky.

Before taking leave of this work it may not be amiss to state, that its author is now engaged in printing an elementary book on the Principles of Botany—a work which has been long and much needed in our country. We are not sufficiently informed as to the precise character and scope of the work to say more; but judging from a small specimen with which we have been favoured, we cannot doubt that it will be of most essential assistance to the student. It will be published in duodecimo form, and be illustrated with a great number of characteristic and well executed wood-cuts.

We inadvertently omitted to mention in the proper place, among the preceding publications on American Botany, three works more especially devoted to its Medical Flora, by Barton,* Bigelow† and Rafinesque,‡ the first two of which, in addition to much useful information concerning the medical properties of many American plants, exhibit, in the accompanying plates, creditable evidences of the progress of the fine arts in our country.

Another work, however, by the first named gentleman is more especially entitled to our notice as its objects are directed to a general Flora of North America.§ The publication of this last was commenced in 1821, and carried on periodically to the end of 1823. It contains coloured engravings, with descriptions of a number of North American plants, not previously figured, many of which are spirited and faithful. S.

*Vegetable Materia Medica of the United States; or Medical Botany: containing a Botanical general and medical history of medicinal plants indigenous to the United States, illustrated by coloured engravings, made after drawings from nature, done by the author. By William P. C. Barton, M. D. &c. 2 vol. 4to. Phila. 1818.

†American Medical Botany, being a collection of the native medical plants of the United States, containing their Botanical history and Chemical analysis, and properties and uses in Medicine, diet and the arts, with coloured engravings. By Jacob Bigelow, M. D. &c. 3 vol. large 8vo. Boston, 1818.

‡Medical Flora of the United States, with fifty wood-cuts. By C. S. Rafinesque, (PH. D.) &c. 2 vol. 12mo. Phila. 1828, 1830.

§A Flora of North America. Illustrated by coloured figures drawn from nature. By William P. C. Barton, M. D. &c. 3 vol. 4to. Phila. 1821, 1823.

PART III

BIOGRAPHICAL SKETCHES

BIOGRAPHICAL NOTICE
OF DR. FREDERICK RIDGELY,
LATE OF LEXINGTON, KENTUCKY

ART. XII. *Biographical notice of* DR. FREDERICK RIDGELY, *late of Lexington, Kentucky.*

Doctor Ridgely, descended from parentage of the first respectability, was born on Elkridge, Annarundel county in the State of Maryland, May 25th, 1757. Having pursued the common course of collegiate studies, at the Academy of Newark, in the State of Delaware, then the most flourishing school in that part of the country, he commenced, in his seventeenth year, the study of Medicine under the tuition of Dr. Philip Thomas of Fredericktown, a physician whose reputation was almost unrivalled.

How long his term of pupilage continued does not exactly appear, but he was no doubt drawn off from the labours of the closet and the shop, by the spirit-stirring temper of the times; for the great political events then brewing, pregnant with the destinies of half a world, found in our young physician's patriotic bosom, warmth and devotedness congenial to the occasion. At the first commencement of hostilities he promptly offered his personal services to his country, in that capacity in which they were most needed; and we have the fullest assurance of the proficiency which he had already made in the acquirement of professional knowledge, when, at the early age of nineteen, he was appointed surgeon to a corps of rifle-men, raised in the upper counties of Virginia, and the adjoining parts of Maryland, and commanded by Captains Stinson, Cresap, and Morgan, afterwards the illustrious General, whose name struck terror to the hearts of our enemy. With this detachment he marched to the North, where the cloud of impending warfare had already burst at Lexington, and arrived before Boston but a few days after the celebrated battle of Bunkers-hill, in June, 1775.

The capital of Massachusetts was at that time in possession of the British, under the command of General Gage: and in the long investment which followed, until the triumphant entry of the American army, under General Washington, Dr. Ridgely continued to fulfil the responsible station, and to discharge the arduous duties of hospital physician, rendered peculiarly arduous by the unusual sickness and mortality which at that time prevailed among the troops.

Adhering to the fortunes of his country, we see him following the army during the perilous campaign of 1776, when the gloom of despondency and the spirit of desertion seem to have seized upon all but the stoutest hearts. In the spring of 1777 his native state conferred upon him an additional mark of her regard, by appointing him surgeon to the 4th Maryland regiment of regulars, commanded by Col. Hall, Lieut. Col. Samuel Smith, the hero of Mud-Island and now Senator in Congress, and Major John Eager Howard, justly styled the Champion of the Cowpens, but whose military skill and prowess were conspicuous in every battle where he fought. United with this band of worthies the Doctor had the honor of participating, so far as his station permitted, in the descent on Staten-Island; the affair of White Marsh, the engagements of Brandywine and Germantown which shed such imperishable glory over the American arms, and gave to the world an earnest of the future darings of her yet unfledged eaglet.

In the spring and summer of 1778 we find our surgeon doing duty in the military hospitals, until October, when the British army having evacuated Philadelphia, and the American troops being about to go into winter quarters, he resigned his appointment; and availing himself of the opportunity which this respite afforded him, he attended a course of Medical Lectures under Drs. Shipp, Kuhn and Rush, then Professor of Chemistry in the Philadelphia College. It is probable that his acquaintance with the last named teacher had commenced at an earlier period, as Dr. Rush was then Physician General to the Hospital department; but certain it is, that during his attendance on that course, he attracted the notice, and won the friendship of that illustrious man, who continued during the remainder of his life, to manifest his affection and respect by frequent correspondence with him.

He was not, however, permitted to remain in Philadelphia, then the chief and indeed the only nursing mother of Medical Science which his country afforded, sufficiently long to obtain the honors of that school; for early in the spring of 1779 he received the appointment of Surgeon, to a letter of marque then about to sail from that port. On board this vessel he made a short cruize off the coast of Virginia; when falling in with an enemy of superior metal, she was chased into the Chesapeake, and after a severe engagement was captured. As his vessel struck her colours the Doctor leaped over-board and narrowly escaped being made prisoner by swimming two miles to shore. On his return he speedily rejoined the army; but our limits will not permit us to follow his progress through the varied fortunes of that glorious contest, to its brilliant termination, and we will only observe that he continued in active service until the end of the war, an highly honored and respected officer of the Medical department.

After the cessation of hostilities he resigned his station in the army, and commenced the practice of medicine in his native country, between Annapolis and Baltimore; where the reputation which he had procured abroad soon obtained for him an extensive business. In this situation, however, he continued but a few years; when captivated by the glowing pictures of a western paradise which then lured many of the inhabitants of the older states from their comfortable homes, to seek a residence beyond the mountains, he joined the tide of emigration, and arrived in Lexington, Kentucky, in 1790.

Here he sat himself quietly down to the business of his life; but it was not long before his country again demanded his services, in her struggle with a new and savage enemy on her borders; the appeal was not in vain, he accompanied the army on one or two expeditions against the Indians; and was appointed Surgeon General to the army commanded by General Wayne, in the decisive campaign of 1794; immediately after which a treaty was concluded which for a long time secured the safety of our border settlements: and on finally bidding farewell to a military life, he again commenced the practice of Surgery and Medicine in Lexington. He soon commanded the best practice in the State, and here for more than thirty years, with but few and short intermissions, he continued to exercise its laborious, important and responsible duties; with what success the inhabitants of this town can abundantly testify. Nor was it alone to the comparatively limited population of this place or county that Dr. Ridgely was known; his fame both as a physician and a surgeon extended itself throughout the bounds of the State, and he was consulted either in person or by letter, on many of the more important cases which presented themselves within an hundred miles.

Meanwhile he devoted no inconsiderable portion of his time, to the purposes of instruction. His shop was always thronged with pupils, and many of the most respectable practitioners of this day in the western country, and among them a distinguished teacher in the Transylvania School, are proud to acknowledge him as their preceptor. The fountains of information which he threw open to them did not so much consist in books, as actual business; not so much in the lucubrations of the study as in clinical labour. They were introduced to the bed-side of the sick; where they were urged to watch the progress of disease, to learn its cause, to note its symptoms, to exhibit the medicines prescribed for its removal and to mark its termination; so that his pupils became instructed in the art of healing from the great source of all correct knowledge, the book of nature.

Dr. Ridgely, though by no means wealthy, was perhaps as disinterested a practitioner of medicine as ever lived. It seemed, indeed, that he devoted himself to this laborious vocation, mainly for the purpose of doing good to others, without any eye to his own emolument. Never did the poor man ask in vain for his assistance; never in the conflict with disease was his hand palsied by the selfish thought, that his exertions would be unrequited; and often have the fruits of his labours among the rich, been poured into the lap of poverty, to sooth the sorrows of the widow, and dry the orphan's tear.

From his first entering into active life, he was at all times too much engaged in the practical duties of his profession, to enjoy leisure for extensive reading, much less for any literary undertaking: nevertheless, upon the first organization of a Medical Faculty in this school, many years ago, he was appointed one of its professors, and delivered to the small class which then attended, a course of public instruction which did him much credit; a fact of peculiar interest in the annals of our University, and one which reflects much honour upon the subject of our memoir, as it proves him to have been the first who taught medicine by lecture in Western America.

Nor was it alone as an active and successful practitioner of Medicine, or as a Medical philanthropist, that Dr. Ridgely was advantageously known. In every project for ameliorating the condition of the country in general, or of this town in particular, he always co-operated and with his purse promoted, so far as his funds permitted. The success of Transylvania University was always dear to him; and for many years he served its interests faithfully in the capacity of Trustee. In this character he, aided by his departed friends and associates, the lamented Morrison, Clifford and Wilkins, and by other yet living members of the board, was eminently active in reorganizing and establishing upon a firm basis its Medical Department, from which he confidently anticipated much benefit to Lexington, and great advantages to the Medical Science of the West. Need I say how fully these prophetic anticipations have been already realized?

Whilst thus pursuing in the evening of his days the enviable path of reputation and of usefulness, our venerable friend had the affliction, in the fall of 1822, to lose the partner of his bosom; the mental anguish arising from which bereavement, together with great corporeal infirmity, disqualified him farther from the duties of his profession: he therefore relinquished it, and on a visit to his daughter, he died at Dayton, Ohio, on the 21st day of November, 1824—"full of age and full of honor."

The extensive circle of his acquaintance and his relatives will pardon we trust, this short and very imperfect sketch of the long and useful life of their deceased friend; whilst with gratitude, the writer acknowledges himself indebted for many of the incidents which he has related, to the kindness of the venerable Pindell,* his earliest and long tried friend, and latest associate in the labours of the profession.

Dr. Ridgely was in person rather below the ordinary stature, but most symmetrically proportioned. His motions in walking were particularly graceful, and even in advanced life, he moved with a step firm and elastic. Possessing, as has been observed of Dr. Rush, "a pleasing figure and an easy address, with great affability and suavity of manners, the intelligent stranger was at first sight, prepossessed in his favour, and that favour soon grew into confirmed estimation." We have already alluded to the early intercourse, and continued correspondence, which existed between these good men; in whose public bearing and private deportment there seems, indeed, to have been a striking similitude. For of no one could it be said, with greater justice, than of the subject of our notice, as the biographer of Dr. Rush has observed of him, that "the sympathies of his heart, the kindness of his manner, and the soothing expressions which he could so

---

* Dr. Richard Pindell, formerly of Hagerstown, Maryland, for the last fifteen years of Lexington, Ky. who at the advanced age of seventy-two, continues to pursue his profession with activity and usefulness.

happily employ, rendered him at all times a welcome visitant at the bed of sickness, and at the house of sorrow. No man knew better than he, how important it is to unite the characters of the physician and the friend, nor could any one with more facility or a better grace effect the union."*

In reviewing the character of Dr. Ridgely, amidst that assemblage of excellencies rarely combined in the person of one individual, there were some with which he was pre-eminently endowed, and which particularly strike our attention. His unwearied assiduities in the discharge of his professional duties; his marked politeness to all persons, and especially his urbanity to brethren of the profession; his charitableness to the needy; his unrequited services to the poor; but above all, his widely extended and general beneficence are worthy of our highest eulogies and our closest imitation. S.

---

*Delaplaine's Repository of the Lives and Portraits of distinguished Americans. Life of Dr. Benjamin Rush, page 33, vol. I.

A BIOGRAPHICAL MEMOIR
OF H. HULBERT EATON, A. M.
LATE ASSISTANT PROFESSOR
OF CHEMISTRY IN THE MEDICAL DEPARTMENT
OF TRANSYLVANIA UNIVERSITY

ARTICLE II.—*A Biographical Memoir of* H. HULBERT EATON, A. M. *late Assistant Professor of Chemistry in the Medical Department of Transylvania University.* By CHARLES W. SHORT, M. D.

(Delivered Nov. 10th, as an Introductory Address to the Medical Class, at the opening of the Session of 1832-3.)

GENTLEMEN:

I APPEAR before you on the present occasion, not for the purpose of delivering to you an address strictly introductory to that branch of Medicine which it is my province to teach in this School, but to devote the first hour of our meeting to a last tribute of respect to the memory of one, who was endeared to me by many ties of friendship—who was highly and justly esteemed by my colleagues—who was well known, and consequently much respected by many among you. The occasion I trust will be deemed a meet one, to make an heart-borne offering before you at the shrine of private friendship, and to express, in this public manner, the respect and estimation entertained by this faculty, for the character and attainments of him, who, although by many years the youngest of our body, and the last who has been added to it, yet in the wise and inscrutable dispensations of Providence has been the first removed from among us.

Indulge me therefore for a few moments, whilst I endeavour to pourtray before you, a brief outline of the life, the labours and the character of HEZEKIAH HULBERT EATON, late assistant to the Professor of Chemistry in the Medical Department of Transylvania University.

The Biography of one so young, whose few and short days were alone devoted to pursuing the noiseless path of Science, cannot be expected to offer adventures or incidents of a kind to catch popular applause, or to engage the attention of the public; but to you, young gentlemen, who, like the subject of our notice, have entered on the same road to knowledge, and look to its pursuit in one of its most honorable branches, as the business of your life, the few circumstances which I may mention in reference to the early life—the education—the advancement and promotion of our late colleague, will not be uninteresting. And here I must acknowledge myself indebted for a portion of what I shall relate to the kindness of a mutual friend, who from longer association and more intimate connexion, knew Mr. Eaton even more thoroughly than myself.*

Mr. Eaton's ancestors were of the first respectability, and among those on the paternal side was the gallant General William Eaton, the celebrated Hero of Derne, whose bold and chivalrous exploit on the coast of Barbary, in capturing by storm, with but a handful of men, one of the strongest holds of the Tripolitans, forms a proud and romantic subject of American military enterprise; and was the first step towards bringing that heretofore indomitable race to terms of peace and amity. The father of our friend was Professor Amos Eaton, well known for his exertions and success in rendering popular the various branches of natural Science, his own predilection for them having been derived, as he acknowledges, from hearing Dr. Mitchell's first effort at the Lavoisierian Chemistry, and Dr. Hossack's earliest essay in Botany. He was moreover about this time a fellow student of the distinguished Washington Irving. Having been stripped by the vilest fraud of an extensive landed estate, he was induced to resort to Science for a living, and being invited to introduce the study of natural history into different colleges throughout New England, he was successively engaged at Williams and Amherst Colleges, in Massachusetts—Middlebury and the Medical College of Vermont, and numerous other literary institutions, until finally he was employed permanently by the Hon. Stephen Van Rensselaer, to conduct the experimental school which that gentleman had munificently founded a

---

*Henry A. Griswold, A. M. Professor of Mathematics &c. in the Eclectic Institute of Lexington.

Troy, in New-York, of which Institution Professor Eaton is now the principal.

At Katskill, in the state of New-York, his fifth son, the subject of our present memoir, was born on the 21st of July 1809. He attended a common school in that place and in Chatham, where he was engaged in the ordinary manner in acquiring the rudiments of a common English education, until about the year 1818, when his father having removed to Albany, was engaged to deliver a course of lectures to the members of the Legislature, in the rooms of the Capitol, on Chemistry and Geology, as applicable to agriculture. Here, though but in his 9th year, the fancy of the son took fire at the chemical experiments and geological demonstrations, and he now first began to collect fragments of rocks and to ask their names. In the following year (1819) we find our young naturalist assisting his elder brothers in the collection of plants for the illustration of the lectures of their father. They carefully labelled and preserved duplicates. They studied together minerals, rocks and insects, and sedulously preserved specimens of all they could collect. In this employment, together with a devotion of part of their time to the more usual elementary branches of education, the brothers continued until the spring of 1823, when the father being called, as before mentioned, to Amherst College in Massachusetts, took with him his son Hulbert as his assistant in Chemistry, Mineralogy and Botany. Though only in his fourteenth year, he was the chief manipulator for this course in Chemistry—he labelled plants and minerals for the students, scarcely one of whom was so young as himself, and in every way discharged his duties to the entire satisfaction of a fond father, and the admiration of the class.

In the summer of the same year (1823) he acted in the same capacity, as assistant to his father, in a course on some of the branches of natural history, at Middlebury College in the state of Vermont; and in the autumn of that year he accompanied his father on a geological tour of three thousand miles, over the western parts of the state of New-York, and some portions of Massachusetts. This afforded him a rare opportunity, under the kind auspices of an able instructor, greatly to extend and enlarge his acquirements in geology and mineralogy. In the winter of the same year, he turned that knowledge to profitable account in the assistance which he rendered to his father in a course of Lectures delivered by him in the Medical College of Vermont, on Chemistry, Natural Philosophy, Zoology and Botany.

In 1824 the Rensselaer school was established—Professor Eaton was appointed to the superintendence of it, and to the interest and advancement of this institution have his labours since been exclusively restricted. Young Eaton entered among the first students of this institution. The intellectual discipline to which he was here subjected resembled that of his previous life. In the words of its founder, the object of the school was "to furnish instruction in the application of science to the common purposes of life." All parts of the plan were strictly practical. In every exercise the pupil was made to take the place of the teacher. He became the lecturer, performing himself the experiments necessary to illustrate and prove the truths of Chemistry and Natural Philosophy. In like manner he was taught to visit workshops and manufactories, to scrutinize the application of scientific principles and to imitate their results in the laboratory. In such a school we may readily suppose that our young friend was perfectly at home—that although nominally a pupil, he was also an instructor, and that acting upon the sound principle, *qui docet docetur*, whilst communicating information to those less favoured than himself, he was constantly adding to his own store of knowledge. Such time, moreover, as was not necessarily employed within the walls of the Institute was industriously devoted to collecting and analyzing subjects in natural history.

In April 1826 he took the Rensselaer degree of Bachelor of Arts, and in the following summer he delivered, unaided and alone, two several courses of experimental lectures on Chemistry, at Black Rock and Rochester; and in the winter one on the same branch of science, in the Female Academy in Canandaigua. In the winter of 1828, when only in his 19th year, we follow our youthful lecturer to a more extended field, where we find him boldly venturing upon a broader arena, and in the literary and scientific circle of Boston, delivering a course on chemistry before the Mechanics Institute, of which a distinguished literary gentleman of that ci ty was president. In this manner he was taught betimes one of the most important and difficult of all lessons—how to act by himself—a lesson absolutely necessary for a life of efficiency and usefulness.

On his return from Boston a highly flattering testimonial of his acquirements was conferred upon him, by his election to a Junior Professorship in the Rensselaer school, in the place of Dr. L. C. Beck, who had resigned it for a situation in the Medical College of Vermont. Having now become a colleague with his father, and being elevated to an honorable post in the halls of his alma mater, the young professor took great pains to improve himself in extemporaneous lecturing—in general literature—in practical mathematics, and especially in extending the bounds of his knowledge in all the natural sciences.

He did not, however, long remain in this situation, for in the autumn of 1829, at the invitation of the Rev. Benjamin O. Peers of this city, he was induced to turn his thoughts towards the west, with the view of making it the theatre of his future action. In adopting this movement he was no doubt influenced in a great degree, by a conscientious persuasion of duty, and a philanthropic reference to the wants of the West, where he was well assured that in his vocation of Instructor, his labors would be rendered more extensively useful. He was certainly influenced too, in no small degree, by an eager desire to explore the natural productions of this comparatively unknown region; and his youthful heart beat high within his bosom, as the extended and boundless valley of the Mississippi opened before him, rich in promise of many a joyful—many a profitable hour spent in the exploration of its treasures—its hills and its dales—its mines and its minerals—its cliffs and its cataracts—its rivers and its lakes—their fishes and their shells—its trees—its shrubs and herbs—its quadrupeds—its birds and its insects. Fired by inducements of this sort the decision was speedily taken and as promptly acted on. Leaving then his paternal roof, and throwing himself on his own resources, he arrived at Lexington early in the winter, and immediately associated himself with Mr. Peers in the management of the school founded by that gentleman, and since known as the Eclectic Institute.

Without some account of the success of Mr. Peers and Mr. Eaton in their philanthropic enterprise, a notice like the present would be very incomplete. Few and unimportant to the public, were the events of his previous life, but the result of this experiment we believe, to be of incalculably more importance to the world, than the achievements of many lives prolonged in years and exalted in public estimation. It was a demonstration that earliest childhood is the proper period for commencing the acquisition of the most useful of all knowledge—the knowledge of things; or rather that the educator, when he receives from the hand of nature, the young mind provided with language and perfect senses, should contrive to employ, as she had done from the first opening of the infant's eyes, those ready ministers of improvement. It was a demonstration that by a philosophic method of instruction, boys of an early age, may know more of the great facts of chemical and mechanical philosophy—more of the organization and productions of the vegetable, animal and mineral kingdoms—more of the growth, manufactures, properties and uses of the objects amid which they live and move, than is known by most men on their entrance into active life. The method of teaching pursued in attaining these results was the peculiar method of the Rensselaer school. There, however, it was employed only with matured minds. Mr. Eaton was the first to make trial of it with boys. In lecturing to them he was remarkable for the clearness with which he presented scientific truth to the young understanding. All truth, indeed, is simple, and, when properly presented to the mind of young or old, it requires no more effort of comprehension than the fact that one and one are two. In the analysis and simplification and illustration of it to the senses, lies the great secret of the teacher; and in that secret was Mr. Eaton deeply versed. By means of it his classes of boys, especially in Chemistry, were enabled to display a knowledge of the subject that produced general astonishment.

To qualify himself yet the more thoroughly for the important duties now devolved upon him, he availed himself of every opportunity afforded him from the labours of teaching others in still further teaching himself. He prosecuted with great industry and earnestness the study of the natural history of this immediate neighborhood, and of the surrounding country, so far as opportunities were offered him for exploring it. During these excursions it was my happy privilege to be his frequent companion, and truly can I bear witness to the amiability of his manner—the instructiveness of his intercourse—the ardor and enthusiasm of his devotion to nature—his admiration of her beauties—his untiring industry in the laborious pursuit of her objects—his patient examination of them—the acumen of his discernment—the accuracy of his deductions—the lucidness of his description—his careful and pains-taking preservation of every thing collected.

One of the most lengthened of these excursions was made in the fall of 1830, and extended one hundred miles north of Lexington. In this tour, which was made chiefly on foot, many interesting objects were examined and considerable collections made. At the Big-bone-lick—that immense—amazing charnel house of extinct and yet existing animals—our friend enjoyed himself superlatively, in examining the different localities of these osseous deposits, and judging for himself of the probable causes which could have congregated into one spot, such masses of the skeletons of the mastodons—the antediluvian horse—the elk—the buffalo—the deer and other animals. In this cemetry of ages long gone by, he gathered many interesting relics; and among the debris of disinterments scattered in profusion around, where the man of science has dug for the sake of science, and the man of mammon for money, our young friend collected several hundred pounds of bones thrown aside by less scientific collectors as valueless. In patiently investigating as far as they could be ascertained, all the circumstances of this odd and interesting spot, he was led definitively to embrace the opinion of those who contend, that the skeletons of the mammoth and other extinct animals, have been buried in this and other analogous situations by fortuitous currents of the great deluge; and to reject the idea of those who suppose that these huge monsters were congregated there by the search for salt water—in the pursuit of which they became entrapped in the morass, where their giant bodies sinking beneath its surface have laid buried for ages.

One little occurrence may serve to show the ardent and enthusiastic manner with which he embraced every opportunity, and employed every moment for extending his knowledge, and enlarging his collections in natural history. On the excursion to which I have just referred we visited the Ohio and Great Miami rivers, chiefly for the purpose of examining and collecting their shells. The time was a most propitious one for such investigations, for the season having been unusually dry the waters of those fine streams were low, and consequently afforded an easy access 'to the shellfish which inhabit them; and of these some rare, and many interesting species were found. On one particular occasion when exploring the treasures of the Miami, some diversity in our objects parted us for an hour, when returning to the quarter where I had left Mr. Eaton, I saw him wading deep in the water—his pockets strutted out with their contents—his arms scarcely able to grasp their collections—his countenance brightened with joy, he exclaimed, "Surely my friend this cannot be reality—I must be dreaming!"

The result of this excursion was published in the 4th volume of the "Transylvania Journal of Medicine," under the title of "Notices of Western Botany and Conchology:" and this paper has been favorably mentioned in some of the Eastern Journals of Science—especially that part of the communication relating to the shells that were gathered, which was exclusively the work of Mr. Eaton.

The next year brought with it an important epoch in the life of our young friend. At the close of the session in the Medical Department of this school, in the spring of 1831, the Chemical chair was left vacant by the resignation of its incumbent, and promptly filled again by the appointment of his successor. Mr. Eaton's preeminent attainments had already attracted the attention of the friends and members of this institution, and at the recommendation of the faculty he was unanimously elected by the trustees Assistant Professor of Chemistry. For one so young this was high honor. He was placed by it in a conspicuous and responsible situation, and he immediately resolved to labor and to study for the enlargement and completion of the means of chemical instruction in this department. Owing to the absence of his colleague it became his duty to make the necessary arrangements and preparations for the lectures of the ensuing winter. He visited the eastern cities for the purpose of procuring apparatus, re-agents, and other means, as well as to examine the construction and fixtures of the best laboratories. How greatly that of this school was improved in point of convenience, utility and arrangement by the information and materials furnished by this visit, I need not here insist on. The session commenced with a large, a highly respectable and intelligent class. The exertions of the assistant professor were unremitted in the preparation and arrangement of the matters called for by each day's lecture; and in the performance of the experiments for their illustration, he was signally adroit and invariably successful.

Through the urbanity of his colleague the subject of Electricity was given up to him entirely, and on this important elementary matter of the science, he delivered a number of highly interesting and instructive lectures, illustrated by apt and brilliant experiments. His efforts, indeed, throughout the entire term gave universal satisfaction to his colleagues and the class; and contributed not a little to the success and popularity of his department.

During the winter he was married to a lady of this city to whom he had been long and devotedly attached. His prospects were now eminently enviable. No young man in the west—perhaps not one in the union—had better reason than he, to look forward to a life of honorable usefulness—preeminent distinction, and domestic happiness. With enthusiastic feelings he not only studied how to discharge the varied and responsible duties assumed by him, but also to promote to the utmost of his abilities the cause of that science, ever near to his heart—the cause of natural science in this portion of our country. In the hope of awakening the attention and interest of the medical class to the value of this kind of knowledge, and thus sending to every corner of our valley a number of active votaries to make observations and collect specimens, he resolved to give them a number of additional lectures, on the outlines and classification of the several branches of natural history. The execution of this project was but just commenced, when he was arrested in his labors by a hæmorrhage from the lungs. By this visitation, alarming at its onset, he was confined to the house until the termination of the session: but by the first of April he had so far recovered as to be enabled to resume his studies, and attend to some of his duties, though in a feeble and exhausted condition. His health, however, rapidly improved, under exercise and regimen, and before the end of the month he was so far restored as to be able to take lengthened excursions on foot, in pursuit of his favorite objects. Again

> ———"with fresh born vigor he inhaled
> The balmy breeze, and felt the blessed sun
> Warm at his bosom, from the springs of life,
> Chasing oppressive damps and languid pain."

Again with the rapture known only to the naturalist, he witnessed the first evolutions of approaching spring—again the song of birds chirping from bough to bough delighted his ear—again was his eye charmed by the anemone and the violet, bursting from their sleep of winter—again were his senses regaled with the vernal odours of the hyacinth, the lilac and the rose; and oft ascended from his honest heart thankful adorations to the giver of all good, for health restored and happiness in prospect.

His friends were now flattered with the hope of his perfect and permanent recovery; and he returned with his accustomed zeal to his varied scientific pursuits. Among these, he was engaged in preparing for the press a work on the ornithology of this neighbourhood, intended as a manual for the student in that branch of natural history: a large portion of this work was already printed, and the examination of subjects, and preparation of materials for the remainder required a considerable amount of bodily as well as mental exertion. In addition to these labors—perhaps too great for his yet delicate condition—he had resumed the duties of teaching and lecturing at the Institute; when, about the 1st of May, a repetition of the bleeding seized him. It was the summons of death! Vain were now the efforts of his skillful physician; vain the untiring, unremitted assiduities of a devoted wife; vain the anxious solicitude of his numerous friends. It became too soon manifest that the canker which healeth not was rankling in his bosom, slowly doing its fatal work but certain to effect it. And although for a while, with that strange delusion, so characteristic of his disease, he still cherished hopes of life and usefulness, yet when his failing strength and his extenuated frame convinced him that his days were numbered, the better resolution was taken; and in the full possession of his intellectual powers, he turned away from his schemes, and hopes, and generous ambition, to prepare for his end.—He died on 16th of August (1832) in the 23d year of his age.

Never was the ruling passion strong in death more strikingly revealed, than in the dissolution of our friend; for in the last moments of his existence—in the delirium of expiring mortality—he fancied himself amidst flowery fields, and called upon his friends to participate in these pleasures with him. He died as he had lived, an ardent admirer of the works of nature, and with full, unwavering reliance on the goodness and mercy of nature's God.

Mr. Eaton's character as a man of science, corresponded to his education. Of his ripe judgement and accuracy of observation, he gave ample proofs in the few papers published by him on matters of natural history. Professor Amos Eaton's Manual of Botany, decidedly the most popular work on this branch of science which has ever appeared in America, received in its 5th edition, material emendations from the hand of his son; who, with the assistance of another pupil* of the Rensselaer school, revised the entire work for the press. His posthumous production on the birds of Kentucky, had he been spared to complete it, would doubtless have proved a valuable acquisition in this department of natural history; and it reflects no small degree of reputation on the character of our colleague, that he should have plumed a wing for venturing a flight over that field of science, which had been enriched by the labours and adorned by the splendid productions of Wilson, of Bonaparte, and Audubon. Mr. Eaton had been elected a member of the Academy of Natural Sciences of Philadelphia, and I believe also of the Lyceum of Natural History of New-York. He was in habits of intimacy and correspondence with many of the first natu-

* "It is proper for me to state, that Dr. WILLIAM AKIN, of Rensselaer school, and Hez. H. Eaton, adjunct professor in the school, prepared the species, after the genus Carex. I assisted no farther than to supervise the work. I decided in doubtful cases, compared their translations with the original authors, examined the proof-sheets, and gave all the new specific names. But they selected, arranged, compared, and transcribed the whole. They compared descriptions with plants in their extensive collections, and suggested numerous valuable improvements." *Prof. A. Eaton's remarks at the close of the 5th edition of his Manual of Botany: May* 13, 1829.

The public will be gratified to learn that a 6th edition of this valuable Manual is now in press, under the immediate supervision of its author, which will embody all the additions to the American Flora down to the present time.   S.

ralists of our country; among whom Professor Torrey, the Linnæus of America, was his intimate friend.

Has his life been in vain? Though removed when his prospects were the most cheering and our hopes the most confident, he lived long enough to prove how rich, and various, and useful, may be the acquisitions of years so rarely devoted to science. And perhaps this moral is impressed more strongly on our minds, than if the achievement of riper years had been allowed to outshine the accomplishments of his youth; for his were not the ephemeral corruscations of precocious youth, soon to be obscured in a manhood of humble mediocrity, but the well-earned and lasting attainments of diligence and zeal, increasing with his days and growing with his years. Such attainments as the most of us may acquire, with the same amount of patient study, and laborious research. Let each one of us, then, gentlemen, be instigated by the bright example of our departed friend, and whilst we mourn the loss of one so highly accomplished, so deservedly esteemed, let us determine to follow in his footsteps until we arrive at the same goal of honour and usefulness.

OBITUARY
[OF CLARENDON PECK, AGED 25 YEARS]

OBITUARY.

Died at Sicily Island, Louisiana, on the 1st of August, Clarendon Peck, M. D., aged 25 years.

Dr. Peck was the youngest son of John Peck, Esq., of this city, and the youngest of four brothers, all of whom have adopted the profession of medicine. The subject of our present notice, even at an early age, manifested traits of character which gave promise of future usefulness and distinction. He rarely engaged in the usual sports and pastimes of his school-fellows, but was found either at home employed in some domestic engagement, or with his books and pencil; or else he was seen in the fields and woods in solitary rambles, denoting thus early an admiration of the works of nature, in the knowledge of which he afterwards became distinguished.

In due time he commenced the study of medicine, and prosecuted it with diligence for several years, under the guidance of a professor in Transylvania University. He graduated in the spring of 1835 with ease and respectability, and shortly afterwards settled himself as a practioner in Louisiana, where his short career had been already eminently successful; when his health, which for several years had not been good, began to feel the influence of a southern climate. Being much engaged, however, during the summer, with professional business, he neglected his own case in his devotion to the interest of his patients, until disease had too firmly fixed itself upon him, and he rapidly sank under its influence.

In addition to his professional attainments, Dr. Peck had made considerable advances in another branch of science, inseparably connected with medicine, although, at this day, too much neglected by medical men—the study of natural history. In this, and especially in mineralogy and botany, he had made respectable proficiency; and from his fondness for the pursuit, his industrious habits, and his neat and accurate mode of preserving specimens, much might have been gained to the scientific world, especially in the knowledge of the natural productions of the interesting region in which he had seated, had his life been spared. Already, indeed, he had commenced a correspondence and exchange with several naturalists in his own country and one distinguished professor in Europe.

In his social relations of son, brother and friend, few men have sustained a more unsullied character than the subject of this notice; for although to those unacquainted with him, his silence, diffidence and unobstrusiveness, amounted almost to coldness and reserve, those who knew him best most highly appreciated the excellent endowments and qualities of his head and heart. **S.**

Lexington, Ky., Sept. 30th, 1837.

PART IV

PUBLIC LECTURES TO MEDICAL STUDENTS

A VALEDICTORY ADDRESS DELIVERED IN THE CHAPEL OF TRANSYLVANIA UNIVERSITY, TO THE MEDICAL GRADUATES AT THE COMMENCEMENT ON THE 12TH OF MARCH, 1828

THE TRANSYLVANIA JOURNAL OF MEDICINE

AND THE ASSOCIATE SCIENCES.

VOL. I.	AUGUST, 1828.	NO. III.

ORIGINAL COMMUNICATIONS.

Art. I.—*A Valedictory Address delivered in the Chapel of Transylvania University, to the Medical Graduates at the Commencement on the 12th of March,* 1828. By Charles Wilkins Short, M. D. Dean of the Medical Faculty.

(Published by request of the Class.*)

Gentlemen Graduates,

You have now received through that official source,† designated by the proper authorities for the purpose, the highest honour which the Trustees and Medical Faculty of Transylvania University have it in their power to bestow; and having reaped that reward in the field of Science to which your la-

---

*Dear Sir, In compliance with the wish of the Medical Class, we would request of you, a copy of the Valedictory Address to the Graduates, for insertion in the Transylvania Journal of Medicine &c.

Respectfully,
N. N. SMITH, of Georgia,
W. M. GWIN, of Tennessee, } Committee.
D. H. MASON, of Alabama,

Professor Short,

March 13th, 1828.

† The Presidency of the Institution being at the time vacant, Professor Dudley was appointed by the board of Trustees to preside on this occasion.

bours and your industry have entitled you—having won that prize to whose acquisition you have so long and so ardently aspired—in whose pursuit you have together so earnestly run the race of emulation, you are about to separate, and parting in a few minutes on this threshold, you are on the eve of bidding to us and to each other, some a long, and others a last farewell.

On this interesting occasion which fills my bosom with emotions scarcely to be suppressed, allow me, as the delegated organ of my worthy associates, your late esteemed preceptors, to detain you for a moment, and but for a moment. The few observations which I have to offer you are brief and desultory, but I hope they will not be irrelevant to the occasion.

The standing which you have heretofore sustained before us has been that of pupil, and although in this capacity you have found the life of a student not without its cares and anxieties, its toils and difficulties, yet these have one by one yielded to the "labor improbus" of perseverance, and having surmounted them all you now assume a new attitude before us. Yet credit me, Gentlemen, when I assure you that the cares, anxieties, troubles and difficulties inseparable from your profession, are not at an end; for as those of the student, when passed over, wane and fade in the distance, those of the practitioner crowd on the vista before you.

The station which you are about to assume in the ranks of society is one of awful responsibility. To your hands will shortly be confided the lives and destinies of your fellow citizens;—the doating husband will repose his hopes on you for the restoration of a beloved companion—the fond wife for that of her only stay and support on earth—the affectionate parent for his only child—the child for the venerable and endeared parent: in short the tenderest ties which bind the human family together, and which cannot be severed but with the convulsive agonies of nature, will hang suspended upon your exertions; and when the demon of pestilence with epidemic rage, sweeps over the land with the besom of desolation, blighting the fairest face and withering the stoutest form, the cries and supplications of a whole community will follow you; the hopes and fortunes of thousands will rest on the energies of your mind, the efficiencies of your arm. To enable you to meet, encounter and overcome these appalling exigences—exigences which none but a madman would encounter without preparation, has been the object of that intercourse between us, which having existed for a term is now dissolved, and thrown upon your own resources, you now launch upon the tempestuous ocean of life.

And here permit me to remark that too many of those who, in the days of their pupilage, have manifested the most devoted fondness for study; who have evinced the sincerest attachment to science for its own sake; and who in consequence thereof have made the most respectable attainments, when they engage in the busy scenes of active life, forget or grow indifferent towards that mistress whom they have so long and so ardently wooed.

Knowledge naturally draws to itself, by ties of strong attraction, all those who like yourselves have been earnest in her pursuit; but by imperceptible degrees, the absorbing duties of life, the imperious avocations of professional engagement, cool this ardour and lessen this attachment. Hence it has followed that many, who have left the academic shades of Science, and the lecture-halls of Medicine, with the highest expectations entertained by others of their future eminence and fame, have too soon disappeared in the shadows of obscure mediocrity, or been lost in the darkness of oblivion. Let not this, we entreat you, be your fate; for although you have honourably gained that object of your immediate desires, to which you have so laudably aspired; and although the ordeal of examination, which you have awaited with such natural anxiety, and have passed with such credit, is over; yet to the eagle-eye of praise-worthy ambition, are arrayed in brilliant perspective before you, laurels of more difficult attainment, in quest of which you must encounter trials of less partial and more penetrating scrutiny. The malicious envy of rivals—the scrutinizing investigation of the public—the detraction of enemies—the calumny of the world may await you. But in return for these you are offered honours and distinctions, wealth and enjoyments. To gain these, fear not to grapple with those opposing obstacles. In this struggle where the prize is so important, and the victory so honourable, let not the faint-hearted mar the progress of the bold. Mount on with courteous alacrity and cheerful fellow-feeling, and having left immeasurably behind you your less venturous compeers, you will have gained an eminence whence your light will shine in comparison with theirs, as, contrasted with the sickly glimmerings of a midnight taper, beams the broad effulgence of a noon-day's sun.

To gain these heights of enviable distinction, we urge you to be students still. However engrossing your duties, however pressing your engagements, devote some portion of every day to reading, study and reflection. Collect around you, as opportunity may offer, those fathers of the profession who have bequeathed to their successors the rich legacy of their experience and observation. Make their writings "a lamp to your feet, and a light to your path," whose illumination will richly reward you for the most studious investigation.

"Nocturna versate manu, versate diurna."

But whilst you call to your aid the intellectual labours of your predecessors, be not too implicitly directed by them. Pin your faith to the sleeve of no man, dead or living. The operations of nature, alike in all portions of the world and in all ages of its history, are as open to your investigation as to theirs. And whilst from the written observations of some—the oral declarations of others, and the instructions of nature as revealed to yourself, you draw your inferences on all subjects, be the motto of your investigation,

"Nullius addictus jurare in verba magistri."

Having yourself derived pleasure and instruction from the lessons of others, it will become you in your turn, to communicate the results of your experience and observation to them and their successors. Cultivate then a habit of writing and composition, and with this object in view, note down at the time of its occurrence every thing worthy of record in the way of your profession. By this means you will gradually become possessed of a store of facts upon which you may afterwards draw with most material advantage, and with far greater certainty than upon the most retentive memory. That strict, unswerving and religious regard for truth, which should be the prime object in every investigation, but illy comports with those inferences which are drawn from the far-fetch'd, distant recollections of memory alone, too apt, at all times, to be perverted by partial views or favourite hypotheses.

A Periodical Journal emanating from your *alma mater*, devoted to her interests and to the cause of science, is now opened before you. Through its pages, as a common medium of intercourse between you, you may communicate one with another, and the results of the experience and observation of any one of you, may be speedily disseminated among all the rest, and throughout the Union.

Cultivate assiduously at all times, by correspondence and personal intercourse, the society and acquaintance of those, from whom you are likely to derive information; but avoid with far greater caution than you would the pest-house of infection, the Bœotian air of sloth, idleness, and dissipation. Labour in your vocation as one labouring for his life, and whatever "your hands find to do, do it with all your might." Whether your bodies be actively employed, or at rest,—whether riding or walking,—whether by the sick-bed or the fire side,—in the chamber of affliction or the social circle,—at the "house of mourning or the house of feasting," let your minds be never unemployed. Be at all times ready to obey the summons of the sick, whether it call you to the seat of opulence and ease, or to the hovel of misery and wretchedness. Be ever willing to pour the fruit of your earnings among the rich, into the lap of poverty—to sooth the widow's sorrow, to dry the orphan's tear.

Scorn as you would the most polluting stain, abhor as you would the very forfeit of your honour, that mean and dastardly disposition which would induce you to supplant a professional brother, by insidious detraction, or by officiously interfering in his business. Despise as contemptible and unworthy of your acceptance, that popular favour which is bought, by sectarian influence or political partyism. Spurn from you as derogatory to your high vocation, that truckling subserviency offered to your aid by tattling gossips, whether male or female. Cast from you as meretricious trappings, all those adventitious decorations, which the misguided zeal of friends, or the ever veering tide of popularity may heap upon you. Rest your claims to popular applause upon more solid and durable foundations—upon your real merit and your professional acquirements. Fear not to have your doings proclaimed from the house-tops; and in all your conduct, and in all your practices, be guided, as your polar star, by that high minded honourableness which should be the characteristic of our profession.

That profession is often accused, and with apparent justice too, of fostering a jealousy among its members, always injurious to happiness, and not unfrequently subversive of reputation; which unfortunate propensity, I hope the rising scions of that body which I have now the pleasure of addressing, will have the magnanimity to dispel from their bosoms. "Let us be excited by a laudable spirit of emulation, not the narrow jealousies which distinguish those, who, conscious of their own inferiority, dread every approach towards reputation in others. All who pursue the same science should labour together for the common good; every degree of assistance, every deserved commendation which they give to each other, is the surest means of advancing their own fame; while every atom of usurped importance, if it does not immediately cover its vain possessor with opprobrium, is almost certain to be deducted, with interest, from his character, by a discerning and impartial public."[1]

Finally, Gentlemen, let me conjure you as cherished alumni, not to be unmindful of your alma-mater; within whose bosom you have sought, and I trust you have not sought in vain, for those intellectual stores upon which you may profitably draw to the latest period of your lives. Whilst you receive at her hands, that testimonial of your qualifications, and that passport to the confidence and esteem of your fellow citizens, let it prove also, a memorial of those hours, (perhaps the happiest of your lives,) which you have spent within her walls. And now, in bidding you farewell, she earnestly prays for you a speedy and a safe return to the bosom of your families and friends—that you may

---

[1] Sir J. E. Smith's Address to the Linnæan Society of London. Lin. Trans. Vol. 1.

soon obtain and long enjoy all that reputation and felicity which you deserve, and when, after a life well spent, and distinction richly earned, you close your career on earth, her genius will drop the tear of sorrow, whilst, proud of the name you have left behind, she will exultingly exclaim, Ecce filios meos! Behold a son of Transylvania!

AN INTRODUCTORY ADDRESS TO A COURSE OF LECTURES ON MATERIA MEDICA

THE TRANSYLVANIA JOURNAL OF MEDICINE AND THE ASSOCIATE SCIENCES.

FOR OCTOBER, NOVEMBER AND DECEMBER.

Original Communications.

ARTICLE I.—*An Introductory Address to a course of Lectures on Materia Medica.* By CHARLES W. SHORT, M. D.

GENTLEMEN OF THE MEDICAL CLASS:—Nearly all the articles of our Materia Medica are derived from the three grand kingdoms of nature—the animal, the vegetable and the mineral: of these the products of *animal* life used in Pharmacy and Medicine are neither numerous nor important; they are rather alimentary than medicinal, for of the few animal substances retained in modern Dispensatories, Cantharides, and the newly discovered substance Urea, alone possess active properties. Castor and Musk, however valued at one time as antispasmodics, are rarely used at this day; while the animal oils are principally employed in plaisters and unguents. Our attention, therefore, is principally directed to *mineral* and *vegetable* preparations, and, of those supplied us by the former, none others equal in utility, excellence and universal employment the preparations of Mercury and Antimony, for without the aid derived from these giant remedies, our art would be stripped of its main resources. It must be confessed, however, that compared with the two minerals just named and their preparations, all other mineral remedies sink into comparative insignificance; and we are compelled at last to seek in the *vegetable* world for that exhaustless store, whence by far the greatest number of our remedies are drawn. This circumstance, then, will be my apology for devoting the present exercise to an address strictly introductory to a study of the vegetable Materia Medica, in which I shall endeavour to point out the importance of the study of BOTANY to the Physician, and to show its close relationship with the study of Medicine.

But here, gentlemen, I must pause, and candidly acknowledge that I almost blush to call the name of my favorite study—so shamefully of late has that name been prostituted. It is known to all of you that within the last few years a sect of empirics has arisen in our land, familiarly known, in popular parlance, as *Steam Doctors*,—in their own self created nomenclature, titled "BOTANICAL PHYSICIANS"! Debasing the noble science of Botany, of which they know absolutely nothing, by daring to associate its name with their system of quackery, these unblushing and ignorant pretenders have raised a popular outcry against Calomel, Tartar and other mineral medicines, professing to restrict themselves to *vegetable* substances, as being more innocent and friendly to the human system; not knowing—or if knowing, knavishly concealing the fact—that many of the most deadly poisons known to us are of vegetable origin—witness the hydrocyanic or prussic acid, the strychnine, the woorara, and many others, of any one of which, a few drops or grains destroy life as instantaneously as a stroke of lightning; and yet these are innocent vegetables!—friendly to the human system!!

These worthy pretenders to the art of healing, as it would seem for the purpose of gaining greater *popularity* to their project in this age of steam, have oddly brought that agent into requisition in their treatment—I will not say their cure of diseases; and by a sort of most unholy alliance, Botany and Steam are blended together in their unique Therapeutics. Happy age! Thrice happy generation!! In which the surgeon's knife is to be wholly dispensed with;—the poisonous minerals, and all chemical preparations are to be utterly exploded; and in their stead the pure element of water, still farther purified by fire, and the unsophisticated roots of the forest are declared amply sufficient for the cure of all diseases and accidents which flesh is heir to.

Spirits of Dalton, of Watt and of Fulton! How little did ye dream that so soon as this, your invisible and all powerful agent would have accomplished so much! That not only would it be made to move the most massive machinery with the rapidity and power of a whirlwind—that it would stem the torrent of opposing rivers with more than a shark's impetuosity—that it would transport us over land with speed outstripping the swiftness of the flight of birds—that the palate of epicures should be feasted on the richest viands cooked by steam—that the purest drink of the men of Temperance, and the fiery potations of the drunkard, should both alike be distilled by steam—that the physic of the regular practitioner, and the panaceas of the quack should each acquire additional virtues from being prepared by steam; and, to consummate the catalogue of good and evil thus teaming upon us, we may, whenever we choose, by the aid of Lobelia, the boiling caldron, and Number Six, be steamed into eternity!

But perhaps I owe an apology to my audience, and especially to you, young gentlemen, for having detained you for a single moment, by a serious allusion to so absurd a mockery. Yet when you are informed of the widely extending influence of the evil—that, originating in the eastern section of our union—the prolific land of universal invention—it has spread, with the insidious and blighting influence of the mildew, over all the west and south; invading not only the retirement of secluded country situations, but obtruding its blushless front into the midst of towns and cities—rearing its standard of presumptuous pretension under the very portals of the sanctuaries of science—even founding a school in a neighbouring state, for the systematic diffusion of its ignorance and errors—obtaining letters patent under legislative sanction for this new mode of murdering; and, worst of all, finding votaries and advocates among men who otherwise have the semblance of respectability and common sense; when, I say, the evil is thus gaining every where, and among all ranks, it behooves us to raise our hands, and our voices too, in solemn protestation against it. If the profession of Medicine is thus to be debased, and losing every attribute of respectability, it is to be followed by the most ignorant hirelings, let every high-minded and honorable man abjure it forever!

From this protest against an abused application of the name of Botany, we return to its proper signification, in which view we regard it as embracing a knowledge of the anatomy and physiology of vegetables, the systematic arrangement and denomination of their various species, together with their economical and medicinal properties.

Perhaps many of the most interesting—certainly to the Physician the most important circumstances connected with the study of plants, are those arising from their analogies and affinities—those relationships subsisting between their external forms, and their internal or occult properties.— Knowing for instance the virtues of one plant, analogy would lead us to infer a like virtue in another, allied to it in form and habit. Those plants which possess similar botanical characters, which agree in structure, and which are consequently grouped together from their affinities, generally contain similar proximate principles, more or less modified: and as their virtues depend upon those principles, their action must in many respects be similar, though they may be modified by some peculiarity of composition and diversity of combination in these principles.

These proximate principles are the products of nutrition and secretion; and as these functions depend on the structure of the different organs of plants, there must be some relation between this structure and the products and properties it gives rise to. This relation has been presumed in many instances from theory, and subsequently confirmed by observation and experiment. Analogy has led many individuals who were furnished with precise knowledge of the virtues of known plants, and an acquaintance with the principles of botanical arrangement, as well as the general structure of vegetables, to make use of plants that were otherwise wholly unknown to them, for the purposes of obtaining their therapeutical or alimentary effects, by observing their similarity to plants which they were familiar with, and whose properties had been ascertained by experience.

Forster, in his voyage with Captain Cook, met with an unknown plant of the natural family *Cruciferæ*, and knowing well the properties of that family, he employed this vegetable successfully in the treatment of scurvy which prevailed to a great extent in the crew.*

Labillardiere, who went as naturalist to the expedition sent in search of the unfortunate La Peyrouse, used several plants as pot-herbs for his crew, because he observed their affinity to those in common use in Europe, though specifically distinct and before unknown.‡ Nuttall, the distinguished traveller and botanist of our own country, whilst exploring the wilds of Arkansas, some years ago, was attacked with intermittent fever; and being destitute of all the usual remedies, he cured himself by using a decoction of a new species of *Eupatorium*—a genus remarkable for its bitter principle, one species of which has been long used in similar cases.§

A knowledge, indeed, of botanical affinities may often become the means of preserving life or guarding against a premature death. Thus a traveller thrown by shipwreck on a desert island, or lost amidst the interminable prairies or forests of our western wilderness, becomes reduced to the utmost suffering by the pressure of hunger, when suddenly he is presented with what promises him a rich consummation of his wants—strange trees and shrubs and herbs loaded with ripened and tempting fruit invite him to a feast of gladness! Now, if he be a botanist, by a bare inspection of these fruits, although before entirely unknown to him, he is enabled to de-

---

*Boott's Introductory Lectures on Materia Medica, London.   ‡Ibid.
‡Eupatorium perfoliatum.

termine with very considerable certainty, which kind will prove innocent and esculent, and which hurtful and poisonous. An instance in proof of this occurred during the expedition to which I have before alluded—that sent by the French Government in search of LA PEYROUSE. Whilst coasting among the remotest islands of Southern Australia, a small party was sent ashore for the purpose of astronomical observation. In this party was RICHE, the botanist of the expedition, who quitting the beach as soon as they landed, soon became enraptured with the richness and novelty of all the productions of that region, which perhaps no human eye had ever seen before, which certainly no observer had hitherto visited. Lured on and still onward by the attractions before him, he presently became bewildered, and losing his course he wandered a great distance inland; nor was he able to find his way back to the landing place for several days, though guns were fired to direct his course, and parties were sent in search of him.* During this long time of anxious solicitude to his comrades, and of ceasless labour to himself, in walking through a region where scarcely a drop of water was met with to allay his thirst; where the fatal Tanghin hung its fruits about him, tempting him to eat and die;—where the fabled Upas cast its gloom o'er every thing around him; and

---

*"A boat was despatched on the second day from each vessel in quest of the lost naturalist, and the admiral ordered guns to be fired every half hour, to enable M. RICHE, if still alive, to direct his steps with the greater certainty, towards the anchoring place: M. LABILLARDIERE himself was of the party.

"The parties traced his course over the sterile waste he had traversed, to the edge of a large lake, which they concluded had a communication with the sea, as its waters were salt. The print of his shoes, observed on the margin of this considerable water, furnished encouragement to proceed in the search, but the marks of naked feet which appeared near his, gave grounds for apprehending that he had been dragged by the savages into the interior country. Moreover, one of his pistols and his handkerchief were found on the sands; and these strengthened in their minds, their apprehensions of his fate. Further on the little smoke that arose from a deserted fire, directed their steps to the spot, and near it they found bits of paper, on which they recognized the hand-writing of the unfortunate man. Around them the dismal waste extended far and wide, but no further trace of M. RICHE was to be found; when, as they were returning towards the landing place, lamenting the fate of their unfortunate mess-mate, and had nearly reached the shore in a hopeless state of mind, they beheld one of the boatmen running to meet them with the pleasing intelligence that RICHE was alive, and had returned!"—*Curtis's Botanical Magazine, No.* 3251, *article Leucopogon Richei.*

where nothing was met with that was not strange and new,—yet was this naturalist enabled to sustain himself on those productions of the country to which he was alone directed by the light of science.

The chemical constitution, as revealed by analysis, is a clue to the knowledge of the properties of mineral substances; but the ultimate analysis of the proximate principles of vegetables is of little use. The knowledge, however, of these proximate principles themselves is of the first importance, both with regard to their *source* and *properties*. They are the products, as before observed, of the organization or structure of the part which affords them. Two plants of different structure growing in the same soil will produce different products; while plants of a similar structure growing in different soils will form similar products. The structure of the nutritive and secretory organs influences the nature of these products. Now, the classification of plants according to the natural system, is the arrangement in families of those which have a similar structure in the flowers and fruit; and as plants so arranged agree in structure, it is reasonable to suppose that their products and properties will also be similar.

That this is the case is proved even by the instinct of animals; for if an animal rejects one plant as food, it generally rejects all the plants of that family. Insects generally have but one kind of food, and are confined for the most part to one species: but if they feed on more than one species, they seldom or never go beyond the species of one genus.* The silk worm thus feeds on the leaves of the mulberry, and wherever domesticated for the product of its thread, it must be supplied with the leaves of some species of the genus *Morus*, or mulberry, and it feeds alike, and with equal avidity, upon the smooth and silken leaf of the Italian mulberry, and the rough coarse one of our country—upon the mulberry of India,

---

*For many of the illustrations of this position, I take great pleasure in acknowledging myself indebted to Dr. FRANCIS BOOTT, late of Boston, now Secretary to the Linnæan Society of London. See two Introductory Lectures on Materia Medica. London, 1827.

and that of Tartary—all distinct and very different species of one genus; although it is probable that the silk produced by the animal when fed on these different leaves, may be somewhat different in texture.

The China Aster, so much admired by Florists, is in this country attacked soon after flowering, by a black insect of the genus lytta, which never appears in the gardens until about the period of the flowering of this plant; and so ravenous are they, that unless narrowly watched, they soon destroy a whole plantation. I was curious to observe, during the last summer, (1833,) the progress of this insect from the exotic aster, just mentioned, to native plants of the same genus, several species of which I had transplanted to my garden, all of which were attacked and devoured in succession; and from them they extended their ravages to the *Chrysopsis*, a native genus nearly allied to the asters; but they proceeded no farther, although other plants of different families, grew in profusion around them.

Sometimes then we find insects which feed on plants of different genera; but even in this case they seldom or never attack plants belonging to a different family. The Cantharis or blistering fly of Spain and Italy, feeds on the ash, the lilac, the privet and the olive, all genera of one natural family; but it is never found on the Jasmine, belonging to a different group, although in Spain and Italy this is generally cultivated with the other trees. The sphinx of the privet again, feeds on the ash and the lilac. The butterfly of the cabbage feeds on the radish and the gillyflower—plants, which although exceedingly unlike each other, yet belong to one and a very natural family. Entomologists fully aware of these facts, generally well know what plants to examine in their search for particular insects. These facts then are strong probabilities that plants of the same family have similar juices; and that the juices of genera associated in families have similar properties.

This affinity between some families of plants and insects is so evident, that we find foreign trees naturalized in our country, not naturally associated with our native plants, are never attacked in the country of their adoption by the insects which infest our own trees. Thus the *Broussonetia,* improperly called Chinese mulberry, since it is no mulberry, and the *Ailanthus,* still more absurdly called the tree of Heaven! both natives of Asia, now very generally introduced into our grounds and walks, are not disfigured by the depredations of insects; when our native mulberries, maples, poplars, elms and ashes, are more or less stripped of their leaves; and instead of being pleasing objects in our grounds and gardens, become loathsome nuisances from the myriads of caterpillars which infest them.

Experience moreover, proves conclusively the resemblance between the properties and the forms of plants. It was formerly supposed that the Peruvian Bark was the product of but one species of *Cinchona;* but it has now been conclusively shown that it is obtained from nearly all the species of this extensive genus, of which near forty distinct species were detected in South America by the late laborious explorations of HUMBOLDT and BONPLAND. Rhubarb, in like manner, was supposed to be the product of but one species of *Rheum,* but it is now known that roots nearly analagous in property are afforded by three or four species. So Opium, entirely similar in action, may be obtained from all the Poppy tribe; turpentine from all the Pines; tannin from the barks of all the Oaks; and gum Arabic from several Acacias. We find that all the Mallows, without an exception, are emollient, mucilaginous and demulcent; all the Gentians are bitter; the Aconites poisonous; the Hellebores cathartic; the Euphorbias acrid and caustic.

If we find a property, of whatever kind, strongly marked in the plants of one genus, we are almost sure to find a similar property, more or less modified, in the genera closely allied to it. Thus the *Pinckneya pubens* of our southern states, nearly allied botanically to the *Cinchonas* of the Southern Hemisphere, like them has been found possessed of febrifuge properties. Many of the *Rumices* or Docks, allied to *Rheum* or Rhubarb, are imbued with similar medicinal virtues. The Chamomile and Tansy, allied to Wormwood, like it are bitter and anthelmintic.

The predominant and characteristic property is sometimes so remarkable, that it is found universally present in all the plants of the most extensive families; thus all the *Gramineæ* or grass-tribe have a farinaceous seed, and a sweet mucilaginous sap in their culms or straw—whence their extensive and indispensable use as food for man, and herbivorous animals. Voyages and travels have shown that nations the most remotely distant from each other, between whom there never existed any intercourse, have used from time immemorial plants of the same genus or family for similar purposes, either as food, or in medicine and the arts.

But it must not be concealed that we find occasionally striking anomalies in, or exceptions to, the general principles here laid down: sometimes meeting with a poisonous principle in one species, associated with principles of an opposite character, in another species closely allied to it. Thus the deadly Hemlock and the medicinal Cicuta, are related to the esculent carrot and parsnip; the sweet potatoe, to the Scammony and Jalap; the common Irish potatoe, to the poisonous Nightshade; the drastic Colocynth and active Elaterium, to the mild Cucumber and the grateful Melon.

But many of these anomalies are in appearance only.— They depend upon certain organs and their products existing in one plant, which are not found in other plants associated with it. For instance, we find the nutritious and feculent potatoe, as just observed, closely allied to the nightshade and bitter-sweet. But this anomaly depends on a part existing in the potatoe, which is not found in the other two, and in our using for these different purposes different parts of these plants. In making our comparisons then between plants, we should draw the resemblance between the organ of one, and the corresponding organ of another: and if in one plant we find an organ that does not exist in another, here our comparison must, with respect to the product of that organ, end. If we attend to this rule we shall never compare the nutritious tuber of the potatoe—a reservoir of fecula—with the poisonous berries of the nightshade, or the acrid stalks of the bitter-sweet. If the nightshade and bitter-sweet were furnished with a tuberous root, as the potatoe is, we have every reason to believe that the roots of these poisonous *Solaneæ* would, like the potatoe, be innocent and esculent—as we know that the apples of the potatoe, like the berries of the nightshade, are deleterious.

The extensive natural family of the *umbelliferæ* presents most remarkable anomalies. This family presents us with the fetid gums—the ammoniacum, the asafoetida, galbanum and others—products obtained from incisions into the roots of these plants. From the same natural family, is derived the carrot and parsnip of our gardens, in the entire roots of which we find a mild nutritious food; here also in this extensive and strictly natural family, is found the *Conium*, the leaves of which afford us a narcotic principle; and lastly, the fennel, the anise, the dill, and the carraway, the seeds of which yield a stimulating volatile oil. This last principle existing in an essential organ, always present, (the seeds) is more or less remarkable in the seeds of all the family.

The same plant even differs in the products of its different parts, as is strikingly illustrated in the root, the leaves and the fruit of the common May apple, *Podophyllum Peltatum*. We need not wonder therefore that the berries of one species differ from the tubers of another; or that the roots of the carrot and parsnip are adapted for food, while the leaves of the Hemlock are poisonous.

It is evident also, if some plants of a family possess an organ, which does not exist, or is imperfectly developed in the others, that the peculiar properties afforded by this organ cannot exist where the organ itself is absent. Thus the laxative property of the *Cassia fistula* and the Tamarind is not found in the pod of the black locust, or in others of the *Leguminosæ*, because the pulp itself, which affords that property, is absent in them. And yet so analogous are the general characteristics of this extensive tribe, that it has been affirmed that no poisonous species exists in the immense family of Leguminous plants; whilst we derive from many different genera belonging to it a multiplicity of important articles in the food of man and of domestic animals. If the property reside in an organ which is essential to the family, we find no variation in the property of all the plants composing that family.—We see this in the farinaceous seeds of all the *gramineæ* or grass tribe—in the saccharine nature of their culms or straw—and the pungent and volatile oil contained in the seeds of all the umbelliferous tribe.

There are certain circumstances, moreover, which remarkably influence the properties of the same plant: and which should be borne in mind, in the explanation of the seeming anomalies which we are now considering. Thus the Celery in its wild state is a native of marshes, and there it is an acrid poison; but cultivated in the dry soil of a garden, and bleached by seclusion from light, it becomes a mild and nutritious vegetable. The Irish potatoe if suffered to grow on the surface of the soil, is a green and acrid root, perhaps little differing in properties from the stems and leaves of its kindred nightshades, but buried in the ground, and secluded from the sun, it becomes one of the most wholesome and nutritious of vegetables.

I have dwelt thus long on the subject of the relation existing between the forms and properties of plants, because it is one of the most interesting and instructive connected with the vegetable materia medica. It gives us the most extensive ideas on the properties of vegetables in general. It thus aids the mind in its researches, and by furnishing us with a leading principle in our investigations, simplifies them, and guides us the more safely through the labyrinth of nature. We have only to ascertain the *general* properties of any plant, and to be familiar with the systems of classification, to appreciate the advantages of the known vegetable world in its application to medicine, to diet, or to the arts.

One other reason may be adduced for urging the claims

of this science to the especial consideration of Physicians.—
It is well known that within the last half century much additional light has been thrown on human Physiology by comparative anatomy—by examining the structure and functions of the inferior orders of organized beings, in connection with the Organology and Physiology of man. In this investigation, the minute and patient study of the structure and functions of the vegetable fabric, has shed a full share of radiance—In proof of which I will cite but one single illustration. Dr. Brown, the long distinguished botanist, and now venerable Vice-President of the Linnæan Society of London, has recently published a learned and lucid essay on the structure and fecundation of a certain tribe of vegetables, which had been supposed to throw insuperable difficulties in the way of the Sexual System of the great Linnæus; but so far from shaking the fabric of the Swedish naturalist, the minute, and patient and laborious observations made on this tribe of vegetables, have not only established its truth beyond all possibility of cavil, but promise to shed much additional light on a very abstruse and difficult subject of human Physiology. There are indeed some facts so very remarkable in the appearances detailed, that Brown, whom no one, who knows his character, will ever accuse of broaching an extravagant or hasty opinion, but who is deservedly celebrated beyond all other observers for the extreme caution with which he conducts and publishes his researches, has given an opinion which we quote in his own words. "I venture to add that, in investigating the general problem of generation, additional light is perhaps more likely to be derived from a further minute and patient examination of the structure and action of the sexual organs in those tribes of plants, (the *asclepiadeæ* and the *orchideæ*) than from that of any other department either of the vegetable or animal kingdom."*

In conclusion, Gentlemen—I wish I could excite in your minds a consciousness of the extreme facility of the rudiments of this most beautiful and enchanting of all the sci-

*Transactions of the Linnæan Society of London. Vol. 16, for 1833.

ences, because I should remove the apprehensions which you may have entertained of its requiring laborious study; and you would then perceive that its pursuit is strictly compatible with the active duties of your profession. The science in its widest extent, is one of the most elaborate, and requires patient investigation and profound observation; for it embraces, as we have seen, not only the external forms and structure of plants, but their physiology, and the functions of their various organs; and some of the most gifted men of all ages have devoted their great talents to its pursuit. Without attempting to give you even the names of those worthies of our profession, who have in all ages of the world identified the study of nature, in this particular department, with the study and the practice of medicine, I will only point you to the illustrious examples of Boerhaave and Haller, whose fame as botanists was only secondary to their celebrity as Anatomists, as Physiologists, and as Teachers and Practitioners of Medicine. The former of these first gave to Leyden its distinguished pre-eminence as a School of Medicine, and whilst pupils crowded to her halls from all quarters of the world, no portion of their time was more profitably spent than that devoted to the instructions of the venerable Boerhaave in the Garden of Leyden.

Of Haller, it may truly be said, that in the midst of all his fame as a statesman, a physician, and a medical teacher, in the University of Gottingen, he still sighed for the charms of his native Alps; and in one of his letters to his illustrious cotemporary—the immortal Linnæus, he thus expresses himself. "Anatomy is now my chief occupation combined with Physiology. To these I am *obliged* to devote the greater part of the year. Your happier fate spares you such interruption to your pursuits. But if ever I can again return to my own country, I shall seek no other pleasure than that arising from the study of Botany. To it, in the investigation of what Switzerland produces, I hope to dedicate the remainder of my life." To Botany as it had been the solace of his poverty, and the delight of his youth, he wished in old age to devote his leisure and his fortune.

DUTIES

OF MEDICAL STUDENTS DURING ATTENDANCE ON LECTURES.

AN

INTRODUCTORY ADDRESS,

DELIVERED AT THE OPENING OF THE SESSION OF 1845—6,

IN THE

Medical Institute of Louisville,

NOV. 3d, 1845.

BY CHARLES WILKINS SHORT, M. D.,
PROFESSOR OF MATERIA MEDICA, &C.

LOUISVILLE, KY.:
PRINTED BY MORTON & GRISWOLD.
1845.

MEDICAL INSTITUTE OF LOUISVILLE,
Nov. 11th, 1845.

AT a meeting of the Medical Class, held in the Hall of the Louisville Medical Institute, Mr. R. L. Scruggs, of Tennessee, was called to the Chair, and Mr. Isaac Hull, of Mississippi, appointed Secretary. On motion of Mr. Henry J. Sanders, of Louisiana, the following Resolution was unanimously adopted:

Resolved,—That a Committee of three be appointed by the Chair to wait upon Prof. Short, and request a copy of his Introductory Lecture for publication.

Whereupon the following gentlemen were appointed: Messrs Sanders, of Louisiana, Peyton, of Tennessee, and Mills, of Kentucky. The meeting then adjourned.

R. L. SCRUGGS,—*President.*

ISAAC HULL,—*Secretary.*

LOUISVILLE, Nov. 12th, 1845.

PROF. SHORT,

  Sir:—

The undersigned, a Committee of the Medical Class, would return their thanks for the Introductory Lecture delivered by you on the 3d inst, and respectfully solicit a copy of the same for publication.

We are, Sir, with great respect,

H. J. SANDERS,
C. W. PEYTON, } Committee.
J. M'. F. MILLS,

LOUISVILLE, Nov. 12th, 1845.

GENTLEMEN:—

Whatever may be my own opinion of its fitness for publication, I do not feel at liberty to withhold from you the Address you ask for; which having been written for the benefit of the Class, is now placed at your disposal.

With the best wishes for the health, happiness and proficiency in your studies of each one of you, and every member of the Class,

I am, Gentlemen, very Respectfully,

Yours,

C. W. SHORT.

Messrs SANDERS,
PEYTON, } COMMITTEE.
MILLS,

ADDRESS.

GENTLEMEN OF THE MEDICAL CLASS:—

As the third in point of seniority of my Colleagues, it becomes my duty on the present occasion to open this session of the College by an Introductory address to you; and in obedience to this call I now appear before you, in the name, and in behalf, of the Managers and Professors of the Medical Institute—of all the patrons and friends of the School—of the Council, and Citizens of Louisville, to bid you welcome to our State—to give you a cordial welcome to this City, and to hail you as thrice welcome to this Hall of Science.

On this occasion, the first I trust of many pleasant meetings between us, I have thought proper to deviate from the course ordinarily pursued in exercises of the kind, and, instead of occupying your time by a discursive essay on some subject, perhaps entirely irrelevant to the main matters before you, to call your attention to things of more immediate interest and more practical utility.

I propose then to appropriate the time set apart for this discourse to some remarks on the manner in which the next coming four months—the brief term of sixteen weeks embracing the ensuing session—should be employed by you. Short as this time may appear, it is nevertheless a period big with the destinies of each one of you; and upon the manner in which you spend it will depend, not only your improvement at the close of it, but, perhaps, the fate and fortune of all your after life. A solemn charge of this kind, in regard to so momentous an epoch in your existence, would, perhaps, come with more propriety, as I am sure it would with more force and effect, from the official organ of the Faculty, the Dean;* but as that worthy officer, in consequence of the multiplicity of his duties and engagements, is properly absolved from this task, I trust he will excuse me if I may seem to trench on his prerogative. That portion of the audience who are not of the Profession, will also pardon me, I hope, if my address should be wholly directed to yourselves; whilst, I am sure, that the fair ones who have graced our hall with their presence on this occasion, will uphold our hands in every effort to promote your interests. The theme before us, however important to those more immediately interested, is one of homely character:—it discloses none of the astounding mysteries of Mesmerism—reveals none of the curious operations of nature in the elements of fire, earth or water—unfolds none of the wonderful works of the Divine artificer in the construction of the universe, our world, or the minutest atom composing it—treats not of the Physiology of organized life, nor the affinities ruling the masses of inanimate matter, and revels not in recondite researches into the magic influence of mind on mind, or mind on matter. These and other exalted topics we leave to those who have the power—the taste, or leisure to pursue them; whilst we content ourselves with the homely but utilitarian task of pointing out to you what we deem your proper course, within the walls of this building—at the fire-sides of your residences, and in the streets, the walks and market places of the city.

In the character of pupils of the Medical Institute of Louisville, your duties, engagements and responsibilities may be ranked under three heads. These are

1st. Those more immediately referring to your connexion with the School, in the capacity of pupils; or your duties to the Professors as your Teachers in Medicine.—

2d. Those growing out of your association with others engaged in the same pursuits with yourselves, or your duties to each other as fellow-students; and

3d. Those arising from your necessary intercourse with

---

*Jedediah Cobb, M. D., Professor of Anatomy.

the inhabitants of Louisville, or your duties as Citizens, though temporarily, of the place.

Under each one of these heads I propose offering for your consideration a few remarks, which I trust will be received by you in the same good spirit in which they are tendered, and which I assure you, from the bottom of my heart, are dictated solely by a regard to your own good: for most fervently do I desire that each member of the class before me, may so pleasantly and so profitably spend this session, that through all your lives, to whatever period in the wisdom of Providence they may be extended, you may look back to this winter as a bright spot in your existence; and that every member of this Faculty and every Citizen of Louisville may long remember the Class of '45-6 as one which has done honor to the Institute.

Twenty-one years have now elapsed since I first became connected with a school of Medicine, in the responsible character of a Teacher of one of its branches. During the greater part of that long time I have acted in the capacity of Dean,—an office which necessarily throws the incumbent into constant intercourse with the members of every class,—thus rendering him intimately acquainted with the character and deportment—the habits and manners—the fate and fortunes—the failure or success of a large number of every class, and especially of those who have been Candidates for Graduation. Having then for so many years possessed—I will not say enjoyed—these opportunities of observation, I may be, in some sense, considered as speaking by authority when I say, that never have I known him who sowed to the wind, reap other harvest than the whirlwind—never have I seen the sober, industrious and attentive student fail in the object of his ambition; but often have I seen the poor young man, struggling against adversities of all kinds, by dint of persevering application, victoriously surmount them, and attain to eminence and distinction,—and too often have I been called upon to witness the bitter tears of anguish and remorse, shed by the presumptuous idler over his blighted hopes and blasted expectations.

We recur, however, to the more particular object of this address, and following the order proposed in the beginning, call your attention, in the first place, to your duties as pupils of the Institute, more especially in reference to your Teachers, its Professors. These may be considered under the threefold head of *Punctuality*, *Attention* and *Studiousness;* under each of which we make a few observations.

I. 1. *Punctuality* in your attendance upon all the Lectures and Demonstrations which lie before you, is a *sine qua non*—an absolutely indispensable requisite—in your proficiency; and without a strict and undeviating observance of it, you cannot derive that benefit from them which otherwise they are well calculated to afford you, and which you have a right to expect from them. Definite hours, with which you will be made acquainted hereafter, are allotted to the Instructions on each particular branch; and it is expected and required that every student who attends that branch will be in his place before the Lecture begins; and all coming in, or going out, during its progress, must be considered as violations of decorum and propriety; for no interruptions more seriously disturb the speaker or listener than these. By a neglect of punctuality in attendance, moreover, you do material injustice to your teachers, for the loss of a single Lecture, or even a part of a Lecture, like the broken link of a chain, may dissever a whole system, and render it a confused and unintelligible chaos. If then such evil results from a casual delinquency in this way, what must be the inevitable consequence of an habitual indulgence in it?—He who is guilty of it, not only loses to himself the advantages which an opposite course might secure, but he perpetrates an act of flagrant injustice to the whole school, and to every member composing it; for, as before observed, no disturbance is more annoying than that arising from entering the Lecture-room, or leaving it during the progress of a Lecture.

It has passed into a proverb that "Punctuality is the life of business." It is no less emphatically the life and soul of our profession; and habits of undeviating punctuality, acquired during your pupilage, will, I can assure you, conduce materially to your success in after life, by infusing system and order into all your undertakings ; and imparting promptness and accuracy to all your engagements.

2. Not only would I urge you by every consideration, to the most scrupulous observance of punctuality in your attendance, but also to the most devoted, absorbing and untiring *attention* to the subjects of every Lecture, and to the instructions which are given from every desk. This may at first be a difficult task to those whose minds have not been properly disciplined to exercises of this kind ; but every mind which is competent to receive instruction, may be drilled into a train of successful attention to the matters presented to it ; and this is mainly to be effected by determinately dispelling from your thoughts, every subject but the one now immediately before them. Make that, whatever it may be, the grand and all-engrossing consideration for the time, and it will eject all minor intrusions. Without this exclusive devotedness on your part to the subject matter of his discourse, the most eloquent and impressive speaker, may in vain essay his utmost powers, upon the most interesting and important subject. If, whilst he reveals to you the intricate structure of some vital organ of the body, and tells you of its intimate connexion with the phenomena of life—its liability to diseased action, and the train of maladies to which its derangements give rise ;—if, whilst he expounds to you the laws of living matter and the affinities of dead ;— if, whilst he points your attention to "the healing balms which swell the tender veins of herbs and flowers," your thoughts are hovering over far-off homes and distant friends,

or wandering with the fool's eye over the ends of the Earth, as well might he have been discoursing to you of "the fall of Empires or the rise of Stocks."

As one means of riveting your attention to the subjects of each Lecture, I would advise you by no means to shrink from the interrogations, or evade the questions, which are daily propounded by the different Professors; but rather to seek for all proper occasions of being examined by them. This is one of the most infallible modes of securing your attention; for the mortification of a failure to answer correctly, from ignorance, is more keenly felt under these circumstances than any other; and the dread of it acts as a most potent incentive to study and application. Moreover, this system of "quizzing" as it is oddly called, renders the Faculty more familiar with your several attainments, even before the end of the session, and consequently does not throw so large an amount of responsibility upon your final examination. If by these preparatory enquiries, and these previous manifestations, your teachers become well assured of your proficiency and attainments, they will be the better prepared to make the proper allowances for any failure which diffidence, embarrassment or timidity may occasion in the Green Room.*

And here I would beg leave to caution you against one error too commonly entertained, and too often the cause of disastrous consequences. It is this.—Students of medicine when attending their *first* course of Lectures are apt to think that great devotion to study, and strict attention to the Lectures, are not expected of them, inasmuch as they have another course or two before them, in which they can make amends for time lost, or opportunities neglected, during the first. They lull themselves, therefore, into the fatal delusion, that they may safely indulge in

---

*To the non-professional reader it may be proper to explain this term. It arose from the circumstance that in the University of Pennsylvania, and perhaps other Schools of Medicine, Candidates for the Degree were formerly enclosed in a screen covered with *Green Baize*, whilst undergoing the final examination; and hence the term is now applied to all places set apart for that ordeal.

relaxation and amusements, attend or not attend as may best suit their pleasure or convenience, leaving the brunt and burden of the day, the toil and study of the night, to the second course members, as they only are Candidates for the Degree. This is a most unfortunate and sad mistake,—one to which more rejections are ascribable than to any other cause; and one against which, here, in the very threshold of your attendance, I would beg most earnestly and solemnly to warn you. As the invariable result of my own observations, and I appeal to the experience of all my Colleagues in testimony of the correctness of the assertion, those pupils who have been most noted for their punctuality, attention and studiousness during the first term of their attendance, have constantly been the best prepared, and have always passed the most triumphant examinations, at the end of the second. Nor is it at all strange that it should be so, but rather the necessary consequence of an all-sufficient cause; for they have enjoyed the full benefit of, and have profited to the utermost by two entire courses of instruction; whereas they who neglect the opportunities offered by the first, assume the fearful responsibility of crowding into one session all the labors of two. This is more than any man of ordinary powers can possibly accomplish; and I charge you to beware how you attempt the unequal race with those to whom you have given the start of half the distance. Defeat and disgrace will most assuredly await you. The goal you aim at is no mean acquisition,—the honor you aspire to is an exalted one; and you will be fortunate, indeed, if after two—nay even three winters, assiduous application, you shall be able to attain it.

Such, then, being the labor,—such the *labor improbus*,— the untiring, the uncompromising labor necessary to attain the honorable end you have in view, and such the infallible, the disgraceful consequences of negligence, sloth and idleness; what must be thought of those young men, who, although matriculated members of a Medical Class and professed aspirants to the honors of the Doctorate, spend their days in loitering and lounging and gossip on the streets—their nights, perhaps, in revelry and debauch; who, when they enter the Lecture-room, do it but to disturb their fellows, by noise and conversation; and who have the unblushing impudence to insult the Professor and his class by reading letters, newspapers, or frivolous books during the delivery of a Lecture! Fortunately, Gentlemen, these outrages on common decency have but rarely occurred within our halls; for the regimen of this school is such, that those who perpetrate them are properly noticed, and cannot escape the merited retribution. Such disturbers of the peace of the community—such nuisances in Medical Schools, do, however, occasionally occur in all large classes. They are especially more frequent in the Schools of our Eastern cities, where young men of fortune or expectation, attempt to while away the tedious years of their minority, or to "kill the time" by *pretending* to study a profession; and it is mainly such as these, that have stampt upon the classes of our oldest School of Medicine, the opprobrious epithet of "Virginia Doctors."

In this connexion, suffer me to enter a protest against that equivocal and noisy mode frequently adopted by Medical Classes of expressing approbation of a Lecturer,—by *stamping and clapping;*—a method of applause which does well enough to cheer on the comic actor, the buffoon, or the harlequin, but which is surely out of place in the sober and dignified halls of Science. Silent attention to what is said, is a much more respectful, and I am certain that to the members of this Faculty it will be a more acceptable manifestation of your approval, than the most tumultuous uproar of the theatre or the circus.

3. The *studiousness* to which I alluded as among your duties to your Teachers, refers more especially to the pursuit of your studies when *out* of the Lecture-room, and by the firesides of your homes and boarding-houses. This constitutes, of course, an important part of your means of

information, and deserves your very particular attention. The books most useful to you, and which should be most carefully read and studied during a term of Lectures, are those which treat of the same subjects which are brought before you in the Lecture-room, and which you should read simultaneously with the oral discussions on them. If, for instance, whilst the Professor of the Practice is lecturing on Apoplexy and other affections of the head, you should limit your reading on his branch to Consumption, or other diseases of the lungs, you surely will not be as much benefited, either by his teaching or your own researches, as if you confined your studies for the time to some good treatise on Cerebral diseases. And so on with all the other departments. To aid you in thus following their courses, the Professors will each indicate to you the different treatises, on their respective branches, which they deem most worthy your perusal; and for the procurement of all such, our city furnishes you with abundant facilities, in several extensive bookstores, the private libraries of Physicians, and the public collection belonging to the Institute. By a proper economy and systematic regulation of your time, even after allotting seven or eight hours to sleep, which is an abundant allowance, you will have an opportunity for reviewing at night all the subjects which you may have heard discussed during the day; and by comparing the observations and experience of the best writers, with those of the Lecturer, you will be enabled to judge the better of their relative value, and to impress the more important points indelibly on your mind.

To aid you in reading to the greatest advantage, I advise you to note down, at the time of their delivery, the more important heads of each Lecture, and to commit to paper those *minutiæ* which the memory is not likely to retain—as for instance, the ingredients of a recipe—the systematic names of substances which are not familiar to you—chemical equivalents, proportions, &c. &c.; but I am not prepared to advocate the extensive note-taking which is sometimes practised. Unless he be an experienced reporter, or an expert stenographer, the student is apt, whilst attempting to write down the substance of one sentence, to lose the matter of another. Strict attention to what is said, and a good memory, are worth more than any mass of notes, however voluminously recorded.

II. We come in the second place to speak of your duties and obligations to each other, in the capacity of classmates and fellow-students. And here it is obvious that much of the comfort and pleasure with which you may pass the winter, will depend upon the good feeling and courtesy towards each other, which may subsist among you, and be extended from one towards another. Where factions prevail, and party spirit of any kind runs riot—where individual bickerings, and heart-burnings, and ill-humor are tolerated, there must be strife, discord and contentions. I am sorry here to be compelled to admit, that it too often happens in Medical schools, that the Professors themselves hold out to their pupils the unhallowed example of envy, jealousy and detraction,—a spirit too readily imbibed by their peculiar admirers, who soon rank themselves under the banner of their favorite teacher or private preceptor: the halls which should be alone devoted to the attainment of knowledge, become the arenas of petty contentions,—partisan dissentions usurp the place of useful instruction, and the demon of discord dispels the mild radiance of the light of learning. Fortunately, gentlemen, no such example will be exhibited to you by us; for I am proud and happy to affirm, that in no College does a Faculty exist—no association of eight teachers can be found, among whom a spirit of greater harmony, good-feeling and friendship subsists, than among the Professors of the Medical Institute of Louisville. If that harmonious concert and concord could but be infused into their pupils, we might safely promise ourselves a pleasant and a profitable co-operation among you, in the one grand object which is equally before us all.

It is not to be expected that, with your time so entirely employed as it should be by your studies, you will have much leisure for the cultivation of extensive acquaintance even among yourselves; and it is more than probable that many of you will part in the Spring almost as entire strangers to each other, as you are at this moment. Nevertheless, this want of personal intercourse and private intimacy, need not, and should not, prevent the prevalence among you of a general *esprit du corps*, nor should it interfere with a free interchange of that civility, politeness and courtesy, which ever characterize the intercourse of gentlemen, whether they meet in the Lecture room, on the street, or in the Forum. But it often happens that intimacies and friendships are formed at College, and as frequently, I hope, at Medical Colleges as in any others, which last through life, and prove the source of much pleasant intercourse and profitable correspondence; and where you meet with individuals worthy of such confidence, I would earnestly advise you to the cultivation of such intimacies. Concert and co-operation with such, in the pursuit of knowledge, will often afford you helps and facilities in the attainment of it, which you might not otherwise enjoy; and with this view, I am disposed to think favorably of those associations or clubs, so frequently formed among students of Medicine, for the purpose of recapitulating the Lectures, and refreshing the recollections of each other by interrogations on the subjects of the different courses. A notable instance of the benefits resulting from these "quizzing clubs," as they are quaintly called, is fresh in my memory. A young man from Mississippi, of rather feeble endowments, and very deficient in his preparatory education, attended, some years ago, his first course of Lectures. Though not addicted to habits of idleness or dissipation, but on the contrary amiable and well-disposed, and apparently punctual and attentive too, he passed through the session to but little advantage; for at the end of it he seemed to have made but small additions to his stock of knowledge. Of this he appeared fully sensible himself, but went home determined to improve himself by industrious reading during the vacation. His summer studies, however, proved even less profitable to him than his winter labors, and in the fall he returned again to the Lecture-room, with many fears and misgivings as to the issue. "To know ourselves diseased, is half the cure." This knowledge, fortunately, our young Southerner possessed, and most fortunately for him, he was thrown into the same boarding-house with a Virginian of very superior mind and far greater attainments. Being room-mates, an intimacy grew up between them,—the Mississippian was kindly introduced by his friend into a club of intelligent and industrious students, whose meetings he attended two or three times every week; and by them he was so frequently and thoroughly drilled, that he passed in the spring a very creditable examination; and is now a respectable practitioner in his native State.

I conclude this part of my address by merely referring to sundry little matters, which, though separately of themselves inconsiderable, yet when taken in the aggregate, may be, if properly appreciated, sources of much personal comfort and convenience among yourselves, or if neglected, on the contrary, of annoyance and vexation. The Halls of this College are free to all who have regularly entered themselves as pupils of the Institution, and have paid the fees of admission to the Lectures: no such thing, therefore, as monopoly, exclusiveness, or favoritism, can be tolerated in any shape or form. And although you will insensibly be led to take the same seat during successive hours in the same room, which on many accounts is a desirable arrangement, yet you will please to remember that you have no privileged right to any one place more than another. True politeness, good humor, and a mutual spirit of accommodation, will reconcile conflictions of this sort, which otherwise might lead to wrangling and to brawls. The same spirit will teach you the impropriety of wearing your hats and caps during Lecture hours—a Quaker custom which, although no doubt not so intended, would seem to imply a disrespect to the Speaker, and is often an annoyance to your fellows, by interrupting the view of those who are seated behind you. The same remark applies to the habit of putting your feet on the backs of the benches, to the inconvenience of those who sit before you,—to the smoking of cigars in the Lecture rooms, to the great discomfort of those to whom the odour is offensive,—to the talking, whispering and laughing together, disturbing the attention of those who are near you; and, in fine, to many other peccadillos which every gentleman will avoid, when he sees the inconvenience or disturbance which they cause to others.

I hope that I may not be considered as descending to particulars too trifling, or as interfering too far with your domestic arrangements, when I suggest to you the economy and convenience of your wearing something like a uniform dress, whilst in attendance at the Lecture room. A loose, plain, and cheap box-coat, of some neutral color, with large pockets for carrying your note-book and writing apparatus—a cloth or fur cap in preference to a hat, and a stout pair of thick-soled boots, with under-garments of warm and comfortable materials, would constitute a much more appropriate and convenient apparel, for the mud and water of the streets, the "wear and tear," the "rough and tumble" of the Amphitheatre, the Hospital, the Laboratory and the Lecture-room, than the ordinary tight and full dress of the present day. Those of you who come from more Southern latitudes should be careful to guard yourselves against the influences of a change of climate, by additional clothing, especially of flannel, and by overcoats during cold or bad weather.

Finally on this head, I beg leave to caution you against the evils so commonly arising from crowding together too many in one boarding-house, and especially too many in one room. So far as my own experience, the result of many years observation goes, two in one room is as many as can with propriety or advantage be put together; and it is far better for you to pay an additional price for such accommodations than to consult the false economy of rooming with three, four, or a half dozen. With the aid and co-operation of a single room-mate, if he be intelligent and industrious,—and you should avoid as you would a pest-house the idler and the sluggard—your labours may be lightened and the acquisition of knowledge essentially promoted. But on the contrary where three or more are huddled together, even although they may all be studiously disposed, yet causes of interruption are necessarily multiplied in proportion to the number; and one noisy idler will effectually mar the progress of all the rest.

III. Our third head brings us to consider your relationship to the inhabitants of Louisville, and your duties as fellow-citizens, whilst you remain among them, of a well-ordered, intelligent and refined community. To this community do we owe the creation, erection and liberal endowment of this School of Medicine; and in this view, if no other, are the authorities of the city, as well as every respectable individual composing its population, whether professional man or tradesman, merchant or mechanic entitled to your civility. Unassisted altogether by Legislative appropriations, or extraneous aid of any kind, the citizens of Louisville have built and furnished this noble structure for your accommodation and for ours. They have watched with parental eye its progress and development, from the little handful which first assembled here, eight years ago, to the large number now collected before them. In each successive year since the first organization of the School they have proudly witnessed its rapid growth, and anxiously participated in whatever concerned its interest. They have freely opened their doors to the reception of its pupils. They have tenderly nursed them when sick. They have heartily participated in their joys, and have feelingly shared in their sorrows. The friends of the Institute throughout this city have watched your coming with anxious solicitude, and feel deeply interested in your prosperity and welfare. Can you do less than reciprocate those feelings, and whilst you enjoy the fruits of their munificence and partake of their hospitality and kindness, will it not be your pleasure to express your sense of them, on all occasions, by mutual acts of courtesy and kindness.

Never, I believe, has the moral sense of this community been outraged by any act of out-breaking violence on the part of our Medical classes, and rarely have the peace and quiet of any portion of the city been disturbed by the noise or disorder of its members. The Citizens now present will bear me witness that the general out-door deportment of the classes has been eminently respectful and orderly. This was, perhaps, especially the case during the past winter, although the number composing that class was the largest ever before assembled in Western America; and we confidently hope and believe that the same sobriety and order, the same decency and decorum will characterize the still greater number now assembling here.*

It may properly be a subject of regret that the time of a Medical Student during his attendance upon Lectures is, or ought to be, so entirely absorbed by a devotion to the business more immediately before him, that he has little or no leisure for mixing with Society or going into Company; for we are all ready to admit that nothing so humanizes our natures, or gives to a young man the easy courteous manners of a well-bred gentleman, as frequent admission into the society of refined and intelligent females. "Such amicable collision, as Lord Shaftsbury very prettily calls it, rubs off and smooths down those rough corners which mere nature has given to the smoothest of us." "Good manners, indeed, however acquired, are the settled medium of social, as specie is of commer-

---

*This address was delivered on the evening of the first day of the Session to a matriculated class of 225. It has now (Nov. 25th.) grown to the number of 337.

cial life. Returns are equally expected for both, and People will no more advance their civility to a bear than their money to a bankrupt."* But, Gentlemen, I am sorry to say that this is not the time, nor this the season, for you to mollify the asperities of your natures in this delightful manner. You have now to hold intercourse with muscles, bones and sinews in a less inviting form. The uncouth technicalities of Anatomy, Materia Medica and Chemistry—abstract disquisitions on Physiology and the art of healing—the cries of the sufferer under the Surgeon's knife, must fill your eyes and ears, and occupy your thoughts, instead of their fair forms, and the dulcet music of a lady's tongue.

Under the present organization of Medical Schools where so much instruction is crowded into so short a space, it is impossible for any young man, or old one either, to go much into the company of Ladies, and successfully pursue his studies. Few minds are so stoical, or so nicely balanced, as to leave a drawing room, filled with fascinating females, and retire to his lonely room, in a mood to trim the mid-night lamp for study. No, Gentlemen, you cannot in this respect serve God and Mammon. You cannot at the same time pour forth sweet incense at the shrine of Pleasure, and render meet offerings at the altar of Science. Oil and water are not so incompatible as are the pursuits of pleasure with the pursuit of knowledge. The simile, indeed, but faintly illustrates the antagonism we refer to; for a bond of union may be introduced between these discordant fluids, and they become converted into one uniform and homogeneous mass: but no play of chemical affinities—no magic talisman—no compromise whatever can possibly amalgamate the characters of a hard student and a man of pleasure. "Choose ye therefore which you will follow." "Cæsar tore himself from the arms of Cleopatra and became the master of the world, whilst Anthony took her as a mistress to his bosom, sunk indolently into her arms, and by his effeminacy lost,

---
*Chesterfield's Letters.

not only his life, but the Government of the Roman Empire."*

A melancholy instance of the incompatibility of the pursuits of Pleasure and Study is still fresh in my memory, although the incident to which I refer occurred in the days of my own pupilage. A young gentleman from one of the Southern States came to Philadelphia to attend Medical Lectures, in the University of Pennsylvania. Being the representative of a wealthy family he brought letters which introduced him at once into the first circles of that polished metropolis. Of fine person, pleasant manners, and good education, he soon became a favourite at all private parties, as well as public assemblies. His nights were consequently spent in a round of intoxicating amusements; and his days were more devoted to fashionable calls than to visits to the Lecture-room. Thus passed his first winter. In the summer, when such distracting dissipations are generally over for a season, we supposed he would have set himself down to the more sober pursuit of his profession; but he had become too deeply enamoured of the life he had just led, to give it up without a greater struggle than he chose to make. He found it much easier to follow his gay and fashionable friends to the watering places and the sea shore, where he whiled away the summer months in the same round of pleasures. Returning to the city in the fall he again became a member of the Medical Class; and considering his reputation now at stake, he determined to devote himself with more assiduity to his studies. But the syren song of pleasure had far greater attractions for his ear than the dry Didactics of his teachers; and consequently more of his time was spent in the parlor, the ball-room and the theatre, than in the Halls of the University. As his friends expected him to graduate at the end of the second session, he madly determined to run the venture, and became a Candidate for the degree; but as might have been expected, he was, of course, rejected. Though high-born

---

*Zimmerman on Solitude.

and well-bred, wealthy, handsome and agreeable—though the ladies' favorite and the "pink of fashion," he could not meet the stern requirements of the Green-Room. In the mortification and disgrace which overwhelmed him, he returned home, and very wisely abandoned a Profession which he had not the industry to acquire, nor the spirit to pursue.

This case you may say is an extreme one, and young men in this place are not likely to be led away by the same overwhelming amount of distracting allurements. Be it so, and fortunately for you is it, that it is so; nevertheless I warn you to beware how you permit your minds to be drawn off, or your attention diverted by any approach to this course; for rest assured, however kindly intended, they are your worst enemies who throw any impediment, however trivial, in the way of your attaining the great end in view: and although you may hardly be at liberty altogether to decline an invitation to spend an evening, or to take a meal, make such interruptions, I beg of you, as few and far between as possible.

In connexion with this head of our subject, you will pardon me if I say a few words on the manner of your spending the Sabbath—the Holy day of rest. If, as I believe, all human testimony concurs as to the infinite Wisdom—the great mercy and absolute necessity, of setting apart one day in seven as a day of rest from labour, that rest is most imperiously demanded by him whose eyes and ears have been taxed to the uttermost, for six or eight hours, of six days in the week, in conveying to his mind the instructions, lectures and demonstrations of seven or eight different teachers; and whose hours of nightly repose have been abridged to the fewest number possible by the mid-night lamp. Indeed, I am confident that I hazard nothing by affirming that your proficiency in your studies will not be at all retarded, but on the contrary essentially promoted, if on this day you do not open a book of Medicine, or revert in your minds to a single Medical subject.

And yet we do not advocate your spending these sacred hours in the sleep and slumber of the sluggard, nor in idly loitering about the streets and commons—to say nothing of more criminal desecrations of the Sabbath; but in that manner ordained by the Author of all our days that His day shall be devoted,—to reading appropriate books, and especially the best of all books, the Bible—to suitable meditations, and in attendance on Divine Worship.

Students away from home and thrown among strangers frequently urge as an apology for their neglect of this latter duty, that they have not pews, or seats allotted to them in the Churches, and consider their attendance as an intrusion on the owners of private property. This is but a flimsy excuse, and one which cannot be pleaded with any propriety in this place, inasmuch as many of our Clergymen have repeatedly extended public invitations to the whole class, and private solicitations to individual members, from their pulpits, and through the Professors, to attend their ministrations; assuring them that seats will always be provided for as many as may choose to come. Indeed from my own knowledge of the courtesy and kindness of the citizens of Louisville generally, I hazard nothing in promising you, that the doors of every pew, in every Church, on every Sabbath in the winter, will be thrown open to you. Many of you, I trust, are members, and worthy ones too, of the different branches of the Christian Church, and here you will have abundant opportunities of worshiping the great Head of them all according to the dictates of your own conscience. Do it, then, I pray you, in sincerity and truth; for you will one day learn that all human learning is nothing in comparison to the salvation of your souls.

And now, in conclusion, Gentlemen, what shall I say but what I said at the beginning, and what I have endeavoured to urge upon you in almost every sentence and every line of this Address—*you cannot sufficiently estimate the value and importance of your time.* Would that I could impress—indelibly impress this one sentiment on the mind of every young man who hears me! When the eye grows dim—the ear dull, and the head silvered with the frost of years, time becomes a matter comparatively of small importance, in regard to the things of this life; for the race is then nearly run, and as the tree falls, so it must lie. But not so in the Spring-time of your existence, and every young man, to whom the ordinary term of years is granted, may, to a great degree, become the artist of his own fortunes.—If he sows to the wind he must reap the whirlwind;—but if he commits good seed to a well-tilled soil,

"He shall confess his sheaves are great,
And shout the Harvest home."

BIOLOGISTS AND THEIR WORLD

An Arno Press Collection

Adler, Kraig, editor. **Early Herpetological Studies and Surveys in the Eastern United States.** 1978

Adler, Kraig, editor. **Herpetological Explorations of the Great American West.** Two vols. 1978

Agassiz, [Jean] Louis [Rodolphe]. **Contributions to the Natural History of the United States of America.** Four vols. in two. 1857/1860/1862

Allard, Dean Conrad, Jr. **Spencer Fullerton Baird and the U.S. Fish Commission.** 1978

Altum, Bernard. **Der Vogel Und Sein Leben.** 1868

Azara, Don Felix de. **Apuntamientos Para La Historia Natural De Los Quadrúpedos Del Paragüay Y Rio De La Plata.** Two vols. in one. 1802

Baer, Karl Ernst v[on]. **Reden Gehalten in Wissenschaftlichen Versammlungen und Kleinere Aufsaetze Vermischten Inhalts.** Three vols. in two. 1864/1876/1873

Barrett-Hamilton, Gerald E. H. and Martin A. C. Hinton. **A History of British Mammals.** Two vols. 1910-1921

Boulenger, G[eorge] A[lbert]. **The Tailless Batrachians of Europe.** Two parts in one. 1897/1898

Brocchi, [Paul]. **Mission Scientifique Au Mexique Et Dans L'Amérique Centrale,... Étude Des Batraciens De L'Amérique Centrale.** 1882

Buffon, [Georges L. L.]. **The History of Singing Birds.** Translated from the French. 1791

Buffon, [Georges L. L.]. **The Natural History of Oviparous Quadrupeds and Serpents.** Translated by Robert Kerr. Four vols. in two. 1802

The Cabinet of Natural History and American Rural Sports. Three vols. in one. 1830/1832/1833

Candolle, A[ugustin] P[yramus] de and K[urt] Sprengel. **Elements of the Philosophy of Plants.** Translated from the German. 1821

Cassin, John. **United States Exploring Expedition During the Years 1838, 1839, 1840, 1841, 1842 Under the Command of Charles Wilkes, U. S. N.: Mammalogy and Ornithology.** Two vols. 1858

Chapman, Frank M. **Essays in South American Ornithogeography.** Edited by Keir B. Sterling. 1978

Cope, Edward D[rinker]. **The Vertebrata of the Tertiary Formations of the West.** One vol. in two. 1883

Cuvier, [Georges]. **The Class Mammalia.** Five vols. 1827

Donovan, E[dward]. **The Natural History of British Fishes.** Five vols. in two. 1802/1803/1804/1806/1808

Duméril, Auguste [Henri André], [Marie-Firmin] Bocourt and [François] Mocquard. **Mission Scientifique Au Mexique Et Dans L'Amérique Centrale,... Étude Sur Les Reptiles.** Two vols. 1870-1909

Flower, William Henry and Richard Lydekker. **An Introduction to the Study of Mammals, Living and Extinct.** 1891

Forbush, Edward Howe. **Birds of Massachusetts and Other New England States.** Three vols. 1925/1927/1929

Girard, Charles. **United States Exploring Expedition During the Years 1838, 1839, 1840, 1841, 1842 Under the Command of Charles Wilkes, U. S. N.: Herpetology.** Two vols. 1858

Grinnell, Joseph. An Account of the Mammals and Birds of the Lower Colorado Valley. 1914

Howard, H[enry] Eliot. **Territory in Bird Life.** 1920

Hume, Edgar Erskine. **Ornithologists of the United States Army Medical Corps.** 1942

Huxley, Leonard. **Life and Letters of Sir Joseph Dalton Hooker.** Two vols. 1918

LeConte, John L. and George H. Horn. **Classification of the Coleoptera of North America.** 1883

Linsley, E. Gorton, editor. **Beetles From the Early Russian Explorations of the West Coast of North America, 1815-1857.** 1978

Linsley, E. Gorton, editor. **The Principal Contributions of Henry Walter Bates to a Knowledge of the Butterflies and Longicorn Beetles of the Amazon Valley.** 1978

Murray, Andrew. **The Geographical Distribution of Mammals.** 1866

Osborn, Henry Fairfield. **Cope: Master Naturalist.** 1931

Peale, Titian R. **United States Exploring Expedition During the Years 1838, 1839, 1840, 1841, 1842 Under the Command of Charles Wilkes, U. S. N.: Mammalogy and Ornithology.** 1848

Phillips, John C. **American Game Mammals and Birds.** 1930

Rafinesque: Autobiography and Lives. 1978

Ray, John. **Synopsis Methodica Animalium Quadrupedum et Serpentini Generis.** 1693

Ray, John. **Synopsis Methodica Avium & Piscium.** [Edited by William Derham]. 1713

Richardson, John. **Fauna Boreali-Americana;** Or the Zoology of the Northern Parts of British America, Part Third: The Fish. 1836

Richardson, John, William Swainson and William Kirby. **Fauna Boreali-Americana;** Or the Zoology of the Northern Parts of British America, Part Four: Insecta, 1837

Riley, Charles V[alentine]. **[Nine] Annual Report[s] on the Noxious, Beneficial and Other Insects of the State of Missouri, 1869-1877** *and* **General Index and Supplement.** Ten vols. in three. 1869-1877/1881

Say, Thomas. **The Complete Writings of Thomas Say on the Entomology of North America.** Edited by John L. LeConte. Two vols. 1859

Schuchert, Charles and Clara Mae LeVene. **O. C. Marsh:** Pioneer in Paleontology. 1940

Sclater, William Lutley and Philip Lutley Sclater. **The Geography of Mammals.** 1899

Seton, Ernest Thompson. **Trail of an Artist-Naturalist:** The Autobiography of Ernest Thompson Seton. 1940

Smith, James Edward. **A Selection of the Correspondence of Linnaeus and Other Naturalists, From the Original Manuscripts.** Two vols. 1821

Stuckey, Ronald L., editor. **Development of Botany in Selected Regions of North America Before 1900.** 1978

Stuckey, Ronald L., editor. **Essays on North American Plant Geography From the Nineteenth Century.** 1978

Stuckey, Ronald L., editor. **Scientific Publications of Charles Wilkins Short.** 1978

Swammerdam, John. **The Book of Nature.** 1758

Wadland, John Henry. **Ernest Thompson Seton:** Man in Nature and the Progressive Era, 1880-1915. 1978

Waterhouse, G[eorge] R[obert]. **A Natural History of the Mammalia.** Two vols. 1846/1848

Weiss, Harry B. and Grace M. Ziegler. **Thomas Say:** Early American Naturalist. 1931

Wheeler, Geo[rge] M., [editor]. **[Reports Upon Insects Collected During Geographical and Geological Explorations and Surveys West of the One Hundredth Meridian During the Years 1872, 1873, and 1874].** 1875

Willughby, Francis. **De Historia Piscium** *and* **Icthyographia Ad Amplisimum Virum Dnum., Samuelem Pepys, Presidem Soc. Reg.** Two vols. in one. 1686/1685

Youmans, William Jay, editor. **Pioneers of Science in America.** Revised edition. 1896